THE KINGDOM OF GOD

THE KINGDOM OF GOD

Paul Sédir

FRIENDS IN SPIRIT

First published in French as
Le Royaume de Dieu
A.-L. Legrand, Éditeur
Sotteville-lez-Rouen, 1926
First English edition © Friends in Spirit, 2024
an imprint of Sophia Perennis
Translation © Friends in Spirit 2024
Series Editor: James R. Wetmore

All rights reserved

No part of this book may be reproduced or transmitted,
in any form or by any means, without permission

For information, address:
Friends in Spirit
Box 931, Philmont, NY 12565

ISBN 978-1-59731-232-5 (pbk)
ISBN 978-1-59731-233-2 (cloth)

Cover Design: Michael Schrauzer

CONTENTS

Biographical Sketch i

CHAPTER I
Power 1

Gospel Quotes 3
Christ and Nature 11
Faith 17
Mastery Over the Elements 20
The Hosts of Man 24
Intuition 26
Checkmate 29

CHAPTER II
Apostolate 33

Gospel Quotes 35
Compassion 39
The Search for the Divine 40
The Harvesters 44
How the Harvest is Gathered 45
Conduct of the Harvesters 48

The Harvester's Toil 60
Courage 62
Gospel Hatreds 65

CHAPTER III
Spiritual Nourishment 69

Gospel Quotes 71
The Miracle 82
The Martyr 84
The Miracles of Bread 85
The Sustenance of the Will 89
The Bread of Heaven 93
The Spiritual Repast 97
Eternal Life 100

CHAPTER IV
Physical Alchemy 105

Gospel Quotes 107
The Mystics' Task 116
Formalism 121
Defilement 125
The Beloved 130
The Ideal 134

The Witnesses of Jesus Christ 138
Renunciation 146
The Transfiguration 152

CHAPTER V
The Disciple and Society 157

Gospel Quotes 159
Cleansing 162
Purification 166
Civic Duty 169
Innocence 171
Violence 176
Christian Fraternity 180
Vengeance 184

CHAPTER VI
The Faithful Heart 187

Gospel Quotes 189
Exile 198
Fatigue 200
Friendship 202
Spiritualism 205
The Will 207

Simplicity of Heart 208
Simplicity of Mind 211
The Gentle Master 214
Pity 221
Death 225

CHAPTER VII
Christian Initiation 229

Gospel Quotes 231
The Disciple and the Material World 250
The Narrow Door 254
Illusions of Piety 260
Martha and Mary 267
Who Are the Disciples? 270
Apologetics 276
The Father's Goodness 277
Special Rules for Disciples 281
The Disciple as Intercessor 289
How to Become a Child Again 293

Acknowledgments

The publisher is deeply indebted to the "friends" of *Les Amitiés Spirituelles*, who have kept Paul Sédir's books in print in French for over a century, and for the dedication of those who have nurtured the vision that one day these books might appear in worthy editions for Anglophone readers. We gratefully thank in this connection Piers Vaughn and Peter Urbanski for the exchange of textual materials many years ago that led to this presents series, Robert Ledwidge for his technical assistance, and especially Madame Zadah Guérin-McCaffery, who nurtured this same vision and worked towards its realization for decades. Her skilled devotion to Sédir's works helped ensure that Sédir's carefully crafted style has been preserved in these Friends in Spirit translations.

Biographical Sketch

VON LE LOUP, son of Hippolyte Le Loup and Séraphine Foeller, was born on January 2, 1871 in Dinan, in the Côtes du Nord region of France. As a child, Yvon suffered the effects of tuberculosis, partial blindness, and a grave leg fracture that troubled him throughout his life. His mother, of Hessian origin, taught him German, which he later spoke fluently. At the age of nine, he made his First Communion at St Augustin's church, then entered the Jesuit school on rue des Francs Bourgeois, where he quickly distinguished himself by his great intelligence. Observant to a fault, he became a fine draughtsman and would have liked to paint. He was drawn to music, drawing, literature, and was extraordinarily dexterous with his hands. In due course, however, he was obliged to pursue a more practical academic course, owing to the influence of his father, an old soldier imbued with discipline who had little understanding for the refinement of this quiet child with lofty aspirations. And so, as soon a Yvon passed his academic exams (1892), he joined the Banque de France. He was twenty-one years old.

A few years earlier, in his late teens (around 1890), a profound shift in Yvon's orientation had taken shape. Not far from the Banque de France was an esoteric bookshop and publishing house (La Librairie du Merveilleux), where Yvon soon met the well-known writer on esoteric matters, Dr. Gerard Encausse (Papus). This led to a great friendship between the two quite different men. Papus set the young Yvon to work organizing his extensive esoteric library and introduced him to numerous personalities from the heady, even feverish, esoteric milieu of the time. One evening, he was taken to the home of Stanislas de Guaita, a nobleman of Italian descent who possessed the most complete esoteric library then in existence. Around this time, Yvon published an article ("An Experiment in Practical Occultism") and made his debut as a speaker on the theme: "Divinatory Sciences and Chiromancy."

In 1891, Papus had formed the Order of Martinists, based on the teachings of "The Unknown Philosopher," Louis Claude de Saint-Martin (1743–1803), and asked Yvon to collaborate. This fraternity took up the ideas of Martinez de Pasqually's Kabbalistic rite, and formed the first initiatory level of Guaita's Rosicrucian fraternity. In these circles, young authors frequently used pseudonyms. Yvon took the name Paul Sédir (anagram of désir), Gerard Encausse became Papus, Dr. Emmanuel Lalande used the name Marc Haven, etc. From the time of his association with the new Martinist Order, Yvon regularly published his work as Paul Sédir.

In 1895, Papus passed his doctorate in medicine and opened a home for the aged. This necessitated Sédir taking on the bulk of the esoteric-hermetic activities on which he and Papus had been collaborating. Every evening he gave classes in Hebrew and Sanskrit, the psychic training of Hindu fakirs, yoga, experimental alchemy, astrology, esoteric botany, etc. He also organized various research groups on related subjects.

Sédir was also much attracted to mysticism, and frequented literary circles such that of the poet Paul-Marie

Biographical Sketch

Verlaine. Meanwhile, in the rue de l'Ancienne Comédie, meetings of the Martinist Order were taking place, where Sédir became acquainted with individuals engaged in experiments regarding which he would later say: "It is here-below that you pay the highest price." His alchemical research did, however, enable him to acquire an ever deeper understanding of the foundations of what is known as the Great Work.

All these early aspects of Sédir's esoteric life reveal an overarching quest for truth that always led him to first experience something before speaking about it. He had by now attained great heights of "secret" knowledge, and even power. But to his great good fortune he had the wisdom to detach himself from these as soon as he realized their worthlessness and danger.

⊕

In July 1897, Gerard Encausse arranged for Sédir (then 26 years old) to meet a most singular man, Master Philippe of Lyon (Nizier Anthelme Philippe), to whom he was introduced by Madame Encausse. Master Philippe was a remarkable healer whom Sédir and others in his circle considered a Christian Master of the highest degree. Shortly after this meeting, Sédir left for Lyon to spend his vacation there. Just what happened at that time remains a private matter, although Sédir gives some inkling of what transpired in his autobiographical book *Initiations*, and also in a remarkable letter of May 1910:

> Together with some companions, I have done the rounds of all esotericisms and explored all crypts with the most fervent sincerity and hope of success. But none of the certainties I eventually grasped appeared

THE KINGDOM OF GOD

to be The Certainty. Rabbis communicated their secret manuscripts to me; alchemists admitted me to their laboratories; Sufis, Buddhists, and Taoists led me during long nights to the abodes of their gods; a Brahmin let me copy his tables of mantra; a yogi imparted to me the secrets of contemplation. But one evening, after a certain meeting, what these admirable men taught became for me like haze rising at dusk on a sultry day. We run after what we think is hidden, but know nothing of our own religion, though its dogma and liturgy are the most complete presentation of integral knowledge on earth. Everything is there in Christianity. The Hindu *trimurti* is neither the Christian trinity nor the Pythagorean ternary; gnosis and the gospels do not lead to the same goal. Read in the texts what is there, not what one would wish to find there. To see that we know nothing; to experience that we can do nothing; to verify that heaven is here within us, and that our Friend constantly enfolds us within his blessed arms—this is the lesson of Jesus. This I have attempted to say by publishing, among other works, five volumes of lectures on the gospels.

Master Philippe had changed Sédir's orientation. *His mission had been affirmed.* He gave up all the esoteric fraternities (and his various ranks and offices in them) in order to devote himself wholly to living and spreading the gospel. His commentaries on the life of Christ are especially notable in that he accepts the intuitive faculty as a means of approaching the Truth. Sédir's literary output was extensive. His best known works are from this period are: *Prayer, Initiations, Mystic Forces, Christian Mysticism, Seven Mystical Gardens, The Childhood of Jesus, The Sermon on the Mount,*

Biographical Sketch

Some Friends of God, The Healings of Christ, The Kingdom of God, The Crowning of His Work, Weekly Meditations, and *The Incandescent Path.* His lectures and books drew many devoted students, and in due course a fellowship called Les Amitiés Spirituelles ("Friends in Spirit") was formed. This organization undertook to publish many of Sédir's books, and though it is much diminished, it remains active today.

Sédir died in Paris. Twenty years later, Breton poet and novelist Théophile Briant of Dinan wrote:

> On February 3, 1926, Paul Sédir died in Paris at the age of 55. The death of this admirable man, with his gospel-inspired heart, went almost unnoticed by the mainstream press, which was more preoccupied with crowning the charlatans and histrionics who were entertaining the public, even as international catastrophes were on the verge of breaking out. Apart from the chosen few whom this Apostle of the End Times had called to the Light, most post-war jabberers were unaware that one of the century's most eloquent voices was no longer to be heard. His was a forerunner's voice, the voice of a herald proclaiming in a wilderness of contentious crowds, a voice that had been devoted for years to spreading the gospel and, at the threshold of the abyss, was raised in dire warning against the multiplied prostitutions of the word.†

---

† This sketch is based on biographical materials provided by Émile Besson and Max Camis (close friends of Sédir), recently published in English in *Paul Sédir: His Life and Work* (Friends in Spirit, 2024).

CHAPTER I

Power

Each chapter begins with a synoptic extract from the gospels that provides the subject matter for the subsections that follow.

S JESUS WAS PASSING along the shore of Lake Genesareth, a crowd pressed around him to hear the word of God. Having seen two fishing boats at anchor near the shore, the owners of which had debarked in order to clean their nets, he boarded the boat belonging to Simon and asked him to steer away from the shore. Then he sat down and from there began to teach the crowd.

When he had finished speaking he told Simon: "Launch out into the deep and let down your nets for a catch." Simon replied: "Master, we have worked all night and we have caught nothing, however, at your command, I will let down the net." Having thrown it, they caught such a large quantity of fish that their nets were breaking. They then signaled to their companions who were in another fishing boat to come to their assistance. When they arrived, they filled both boats to such an extent that they were on the verge of sinking. Simon Peter, having witnessed this, threw himself at Jesus's feet and said to him: "Lord, leave me, because I am a sinful man." In fact, because of the great quantity of fish that they had caught, fear had gripped him, as well as the others who were with him, including James and John, the sons of Zebedee, who were Simon's companions. Jesus then said to Simon: "Do not be in the least afraid; henceforth, you will be fishers of men." Having brought the boats back to shore, they left everything and followed him.

THE KINGDOM OF GOD

⊕

Then Jesus boarded another boat, followed by his disciples. Suddenly a violent storm arose over the Sea of Tiberias to the point that the boat was being inundated by the waves. Jesus was asleep. The disciples approached him, awakened him, beseeching him: "Save us Lord, we are sinking!" He answered: "Why are you afraid, men of little faith?" Then he rose, admonished the wind and commanded the waters: "Silence, be calm!" The wind dropped and the sea became calm. These men, full of admiration for him, wondered: Who is he whom the winds and the waters obey?

They crossed to the other side of the sea, to the country of the Gerasenians. Just as Jesus was debarking, a man possessed by an unclean spirit came from among the sepulchers to meet him. He was so dangerous that nobody dared to venture upon that path. This man had not worn clothing for a long time; he made his home within the tombs and nobody had been able to tie him up, even with chains. Several times he had been chained and steel shackles had been placed on his ankles, but he had broken both the chains and the fetters, and nobody possessed the strength to subdue him any more. Day and night he roamed ceaselessly, howling among the sepulchers and in the mountains, cutting himself with stones. He saw Jesus from afar, and ran to meet him. Prostrating himself before him, he shouted with all his strength: "What is there between you and me, Jesus, Son of the Most High? In the name of God I beseech you, do me no harm!" So Jesus answered: "Unclean spirit, leave the body of this man." Then he questioned him: "What is your name?" "My name," he replied, "is Legion, because we are many." And this legion of demons begged him not to expel them from the region. Browsing on the mountainside nearby there was a herd of swine, and the unclean spirits demanded of him: "If you chase us out, send us into the swine so that we may live in them." Jesus agreed to their demand. Then they departed from the man and entered into the swine, whereupon the herd stampeded into the sea. There were about two thousand swine, and they all drowned amid the billows. The herdsmen took flight to the city and the surroundings to spread the news of what had happened. The inhabitants came to see what had taken place. They approached Jesus and found the demoniac, who had been possessed by the legion, now dressed and sane, sitting at his feet. Seeing this, they became afraid. Those who had witnessed the event told them what had happened to the demoniac and to the herd of swine. The inhabitants then begged Jesus to leave their region. As he was boarding the fishing boat, the man who had been delivered from the demons asked his permission to stay with him. Jesus declined his request but told him: "Go home to your family, tell them the great things that the Lord has done for you and how he took pity on you." The man left and set about proclaiming in the Decapolis the great things that Jesus had done for him; everyone was struck with admiration.

When Jesus had returned by boat to the other side of the lake, a rather large crowd assembled around him. While he was still on the shore, the head of a synagogue, named Jairus, came looking for him. Having found him, he threw himself at Jesus's feet, urgently beseeching him: "My little daughter is very near death. Come, lay your hands on her and heal her, so that she might live." Jesus went with him, followed by a large crowd which pressed close to him on all sides.

There, among the people, was a woman who for twelve years had suffered constant hemorrhaging. She had suffered much at the hands of numerous doctors, having spent all she possessed seeking a cure, but to no avail. On the contrary, her condition had in fact worsened. She had heard people speak of Jesus and, having joined the crowd in the rear, she approached him and touched his robe because she had thought: "If only I touch his cloak, I shall be healed." Immediately the hemorrhaging ceased. She felt that her body had been cured of its infirmity. At the same instant, Jesus knew that a force had left him from within. He turned to face the crowd and asked: "Who touched my cloak?" His disciples answered: "See how the crowd presses in on you closely from all sides and you ask who touched you?" But Jesus was looking around him to find the one who had touched his cloak. Then the woman, quite afraid and trembling, aware of what had happened to Jesus, came forward, threw herself at his feet, explaining to him what she had done and why. Jesus said to her: "My daughter, your faith has healed you. Go in peace, you are delivered of your infirmity."

He was still speaking when friends of the ruler of the synagogue arrived in haste, telling him: "Your daughter is dead. Why trouble the Master further?" But Jesus, ignoring their news, said to the ruler of the synagogue: "Have no fear whatsoever, just have faith." Then, permitting only Peter, James, and his brother John to accompany him, they went to the house of the ruler of the synagogue. On their arrival they found a large number of people in mourning, grieving and wailing loudly. Having entered, he asked: "Why is there such a tumult here and why all these tears? The young girl is not dead, she is just asleep." They ridiculed him, knowing full well that she was dead. But Jesus, insisting that everyone else leave, took with him the girl's father, mother, and the three disciples who accompanied him, and entered the room where the child lay. He took her hand saying: "Talitha, koumi!" which means "Little girl, I say to you, arise." The little girl, who was twelve years of age, immediately arose and began to walk around. All present were completely astonished. Jesus asked them expressly not to speak to anyone about what had happened; then he asked them to give her something to eat.

⊕

As Jesus was leaving, two blind men followed him, begging him: "Have pity on us, Son of David!" He entered his lodging and the two blind men followed him. Jesus asked them: "Do you believe that I have the power to do such a thing?" They replied: "Yes, Lord!" Then, touching their eyes, he said: "Let it be done according to your faith." And their eyes were opened. Then, in a stern tone, Jesus added "Take care that no one finds out!" But when they had departed, they broadcast his reputation throughout the region.

After they had gone, a dumb man possessed by a

demon was brought to Jesus. After the demon had been cast out, the man began to speak. The crowd expressed their admiration, acclaiming: "We have never seen anything like this in Israel." But the Pharisees dismissed it, saying: "It is through the power of the prince of demons that he casts out demons."

Nevertheless, Jesus visited all the cities and villages of the region, teaching in their synagogues, preaching the gospel of the kingdom of God, healing all sorts of diseases and infirmities. Seeing the crowd, he was moved with compassion, because they were like sheep without a shepherd, worn out and without a place to rest. Then he said to his disciples: "The harvest is great but the workers are so few. Pray, therefore, that the Master of the harvest sends workers to gather it."

Filled with the power of the Holy Spirit, Jesus returned to Galilee. His reputation had spread throughout the country. He taught in the synagogues of the region and everybody marveled at his accomplishments. Visiting Nazareth, where he had been brought up, he began to teach in the synagogue, which caused great astonishment among his compatriots. They said: "From whence did he obtain such abilities? How is it that such wisdom has been given to him, and that such great miracles are accomplished through his hands? Is he not the carpenter, the son of Mary, and are James, Joseph, Simon, and Jude not his brethren? Are not his sisters living among us? How has all this come to him?" Jesus was causing a scandal. He was unable to perform any miracles except for laying hands upon a few and healing them; yet Jesus was astonished at their incredulity.

Power

On the sabbath day he went to the synagogue, as was his custom. When he rose to read to the assembly, he was presented the Book of the Prophet Isaiah. He opened it and found therein a passage in which it was written: "The spirit of the Lord is upon me. He has anointed me to announce the gospel to the poor; he has sent me to announce freedom for those in captivity, sight for the blind, deliverance for the oppressed, And to announce a year of blessings from the Lord."

He closed the book, gave it back to the servant, and sat down. Everyone in the synagogue had their eyes fixed upon him. Then he began: "Today, this passage of the Scriptures that you have just heard is being accomplished..."

Everyone present acknowledged him and marveled at the words of grace he had just uttered. But they were wondering: "Is this not the son of Joseph?" Then he said to them: "You will even go so far as to apply to me the proverb "Doctor, heal thyself." "Everything that you have done at Capharnaum and of which we have heard spoken about, do it here as well, in your own home town..." "Let me tell you," he added, "that no prophet is ever well received in his own country, in his own family, or his own house. Truly, let me tell you that in the days of Elijah there were many widows in Israel, when heaven was closed for three and a half years and there had been a great famine came across the face of the entire earth. Nevertheless, Elijah was not sent to any of them, but rather to a widow named Serepta, who lived in the land of Sidon. In the days of the Prophet Elisha, there were many lepers in Israel, yet none of them were healed. He who was healed was a

THE KINGDOM OF GOD

Syrian called Naaman. These words of Jesus so angered all who were present in the synagogue that they rose up and chased him out of the city. Then they took him to the edge of the hill upon which their city was built in order to throw him off the cliff. But Jesus, passing through the midst of them, left and descended to Capharnaum.

Next they went to Bethsaida, where they brought a blind man to Jesus, asking him to touch him. He took the blind man by the hand and, having led him outside the village, put some saliva on his eyes, imposed his hands upon him, and asked him if he could see anything. The blind man looked about him and replied: "I see some men and I see them walking, as if they were trees." Then Jesus again placed his hands over his eyes. The blind man, looking around, found himself to be healed, seeing everything quite clearly. Jesus sent him back to his home, telling him: "Do not return to the village."[1]

---

[1] Luke 5:1–11—Matt. 8:23–27; Mark 4:35–41; Luke 8:22–25; Matt. 8:28–34; Mark 5:1–20; Luke 8:26–39—Matt 9:18–26; Mark 5:21–43; Luke 8:40–56; Matt. 9:27–31—Matt. 9:32–34; Matt. 13:53–58; Mark 6:1–6; Luke 4:16–30—Mark 8:22–26.

Power

Christ and Nature

NO ONE I KNOW OF has studied the connections between the actions of Jesus and the particular regions where they took place. A few celebrated authors have drawn beautiful pictures of the Palestinian countryside—the mystery may have spoken to their souls. But one would need be a Fra Angelico or a poetic St Jean-Marie Vianney to do this mystery justice, since all I can do is to depict a new horizon to the soarings of your love. To believe that the Word incarnates only for the salvation of humankind would be sheer presumptuousness. Of course, men are in the forefront of his preoccupations, but all creatures are dear to him as well. Although the human being is the central vessel into which the fountains of divine graces are pouring, and from which immeasurable channels will subsequently distribute them to the immeasurable non-human spiritual hierarchies, the Word who took a physical body never fails to heal, to enlighten the forms of the terrestrial nature with which the apparently unforeseen occurrences of his existence put him in contact.

The stone upon which the foot of the divine Voyager steps, the spring that refreshes his lips, the stalk of wheat, the fruit, the meat from which he pretends to restore his strength, the summit upon which he finds isolation, the plain, the lake, the public square where he teaches, the sun that does at times not recognize him, the nocturnal stars that regret his departure, the others still awaiting his coming, the wind, the clouds and the rain, the wild beasts of the desert and of the forest, the birds, the water-sprites—one and all receive from his hands the blessing they are yearning for.

THE KINGDOM OF GOD

Our nurturing Mother Earth, from which we extract our sustenance, imposes structures analogous to her own upon her children. From her mountains comes the bony system of the vertebrates, from her oceans the heartbeat of our hearts, from her rivers, whether visible or subterranean, the arterial and venous circulation. The vegetable kingdom is her head of hair, the animal and human kingdoms her twin nervous system. And just as men and animals come and go, pulled by the invisible attractions of their needs, of their desires and hatreds, so does our planet circulate among the myriads of stars, drawn by the invisible threads from which astronomers have not yet been able to isolate but a small fraction. However, this general analogy entails particular differences.

Scholastic philosophy sets forth that the intelligence of the angel differs from the intelligence of man, not only because of its perfection, but also because of its nature. However, the angel and man are not the only ones gifted with intelligence. All beings possess the quadruple faculty to feel, to understand, to will, and to love, each according to his nature. The rock perceives, desires, thinks, decides, just as do the tree, the animal, or the phantom and the elementary spirit, the genii or the god, but each follows the modes peculiar to its own species. That is why the kingdoms of various creatures seldom communicate with one another. The grass does not understand the clod of earth from which it feeds; the steer does not understand the grass; neither does man understand the steer; and when the invisible creatures brush against us we are afraid, at least as much as are the primitive tribes when some unknown explorer beyond their ken suddenly appears among them.

Jesus alone understands all beings and knows how to

Power

speak to them. Jesus alone knows how to tell them what suits them; Jesus alone knows how to heal and console them.

An orator makes himself understood when he uses the language the audience possesses. But foreigners do not comprehend his discourse any better than do the walls of the assembly room where he delivers his lecture. Thus, in our spiritual penumbra, we communicate with the rest of nature but in a confused and vague manner. Making use of certain rather illicit and artificial methods may lead us to have particular, precise connections; some individuals possess from birth the privilege of seeing and hearing some invisible beings, but solely the gift of tongues coming from the Holy Spirit permits pure hearts to have true and normal connections with extra-physical worlds and their inhabitants.

This was the case with Jesus. Each of his actions, down to their smallest details conceived and organized by his omniscience, is addressed not only to human auditors, but also to innumerable hidden eyes, to the innumerable secretly listening ears that are in need as ours are, of light and harmony. When Jesus arrives at the shores of the lake of Genesareth on a certain day, at a certain time; when the fishermen he calls are particularly Peter, James and John; when the nets are filled to overflowing at such and such a place in this lake and not at another: it means that this lake, these boats, these men, these fish were on that day, at that very minute, ready to understand the Word and to see the light.

If Simon and the sons of Zebedee recognized their Master at that miraculous hour, it was because their souls as well as other souls had perceived him long ago in previous times; but it was also because, since that immemorial perception, they had desired that it would recur and be fulfilled. Heaven shows itself to each creature once, twice, even seven times, to kindle within the depth of their spirit the nostalgia for its splendors. But for the Master to seize and grasp these indocile children—for him to bring them back to the right path, they must affirm through a decisive gesture their hunger for the light. In one way or another we must, as did the fishermen of Genesareth, "leave everything to follow Jesus."

Stray impulses accompanying our slight inclinations, regrets and sighs intermittently offered to God, are not sufficient for him to take us. There has to be a perpetual desire, intensifying each day. This is the only way to agglomerate within us the one thousand scattered forces whose unanimous élan will be necessary on the day of the final choice.

No one in the world imagines how grave is that choice, because no one can imagine God, his Son, his Spirit, the Virgin, or the Kingdom. From that choice, whether hastily taken, or delayed depends our fate and the fate of thousands of beings here and there throughout the universe. Awaiting the Lord should be at the basis of all our concerns. This expectation palpitates within us anyway, but is so weak, so hidden, that we are hardly aware of it; it reaches our conscience after so many deformations that it is unrecognizable beneath the forms of desires for happiness in which our fugitive delights so bitterly wallow.

Were we wise, knowing that our only thirst is immutability, that our only hunger is certitude, would confirm to us that it is in God alone that we will find our plenitude, that ever renewed youthfulness that will develop our being pacifically amid the numberless spheres of the uncreated Glory.

Power

Libraries have been filled with works on predestination. But think! Would our Father be our Father had he not predestined all his children to become perfect? Would he be the Creator, had he not organized the universe down to the last detail for the greatest good of each of its inhabitants? For long periods of time they bustle about towards immediate results: to feed themselves, to take care of themselves, to conserve the species, and dominate their fellows. A great deal of experience is necessary not to see their efforts as merely a goal in itself, but a means, an exercise, so that the idea for the veritable goal will surge from within—which is the fulfillment of the designs of the Creator. After having conceived that ideal, they need a long training period to adapt to this discipline the total ensemble of their physical and soul faculties. During the stage of this last schooling, they will become disciples, then apostles—which means beings who, while attending to all the tasks of their destiny, bring everything back to God. They will teach others to remember God. And God will enlist them as his workmen.

Creation is so vast that never will our intelligence encompass the ensemble of its plan. That is why, to reason alone, it seems to be a fluky imbroglio. What we perceive of Creation is never but a tiny circle. Neither do we comprehend the disparate mixture of beings who swarm beneath our eyes, because in each of these premises are to be found representatives of all other places—provided, of course, that they be tolerated there. Hence, any creature who seeks for the light can find it, and no one can hold the Father responsible for the ignorance wherein it gropes.

Neither must we believe that those three fishermen at the lake of Genesareth, nor the others, were chosen because they happened to be there, or because one of them, all of a sudden, accepted Jesus as his Master. There was a crowd on the shores of the lake, but these three alone found strength to forsake everything. It is because they alone had longed for this meeting from birth. It is because, during the course of the mysterious migration of their spirits for centuries, they had desired for, hoped for, begged for it. It is also because, from the time of the first exile of their souls outside of the eternal Fatherland, they had kept the memory of the immemorial smile. Moreover, this long apprenticeship will preserve them later, during the terrestrial night, from succumbing to doubt, to fear, and to pride.

The inestimable value of the light is such that no amount of work would suffice to assure us of possessing it. Light is beyond price! The highest value of nature, the sublimest treasures of genius or of the human will, remain infinitely disproportionate to it. In the universe there is no measuring stick in common with it, and our costliest sacrifices enable the light to hover over our heads only because they move it's compassionate heart.

The justice of God is always vanquished by his love. And yet, never does it intervene directly; it leaves free reins to the natural interplay of reactions. We are never punished, either for a while or for eternity. When we have disobeyed, we are swept along by the law of disobediences and we remain enchained until the greater part of the damages has been redressed. Naturally, these atonements might take a long time, and seem that much longer, since time lags when one suffers. But they all come to an end. Because of Jesus who offers us recourses through unending graces, we may even hasten that end.

But we must first understand the enactment of the divine encounter. Let us imitate the fishermen chosen. Peter,

Power

James, and John, although consumed by the desire to see the Lord, awaited him in the vicinity of their native lake, performing their humble village tasks. In such a small country, where news spread so rapidly, no doubt they had heard of the child welcomed by the Magi, of this young prophet, of his doctrine, of his miracles. They had not run hither and thither to meet him. Their faith knew, their hope was unquestionable: they had remained home. With such concentrated energies, so much ardor burning silently, so much humility clarified their eyes and rendered their hearts translucid. Beyond the words of the unknown prophet they had heard the Word; beyond the miracle, they had seen the splendor of the Almighty. Let us pray as they did, let us work as they did, and may the Father see that it befalls us as well.

Faith

TRUE ARE THE ancient beliefs (which popular sanction has kept to our day) that they affirm the existence of the genii and of spirits within elements and objects and within mineral or vegetable forms. In fact, everything in the Invisible possesses not only its electric aura, not only its magnetic double, but also its spiritual archetype, its soul endowed with intelligence, sensitivity, and free will. For instance, the alchemist acting upon the mineral reaches its aura; the magnetizer reaches the doubles; the magician orders the spirit of the creature, either by force or by scientific ruse. The only one who commands legitimately is the free-man.

The mountain, the rock, the field; the state, the province, the hamlet; the spring, the brook, the river; the grass, the seed, the forest; the gulf, the ocean, the lake; the house, the room, the furniture; the tool, the book, the letter—all of them constitute the physical body of an invisible being. The various polytheisms are the recognition of these agents and of their power, and the search for the means proper to capture them and to conciliate them. Theoretically, the polytheistic priest needs to acquire a very complex science and an unshakable animic force. Practically, he labors as best can be with its fragmentary knowledge and its fragile will.

To calm a tempest can be done in several ways. One is to use a physical means such as oil and cannon shots. Then there are the fluidic means: since we know about the electro-telluric currents, we must identify the poles of the perturbating whirlwind and annul them by opposing other artificial ones working counter clockwise. Then again, there are (might we say) the idolatrous means, such as the promise or the threat the seaman makes to his God, to a saint, or to a sanctuary of his country. The magician determines the kind of demons that cause the meteorological upset, and sends other agents to combat them: thus is it dealt with on the Barbary coasts and the China seas. There is also the pure and simple prayer addressed to God or to the Virgin. Lastly, there is the procedure of Christ—the effortless command, possible solely to the free-men.

This latter attitude is the one toward which we, his disciples, must aim. For this, there is but one method to follow: by cultivating faith. "Fear and doubt exist that we may not become puffed up!" so says the sage Zhora: one can surmount fear through pride or humility. We must place our confidence in God. Nothing happens to us except through his permission. Moreover, we are all brothers, hence altruism demands that we be happy if trials come upon us rather than upon our brothers. But such abandonment is difficult:

even the infusoria fears for its ephemeral existence. As far as we are concerned, our whole life is but a succession of unjustified fears. This is what we have to react against.

Within us is the germ of faith. For it to grow, let us first, understand the all-divine power. Secondly, let us give our all to each effort. And thirdly, let us realize that when we think we have given our best, we still have a last effort to attempt.

Faith is a substance that exists only in heaven. Its biological mode is supernatural. Intelligence, muscular or magnetic forces, and reasoning have nothing in common with it. Among the forces of the human spirit, only passion and will power have a few points of contact with it. Faith is ignorant, illogical, unlimited; it is the lightning bolt in the dark of the night; it is life where there was none; it is the impossible incarnating upon our demand.

But Christ does not give commands only to the tempests over our seas. Within each being there is a "watery" function. In man, it is his circulatory system; in society, it is commerce; in the Church, it is the edification of its doctrine. Or again: in physiology, Christ is the heart; in our present society, his place is taken by Mammon; in the Church, he is the Mass; in the mathematical sciences, he is called number; in physical nature, the Brahmans call him the black sun; in philosophy, he is verity; in art, he is expression. The tempests that he calms within each of these worlds are disease, error, insignificance, and the indefinite. And everywhere, for everything, and in everything, man must solely rely upon faith to re-establish harmony.

THE KINGDOM OF GOD

Mastery Over the Elements

THE EVANGELISTS have often confirmed the power that Christ exerted over the forces of Nature; for the moment we will merely probe the miracle that took place at the lake Tiberias. Travelers relate many similar feats, and when we check their multiple stories, it seems that there are men on Earth who have command over the clouds, winds, rain, storms, hail, and tempests. Tibetan or Mongolian Lamas, Taoists, Indian fakirs, Arab and Black enchanters, European sorcerers, all seem to possess that power. But there is an essential difference between their procedures and that of Christ. They operate in virtue of a pact, a particular or a tacit one. Most of them give something to some genii or other and in return these genii place themselves at their disposal—this is what is known in popular legends as "selling your soul to the devil."

Even those thaumaturgists who believe they owe their power solely to the rational development of their soul forces, unconsciously clinch a pact with the demons of the mental plane. The mystics alone, by which I mean those men who, whatever be their religion, confine themselves solely to charity and have recourse solely to prayers, can realize legitimate and normal miracles: they ask, and the form of the Word particular to their race grants their request.

Being the supreme Master, whenever Christ (who knows the language of all the categories of creatures) gives a command—they obey. You might answer: "Yes, but, he spoke Aramaic; do the genii of the tempest understand Aramaic?" Of course not; for example, let us take an ordinary man, an orator, a writer. If the sentences he pronounces are but an assembly of words (no matter how clearly expounded), he will make himself understood by the auditors, but he will not sway them, arouse them, or move them. Words alone cannot spark enthusiasm. The orator's exaltation will exalt the audience, will transport them beyond themselves, will stir the fires of spiritual life deeply within them. The more vigorous and rich is the soul of a man, the more it awakens the real intuition and intelligence within other souls. The soul of Christ was teeming in experience, powerful in the triumphs throughout his long incarnation; all he had to do was to address any creature, using any words at all, in any tongue, to be recognized by it and to be obeyed. His physical body, living in any country whatever, used the idiom of the country, just as he wore their garb and followed their customs. But it was his inner being that vitalized these forms of his outward personality—inert by themselves—to make them perfect organs of his will.

Contemplating our contemporaries, we notice that we all dress according to the fashions of the day. And yet some, who wear designer clothes, nonetheless retain a plebeian appearance, while others who wear common, ready-made garments, seem elegant. Many beautiful women wearing fashion designs cannot hold a candle to the simply-attired ones whose demeanor exudes good breeding. I am not giving a course on dandyism, but calling attention to "that something" which may add prestige to individuals physically disadvantaged. In the eyes of an artist, a simple earthenware water jug made by the village potter is often of more value than the vase wrought by a goldsmith. This mystery, in which dwells the essence of beauty—this ineffable quality that permeates the poor terrestrial objects, is one of the reflections from the eternal splendor, the magnificent totality of which is found in Jesus.

THE KINGDOM OF GOD

For the being who has received the Spirit, a miracle is a simple act, as simple as walking and speaking is for us, for that being lives "at one": in unity. He does not, as do many great poets or profound thinkers, have his feet on earth and his head in the clouds—no, all of him is at one on earth as totally as he is at one in the skies. He carries heaven within himself no matter where he goes or whatever he does. So, Jesus did not make any effort to heal, to resuscitate, to change the course of the worlds, to stop the storm, or multiply the bread: he gave an order—his creatures obeyed him.

He to his distraught disciples, "Why are you afraid, you men of little faith?" In fact, our lack of faith in the sole cause of our fears. We are not concerned here with "theological" faith. The faithful believes in the Trinity, in the Immaculate Conception, and in all other dogmas because men in whom he had faith told him that such was the truth. But let these same men, the priests, tell him that Christ can heal or save him from ruin, he does not believe anymore. We accept dogmas that do not offend our terrestrial sensitivity, or agitate us overmuch. But when it comes our health, our savings, or some peril, our material being spins wide, foreseeing nothing but a menacing catastrophe: and faith evaporates.

Accepting certain truths, incomprehensible to our understanding, but which we admit upon authorized testimonies—such as Councils—does not penetrate to the depths of our being. To realize the affirmations of the Apostolic Creed down to their basic material meaning, that alone is faith: "I believe in God, the all-powerful Father"—that if he is all powerful, he can heal me, save me from a fire, stop the bankruptcy; that if I believe him to be my

Power

Father, he will heal and save me; that if I am not convinced that he can do those things, I do not have faith; and that the only sign of my conviction will be the serenity with which I face the perspectives of suffering, of ruin, even death; that if I am perturbed by theses eventualities, I do not have faith.

Let us adhere firmly with our whole will with the total fervor of our love to the words of Christ. This centralized adherence will illuminate our intellect little by little, so that we will eventually understand what at first seemed obscure. Besides, if we succeed to force our body and its instincts to obey the words of the Creed, our faith will start growing, will be alive. Mental belief is not sufficient, animic acceptance is not sufficient. For faith to operate miracles, it must be alive in our corporal being—faith without works is a dead faith.

This veritable faith is susceptible of unlimited developments. It gives us peace of heart, comprehension of mysteries, and thaumaturgical power. But do not confuse this divine force with its caricatures: autosuggestion, mentalism, and an artificially developed will. A religious sect in America claims: "Believe that evil does not exist and you will be healed." That is a philosophical sophism and a volitive illusion. Another religion in Belgium proclaims "Nothing exists unless we believe it to be." Another sophism of Oriental origin, another illusion.

I hope this has been expressed with adequate clearly for you to have sufficient evidence of the antinomy that exists between the faith that Christ offers us and its human counterfeits. May the time and minutiae spent for the training needed to render our personality capable of receiving this divine force not discourage us. Think how much confidence an athlete must have to develop his muscles fiber by fiber; for the virtuoso to limber his fingers, the singer his larynx; for the shopkeeper to amass his fortune one dollar at a time. Let us begin our task, and never stop. once we have started.

The Hosts of Man

WITHIN US there are virtues: powers expressed by invisible, supernatural organs. There are also natural forces such as our mental faculties: these are properly speaking our working tools. There are also the organic forms of the self: vices, faults, passions, the results of past lives, which we have to ameliorate presently. Lastly, we lodge within us hosts and visitors, good or bad—devils for the most part. All these powers grow only through works and are ameliorated only through the purification of the heart. It is useless to know more, needless to try to find the real cause of our sufferings. In fact, we do not know ourselves; what we see of our selves is merely the effect of the internal forces upon the plane of our conscience. The external symptom is the only controllable one.

Any force, having attained its goal, will tend to return to its point of emission; any desire returns to the heart that has generated it. And, as every thing is a being, if our desires are wrong, they end up bringing us the visit of demons. That is why we find obsessed people. On the other hand, to be obeyed, one must prove one's superiority. Hence an evil being will only capitulate to the one who shows that he is the stronger, and a devil heeds only the one he has never been able to disconcert. That is why it is so difficult to cure mental derangement, and how Christ drove out the devils.

Power

Yet the Evangelists relate how the unclean spirits that obsessed the Gadarene man entered into a herd of swine that rushed at full speed down into the sea. Yes, the human spirit is worth much more than that of animals. But such a procedure seems rather illicit, since true healing does not consist in dislodging the evil, but in transmuting it. Though Jesus, Master of life, had the right of taking it away or of changing its form at his good pleasure, he granted solace to the demoniacal legion by not throwing it back into the infernal hells. The animals that were precipitated thus into death benefited from a more rapid evolution, the owner of the herd paid one of his debts, and other men were thus preserved from the long delay that an obsession inevitably causes.

Contrary to his habitual silence, this is one time that Jesus ordered the man to tell about the miracle of which he had been the beneficiary. The reason was that when we speak, not only men hear us another multitude of ears is open, on watch, trying to overhear the marvelous things we say, which might be of benefit to them. It was essential for the spirits of the waters to learn about the presence of God, and for other beings also—for whom we are gods. This is one of the reasons that when we converse upon serious, profound subjects, we must pay attention to our words. In fact, but a few hours later, in the presence of five persons, Jesus—having resuscitated the daughter of Jairus—ordered all of them to keep it secret. And he did so again shortly after in the case of the two blind men.

This different conduct was dictated by the state of the milieu: to prevent scandal, to spread the light only in the measure wherein the auditors are capable of it, and not to use means that bring about human glorification. In that way, heaven acts as if it were not acting, allowing all men their free-will, thus offering them the chance of being more meritorious. Man need not, then, be consciously concerned with his invisible hosts: he needed only act wisely, and all his inferiors will participate in the benefits of the light that increases within him.

Intuition

MAN MAY RECEIVE communications from very distant or from secret places—or rather, we should say it is his spirit that communicates with the rest of the world. But only a part of the messages received by him reaches his conscience, because perception does not take place unless there exists a magnetic correspondence in the nerve cells of the receiver to which it addresses itself. This correspondence is but the result of the intellectual perfecting of the said nerve cells—or better still, of their spiritual purification. The individual cell, just as the individual man or the individual planet, acquires true knowledge only in the measure wherein it frees itself from sin, that is, frees itself from the tyranny of the self. The same goes for all modalities of universal life: the stones, plants, animals, fluids, genii, spirits; arts, sciences, religions, philosophies, societies, and stars evolve in like manner. There is no need here to offer additional detail concerning this development—you will find them easily by yourselves, if it is necessary.

But let us return to the individual man. If he is conscious of but a minimal part of the messages that the physical, soul, and intellectual worlds send him, then the field of his receptivity will broaden in proportion to the number of walls he himself will have pulled down—walls that his selfishness built. So will he pay the debts that his lack of foresight contracted and compensate for the havoc he wrought round about him.

Evolution goes from bottom to top, from the periphery towards the center; the higher one climbs the broader the horizon; the more we live interiorly, the more secrets are revealed to us.

As the life of the individual tends towards the life of the universe; as our spirit is assigned to lower or higher abodes according to its qualifications; as it cannot pass from one to the other without crossing the gates of death—it follows that its relationship with the rest of the world grows subject to the essential altitude of its residence. Hence, in the end, the perfect man inhabits in the center of the world, the place where everything is similar, coordinated, synthesized, and unified. From then on, his connections are only with the real "types," the real figures of creatures, instead of settling with their apparent forms. He understands the language of things and of beings and can answer them all. At the same time, he possesses authority and makes himself obeyed because he never wants anything but the will of God.

Christ is that free-man—everything in him possesses a clear, pure, exquisite conscience. All the points of his body are just so many brains (so to say) obedient and swift. Each cell is a love filled with a heart filled with a vivifying virtue. And all—receivers and distributors—fulfill their roles in a perfect spirit of abnegation.

Therefore, there was nothing startling in the healing of the woman with the flow of blood. I have been a witness to two analogous cases. One evening, someone came and said to a man I know, "Sir, I have a tubercular friend. She cannot get up anymore, neither feed herself nor sleep. The physicians say she will not last a week. I beg you to do something for her." That man affirmed to me that he had not even thought of asking for her healing at that moment. And yet the next day someone came to tell him that she was up and about—and she has lived in excellent health for the past twenty years. Another time, someone came to beg this same gentleman to see to it that the removal of a cancer to a stomach be successful. The operation was booked for the next morning. As in the preceding case, nothing was asked, and yet the patient was up and about the next morning to receive the doctors and to send them away because, as he asserted, he did not suffer anymore—and the fact is that no symptoms of the disease ever returned.

It may be also be that the force of the Spirit acts independently of the will of the transmitter whom it chose. Thus it was that the woman cited in the gospel (Luke 8:43–48; Mark 5:25–34) was healed before Christ could speak to her, which is why he told her: "Thy faith has brought thee recovery," alluding most likely to the moral cure rather than to the pathological cure.

Let us note how faith functions. This woman knows she is incurable. She has tried everything and is ruined. She has no more hope. She knows Jesus only by reputation but she comes to him alone without friends. She does not expect to receive a word from him or to ask him anything, not even to look at him face to face. She comes up behind Jesus, touches his cloak, and says to herself "I shall be healed," thus hoping for the impossible, dominating her fear.

Now, timidity is often quite difficult to overcome. It might have profound roots in us due to a fear of our spirit, accustomed as it was to a different world, and now put in

Power

contact with forms, beings, and customs totally foreign to it. That is the reason we must overcome this weakness each time the occasion presents itself. Is not heaven with us? Do we not have to experience criticism and jeers, scoffs and mockery?

Checkmate

IF THE LIGHT is a triumphant flame, it is always repulsed, as is the assault to the waves striking the reef; how many times has a rock reduced a billow to a powerless foam? But the dark night is close at hand when, undermined in the deep, the rock will be shattered to dust in the gulf of its patient enemy.

Cycles after cycles, races after races, years after years, minutes after days, heaven offers itself tirelessly to man and to the devil; and both avidly grasp this food and drink using their rejuvenated forces to satisfy their wellbeing.

But love, ceaselessly immolated, struggles in these shadows of selfishness, until the day comes when the creature feels something within—it is remorse, the dawn of the triumph of love. This sun might take thousands of years to pierce through the clouds but it will pierce through them.

To predisposed eyes, the victory of heaven wears the mantle of defeat; because its operation surpasses understanding, it seems to us incomprehensible and unreasonable; that is why it belonged to the domain of faith and why the incredulity of the compatriots of Christ prevented the miracle.

In fact, faith rests upon mystery and the unknown; a thaumaturgist whom one has seen playing games with his child on a public square, whose home and family are

THE KINGDOM OF GOD

known to us, loses his prestige. The reasoning mind of spectators shuts the door to intuitive secrets; they are scandalized at this derogation of their habits, of this upset to the established order; they build a dike to divert the bed of the river of grace away from themselves.

What is the work of the missioner, the one chosen for a mission? As Isaiah explains it: it is sextuple. The one who has received the baptism of the spirit must restore courage and hope to those who vegetate in privations, those that no one seems to take out of the mire of poverty, of ignorance, of solitude—to them, he brings the key of the celestial treasure.

In those who suffer from a broken heart, he awakens desire, enthusiasm and faith; he enables them to go back to work; he gives them the prescience of beatitude so as to obliterate the acerbity of the temporal loves they lost.

To those who have neither moral nor meritorious credits, those whom the police forces to labour without salary so as to pay off their debts, he donates the salary of his own sufferings, he enables them to start working for their own benefit.

There are others who have turned their sight, their eyes as well as their hearts away from the light; just as an unused organ atrophies from lack of use, so they have lost the faculty to see. It is a difficult cure to operate and is possible only to the veritable therapeut.

The unjust persecution, which a small number of "men of goodwill" are subjected to, those who have refused to render a cult to the gods of money, glory and ruse must be made to cease. These men who are the obscure, unknown servants of heaven have the right to some respite from time to time; a time of rest; a shelter must be prepared for them not only in thought but physically; a small corner of the earth, an oasis must be arranged for them to live in peace with their family.

Lastly, heaven is not concerned only with human beings, there are innumerable hierarchies which demand Its assistance. The refection of all these beings, reorganizing them, revamping the directive forces, cultivating spiritual lands, finding the men whose names are inscribed in the Book of Life, allocating them into the appropriate families, choosing an expedient science, such are the few aims which he, whom heaven has chosen to establish the foundations of his reign, must regulate.

To fulfill such a formidable task, a solid organism and an iron constitution are essential. Yet, human nature could not resist to such pressure were it is not aided—but that is not our concern. Let us look around us and find someone who is calumniated by many people, there is a great possibility that he is an envoy of God.

CHAPTER II

Apostolate

HEN JESUS BROUGHT his twelve disciples together, he sent them two by two to preach the kingdom of God, giving them power to cast out the impure spirits, to heal all diseases and all infirmities. He sent them forth after having given them these instructions:

"You do not have to go among the Gentiles or pagans, nor enter into a city of Samaria; but rather, go to the lost sheep of the house of Israel. During your travels, proclaim that the kingdom of God is at hand. Heal the sick, raise the dead, cleanse the lepers, cast out devils.

"Give freely as you have been freely given.

"Take nothing along for your journey; take neither gold, silver, nor change in your pockets; neither a knapsack nor bread for the road, neither two coats nor shoes, nor staff; for the workman is worthy of his maintenance. Whatever town or village you enter, find out who is worthy of sheltering you and lodge there until your departure.

"Upon entering the house, wish it well and say: Peace be upon this house. And if the house is worthy of it, peace shall descend upon that house. But if the house is not worthy of it, the peaceful blessings will return to you.

"If you are not made welcome and your words are not heeded, shake the dust from your feet upon leaving both the house and that city. In truth, I say unto you, the fate of the cities of Sodom and Gomorrah will be preferable to that of the city you left, on the day of judgment.

"I am sending you as sheep among wolves; therefore be as prudent as serpents and as innocent as doves.

"Be wary of men; they will deliver you to the tribunals; they will scourge you in their synagogues and you shall be brought before their governors and kings because of me, for my sake, to be a testimony against them and the Gentiles. But when they hand you over, take no thought of how and what you shall say. All of that will be given you at the time, as it is not you but the Spirit of the Father who will speak in you.

"A brother shall deliver his brother to death and a father his child; and the children shall rise against their parents and will cause their death; you shall be hated by all men for my name's sake. But he who perseveres to the end, that one shall be saved.

"When they shall persecute you in one city, flee to another; for in truth, you shall not have ended your task throughout the cities of Israel before the arrival of the Son of Man.

"Verily, I declare that the disciple is no better than his master, nor a servant than his Lord. It suffices for the disciple to be like his master and for the servant like his Lord. Be happy that you are aware of these things, provided that you put them into practice. If they have called the head of the household Beelzebub, won't they call the members of his household doubly so?

"Do not fear them, because anything which has been veiled will be revealed, and anything hidden will be made known. What I tell you under the cover of

Apostolate

darkness, bring it out into the light; what I have told you secretly in your ear, proclaim it from the housetops.

"Do no fear those who kill the body, because they cannot kill the soul; but rather, fear the one who can destroy both the soul and the body in Gehenna.

"Are we not able to purchase two sparrows for less than a penny? Yet not one of them can fall upon the ground without the Father's will. As for you, every hair on your head has been counted. Hence, have no fear; are you not worth more than a lot of sparrows?

"Any man who acknowledges me before men, I too shall acknowledge him before the Father. But whoever shall deny me before men, I too shall deny him before my Father in heaven.

"Do not think that I came to bring peace on earth; I did not come to bring peace but the sword. Because I have come to set discord between a man and his father, a daughter against her mother, a daughter-in-law against her mother-in-law. So a man's enemies will be those of his own home.

"He who loves his father and mother more than me is not worthy of me; and he who loves a son or daughter more than me is not worthy of me; and he who does not take up his cross to follow me is not worthy of me.

"He who secures his life will lose it, while he who loses his life because of me will save it.

"Whoever welcomes you welcomes me, and whoever welcomes me receives him who sent me. Whoever heeds you, heeds me; he who rejects you rejects me. And whoever rejects me, rejects the One who sent me.

THE KINGDOM OF GOD

"Whoever welcomes a prophet in the capacity of a prophet shall receive the recompense due a prophet; and who welcomes a just man in the capacity of a just man, shall receive the due to just men.

"And he who gives merely a glass of water to any of these little ones because he is a disciple of mine, truly, he shall not lose his reward.

"You, you are among those who have persevered with me during my tribulations. Thus I am inclined in your favor to the kingdom, just as my Father inclined in my favor; so that you will be able to eat and drink at my table, in my kingdom, and for you to be seated upon thrones to judge the twelve tribes of Israel.

"I am not referring to all of you. I know those I have chosen; but it is essential that this word of the Scriptures be fulfilled: 'He who has shared my bread has lifted his heel against me.'

"I am telling you this before it comes to pass, so that when it has occurred, you will acknowledge who I am.

"Whoever loves his life shall lose it and whoever hates his life in this world, will keep it to live eternally. Let him who wants to follow me become my servant! Because there where I am, so shall my servant be. If anyone serves me, my Father will do him credit.

"Whoever believes in me, it is in him who sent me and not in me he believes, and whoever sees me, sees the One who sent me."

When he had finished giving his instructions to the twelve disciples, Jesus left them to go to teach and preach in the towns of the land. Then they left, going forth from town to town announcing the Good Word. They were preaching repentance. They continued

Apostolate

driving out many demons, anointing many sick people with oil and healing them.[1]

Compassion

WHY DOES THE MISSION of Christ assert itself besides words through his healing of diseases?—Because man is still enmired in physical matter; his body absorbs a lot of his attention and if as the proverb says: "It's no use preaching to a hungry man," so the person suffering from hunger pangs will not heed a preacher's discourse.

For physical words to penetrate into our heart, the heart must be open; if it is concentrated upon a subject, especially if crushed by sorrow, this temporary monodeism shuts it in and our ears are closed.

That is why the person who speaks to the sick must be a radiant being if he wants the drug, or the fluid to operate fully; if he wants divine force to restore, to reconstruct the missing organ, if he wants the Consoler to transform corner of hell into a paradise.

He must be as compassionate as his Master, he must understand the distressed, their qualms of conscience, groaning inwardly with them, yet maintaining a serene, smiling face. Let his heart become a vast hostel wherein any wayfarer finds comfort and solace. There must be a room in that inn reserved for the Friend, but the rest is at the disposal of the travelers. Such a man must never regret spending his time, efforts, intelligence, and kindness; neither

---

[1] Matt. 9:35–38; Luke 10:2; Matt. 10:5–11:1; Mark 6:7–13; Luke 9:1–6; 12:4–12; 6:40; 12:51–53 17:33; John 13:16–17; 15:20; 12:25–26, 44–45.

must he expect anything in return for his work. He must labor through obedience; he must love all beings and all things because they are children of his Master. Today, he has to take care of these. Tomorrow, there will be others. In the measure wherein he remains impersonal, anonymous, and serene, will his work be perfect.

The Search for the Divine

THE RESTLESS MINDS that neither philosophy nor science can satisfy seem to abound more and more in our days.

Desire for the Absolute, thirst for the Infinite, fervor toward Perfection, rise up within us imperiously with such energy that, in spite of ourselves, we start our march toward the Ideal. What things does desire—father of the will—have to worry about? There are three.

In the first or lowest category one finds matter, comfort, laziness, sloth, rest, inertia, sleep—in short, the *far-niente* upon all planes, the physical as well as the intellectual.

In the second category one finds the thirst for possessions, conquering, enjoyment, discovery, conflict—in short, it is the exaltation of the self such that we work ceaselessly without rest, and learn to sacrifice some pleasure to obtain another, whether in the religious, social, economic, or individual domains.

The third category is unveiled only at the gray dawn of satiety—in short, when the self finds that inertia is suicidal, and activity *per se* but an illusion, it seeks life and reality elsewhere. Having realized that work is necessary and obligatory, the searching self begins to inquire after an eternal goal, since all temporal goals have dwindled away more or less quickly. And so the self finds this goal above and beyond

Apostolate

money, power, glory, science, love, and other beings—in God alone.

The prudent ones then return to their natal religion, to the dogmas and rites in which they find consolation and solace. The adventurous ones veer toward schools of liberal spiritualism.

The spiritualistic theories currently in vogue are tied to ancient esoteric mysteries. They fatally abut upon Oriental non-activity or non-performance. The adepts of said mysteries say: "Before being able to help my brothers, I must first attain perfection." In saying this, however, they forget that because man is a child of God, his real possibilities lie far beyond the Relative, and that everything he shall be capable of achieving by himself will naturally reach limits no matter how vast they may be.

None of our achievements will fill the infinite void of our heart. Only one issue will take us out of this impasse—being children of God and his heirs. All we need do to await our inheritance is consecrate our days to the usual tasks the forms of which are multiple but whose conscience will always bring their characteristics back to the essential quality of moral perfection.

Only one method exists that suits all intellects, all good wills, in all situations: it is the gospel.

The gospel is the principle of Christianity whose unique dogma is faith in the divinity of Christ, and whose unique law is love for one's fellowman.

Of all Christian doctrines, the Catholic path offers the truest teachings and the richest blooms, the most vigorous methods. But there are hearts that find its prudent economy seemingly too slow, its dogmatism too rigid. Can we criticize their impatience for freedom? No, because it urges them to action. Christ will not reject them because of their daring; has he not said that the kingdom of God belongs to the violent? If these enthusiasts climb the slopes of the mystical mountain, choosing the paths of the sheep-herders, would Jesus, from whom comes all flames, abandon them?

Quite to the contrary, he will send them an extraordinary guide, since in order to come to him they have not feared using extraordinary means. They do not comprehend the language of theology, only the one of experience. They will not heed the elemental spirits nor the gods, but only he who, descending from the summit, comes to meet them, proves his mission to them, and wins their trust.

The only one who can lead men is he who by experience knows their needs, their weaknesses, their desires—he who has nurtured the same hopes and trod the same paths. The only one who can lead men is the one whom the Father authorizes to draw from his Treasure, who can hold the princes of darkness at bay and shoulder the load of many; he who possesses perfect purity along with liberty; in short, he who is God as well as Man.

How can we meet this Unknown? Balzac explained it: "Science is still searching for what love has found."

In fact, we enter here into the domain of the irrational Impossible. It is inconceivable that the Absolute may manifest itself in the Relative. Intelligence, whose movement is essentially logical, will never cross the boundaries of the finite. Sentiment alone is capable of it, provided that a severe and persevering discipline sublimizes it, for usually it sidles along, deforming itself according to the innumerable phantoms of egoism; but it is possible to pull it pull it out of the swamp by it to ignite only for universal objects and

Apostolate

ends. It then becomes love, and nothing in the world can stand in its way.

If the essence of the human soul is liberty, its characteristic attribute is the act. Consequently, as action is that which demands the greatest output of energy, and as the purest energy is the one that thwarts our selfishness, no matter what label we adorn it with, the human being will never attain his true stature or fulfill its law unless he dedicates himself wholeheartedly to the works of that pure love whose commands and fruits are delineated in the gospel.

The singular merit of the gospel, far from establishing a debilitating doctrine (as the devotees of the self strongly claim), offers a most rigorous code such as no religious legislator ever before dared promulgate. Wisdom in ancient times proclaimed that the greatest victory is over the self, and never showed indulgence toward the weak. The gospel demands that we battle against this self, which is our fulcrum or base of operation. As the effort exerted for this battle is superhuman, man must find another support upon which to rely, something other than himself; moreover, this base of support cannot be the world because that is exactly what we have to overcome. So, what remains beyond man and beyond the world, if not God?

That is the indispensability of Christ, for Christ is the tangible form of God. Therefore, unless it be founded upon and directed towards him, any inner effort will only result in some wisdom or some virtue whose fruits will never ripen under the sun of the living eternity.

The universe appears to be an extremely complicated network of crisscrossing roads of communication traveled by all creatures; their junctions are so close together that at a moment's notice travelers must choose between two roads: the narrow or the broad. The first is the path of the gospel: the sacrifice of self in the name of the Word, Jesus. The second includes all the other methods: whether laical morals or religious ritualism (albeit in the latter category there are some shorter, hence better, roads than others).

But, whether we choose the first or the second path, we will have to march. Marching, spiritually speaking, means making an *effort* toward God. This is why all religious codes resemble one another. There is, however, an art to walking, which is where religious forms differ. There are also states of soul that make of the voyage either a fastidious ordeal or a fortifying, outdoor exercise out in the pure air of life. There is also a third characteristic in this true search for the divine: joy or cheerfulness.

The first is application of intensity in the effort. The second is certitude in our succeeding, because of the interest God bestows upon our effort. As for the third, mystical buoyancy or joy, it constitutes a criterion as to the quality of our effort. In fact, the optimism essential to our success is a mental attitude based upon having confidence in our good star, or in self-confidence; but joy or cheerfulness is based upon our faith in God—in God alone.

The Harvesters

CREATURES, CREATED BEINGS do not always follow their same tasks; from time to time spiritual nations, are remolded, recast, and their citizens allocated to new places in different frameworks. These reorganizations, these judgments among other goals, are to separate the servants of God from the servants of the devil. This is what Jesus calls a harvest; and the harvesters are the soldiers of heaven. They

Apostolate

have an arduous task. They must seek here and there for those they must lead, care for them, teach them, guide them, and keep them clear of wide-strewn, sharp-toothed traps; they must assemble them, plan their invisible itineraries, prepare the site of the future paradise, complete the action of divine mercy, through prayers wrest a few more souls away from error. They are the incarnation of the Father's solicitude, because the coming of the kingdom of God is not a metaphysical concept, but a most visible, material, and social reality.

Crops, however, cannot be harvested before all ears are ripe. The divine Farmer visits his fields and orders a surplus of fertilizer to be spread over the tardy, late harvest. His valets come and go in the world, helping one, healing another, teaching a third, bringing to still another a salutary test. But do, please, understand that they are merely instruments; they wear no other distinctive signs than that of their humility, and are generally mocked; they do not act of their own accord; they are moved by the Spirit, and are seldom are aware of being missioners.

These unknown servants are the greatest among men, yet unaware of their roles. You will not be able to reach them by taking on the visible appearance of their prerogatives; we must patiently and in faith await the order that the Father will send us, either through a set of circumstances, or (in a more precise but less frequent manner) through the voice of one of his Friends.

How the Harvest is Gathered

THE FARM-HANDS of the Farmer, though they work hard, do not have a task beyond their strength. One does not reap all the wheat of a country at one time; and in a field, the workers enter on one side in the morning and exit on the opposite side in the evening. This is how Jesus sends his apostles: first in Israel, then later to the schismatics and to the pagans. However, the action of heaven always conforms to the comprehension of creatures, and to that end submits to the laws of space and time.

In this order of Christ, we notice that our spiritual influence spreads similarly to any radiating force. Any man in whom heaven revivifies the divine flame must first revive those around him. This flame is the center of a sphere, the circumference of which expands from day to day. It starts with the intellectual faculties, then the physical force, then the etheric-fluidic powers that begin to feel the warmth of that hearth; it then permeates the objects, the beings, and our immediate surrounding, which benefit from it; then the action spreads to our fellowmen, our compatriots, all our brothers, in both in the visible and invisible spheres.

Whether we look at created individual and social beings, or at scientific, esthetic, philosophical, religious, or cosmic creatures, we notice that wherever the divine Sower drops a seed, it is exactly the one meant for the characteristics and particular virtues of that field or plane: everything in the universe follows a preconceived plan and is regulated in an impeccable manner, down to its least detail.

Why does Christ send his disciples forth two at a time? Apart from motives of prudence or material convenience, there had to be, following the promise he had made to be present when two people met in his name, an initiatory reality. The presence of the Word in a physical, hyperphysical, or psychic spot causes such a powerfully dynamic discharge that, in order to produce its full effect on earth, it

Apostolate

needs a support, a corporeal organism capable of receiving its smallest fragments in full. That is why men who may be used as channels to divine action are so rare.

All the cells of their body, all the currents of their ethers, all the sparks of their thought, must become *in toto* docile instruments of the power that has chosen them. Such perfect receptivity is so difficult to find, that the angels who transit the energies of the Father (which are the energies *per se*) generally give but one power to each of the soldiers through whom Jesus manifests himself on earth. One teaches, one heals, the third consoles, another prophesies, another invents; in spite of the work thereby shared, the force of the Spirit soon consumes their organisms, which are nevertheless the purest among the pure.

The Savior therefore matched, or rather paired off, his missionaries by harmonizing their individualistic capacities so that each couple would continue representing the two poles of a terrestrial current ready to answer the call of one of the powers of the Holy Spirit—the Master, himself personally concentrating, distributing, and radiating the seventh or supreme gift.

The work of these harvesters is one: it is to put light in the darkness; and triple: it is to re-establish harmony in the domain of idea, in the domain of the body, and in the domain of the invisible. You are already aware of all that matters regarding teaching and the healing of diseases. As to the third work—chasing away demons—thus far we have only studied that power in the spirit of man. But there are demons everywhere.

Our body, our spirit, our thought, the three kingdoms of nature, localities, houses, the atmosphere—all are inhabited by demons who act therein as in conquered lands. To send them packing is not an easy task, but those who have been assigned this work are taught and armed for this purpose. It is needless for us here to expand on methods useful toward this end.

Conduct of the Harvesters

THE HONEST LABORER accepts a salary only from the man who has hired him. In a similar manner, when heaven puts a power into our hand, within our eyes, or upon our lips, we are obligated to develop it, not by using more or less esoteric methods, but by *exercising* it.

If we are very brave, let us seek out the sick, the hopeless, the ignorant, the unbelieving, and try to heal them first by our strength, our hope, our science or our faith, and then by prayer. If we are less brave, if we fear the inevitable backlash which the descent of the light into the darkness will provoke, let us wait until the sickly, the needy ask us for help.

But it may be that whatever we do, the disease will contaminate us, that despair and doubt will overcome us. It matters not; let us pray secretly, then all the strength and courage we possess will be restored.

The one who acts by virtue of heaven does not have the right to demand a salary for his cures or lessons. Since he did not acquire his powers or knowledge through his own efforts, he must share them at no charge; at the very most, he may accept money *offered* him.

Let us understand that these regulations, and those following, apply to the men who have received an order personally from the mouth of Christ incarnate. Do not rely upon your own clairaudience or clairvoyance, for discern-

Apostolate

ment within our minds is a rare faculty and we cannot know the origin of our hyperphysical sensations with certitude. Let us be content, we the masses, to fulfill our duty upon earth. To want to follow the lifestyle of the "soldiers" of Christ is far too difficult: with the best of intentions we would deceive ourselves and cheat others.

But the one into whose ear God speaks directly need have no cares. Let him not be concerned with money, raiment, or housing: nothing in him must belong to the prince of this world. There are beings from the invisible worlds who are committed to preparing everything for him in advance; and if the chosen hosts do not conduct themselves worthily towards the workman of the Lord, they will be held accountable on account of the eminence of the Master. Remember, it is not the form of the act that matters, but its direction; and the least visit from heaven is worth more than all treasures in nature.

In the midst of the world, the apostles are like "lambs surrounded by wolves." Material life is to cut each others' throat, to enrich oneself at any price. Nature's children covet all forms of energy, and more especially so if they gather them with an eye to being as splendid as those belonging to the servants of God. In truth, their effort to despoil them so relentlessly belies a striving to smother their own conscience.

As our duty is the care of our body and of the forces for which it is a vehicle, one must be prudent. Look at the world—things, beings, sciences, opinions, phenomena—everything is a sign. Open your eyes and ears, study, weigh-up, analyze, then ask heaven to clarify your diagnosis.

It is not too difficult, but nonetheless essential, to remain simple. Our unity, our oneness, proceeds from our simplification, and our power proceeds from our unity. Man's role is important: superior powers flow into and through him; inferior forces stream towards him; he is the crossroads wherein involution meets evolution. He must be able to receive from the six corners of space, as the ancient hierograms state; he must be a city that is both open and diligently defended, for he can only transmit upwards or downwards after tinting with his own light what has been received from below or above.

And if all the avenues of the human beings and all the monuments of the city-with-the-seven-doors can see nothing but visitors animated from the same spirit, it is by practicing simplicity that man will obtain this peaceful inner harmony. What undoes us is not variety of work, but diversity of will. Accomplishing twenty tasks with one intention in view unifies; switching goals twenty times for one task disperses and dilapidates our energies.

Conforming to the exigencies of life while maintaining deeply within us a sole passion for heaven is the simple man's most dignified behavior; by this means he retains the clearest intellectual lucidity and the most realizable, powerful energy.

The ewe surrounded by wolves feels lost, is panic-stricken, and behaves just as expected so as to be outwitted and then devoured. The prudence and simplicity Jesus recommends are in such cases our best protection. Foremost comes prudence, since we should not awaken the hostile covetousness of those who do not belong to our Master by permitting them to perceive our intimate and mystical privileges. And then simplicity, because it is the means that best foils the pitfalls of cunning.

The first practical application of this advice is that our

Apostolate

quality for discipleship or as an apprentice-disciple does not permit us to be exploited, because it is not only we whom our enemies strike: indirectly, it is those left in our charge; and directly, it is our body and the diverse faculties that were entrusted to us and that on Judgment Day we will have to return in accrued and enriched forms.

Many good people imagine that all one has to do is sit and wait for a fortune to drop in his lap from heaven. Others believe that all they have to do is spend the minimum of time earning a living, and are discouraged and surprised that heaven does not add a surplus to their bare necessities. All of which adds up to a false mysticism; it is quietism.

It is a duty, a strict obligation to work hard, to exert ourselves doing manual labor, to bestir ourselves in commercial ventures, to invent and scheme in liberal profession—even more so than do the positivists and utilitarian minds that rely upon themselves to become rich and to accumulate honors. The disciple must not limit the benefits of his activities in the practical world, because, were he to do that, he would limit the possibilities of the material and intellectual status of his family, of his servants and employees; he would restrict the small ambit of the sound life over which he has influence, and, almost always, such is but laziness fearing the effort. Yes, it is far easier to sigh than to perform physical labor or to tire our brain with sustained mental effort.

Our duty as disciples is not to live at the expense of anyone; aside from those who beg or whose low economic state must be subsidized by welfare societies, anyone who does not augment the monetary, industrial, commercial, intellectual, or artistic capital lives at the expense of society. Try to earn a little more than bare necessities. When your wife and children have all their reasonable needs met, and you have provided for their essential comfort, education, and instruction according to your standing, then the rest will be for your charitable interests. Be as ascetic as you want, but do not let your family suffer from it.

Your duty as a disciple means that your charities be at the expense of your own comfort, and out of your own purse; and that you do not have someone else do it, for you have seen kind-hearted souls who naively had friends donate money to notorious cadgers who geared others to buy worthless paintings, to find jobs for incapable people, resulting in those donors deeply resenting being thus taken in and who on that account become forever disgusted with charity. These so-called spiritual amateurs, lacking common sense, thought they had done a good deed. It never entered into their mind that because they lacked a few dollars they could have endured personal privations in order to strengthen their prayerful demand in favor of their protegés. Yet, are we not aware that prayers can provoke physical miracles when this prayer is valid; some of us have experienced it.

Your duty as a disciple, following the same economic line, is not to bury what you have in excess of your needs, but on the contrary, to make it fruitful either materially by furthering new enterprises, or spiritually by giving alms. The will of heaven is that we augment life in all fields.

In a word, take much trouble, like the most ambitious of upstarts, while depriving yourself personally like the avaricious, detaching yourself from success like the ascetics, while being generous, as if what you are giving had not cost you anything to acquire.

The habit of such a frame of mind is the best way to

Apostolate

learn prudence and simplicity. Generally speaking, you are simple in the good sense of the word, but you lack prudence and a sense of practicability. You launch yourself into businesses without having analyzed them fully: you are unaware of the techniques needed for their realizations, what others have done in similar cases, what are the means of success, and who the possible competitors are. This denotes laziness. Unconsciously, you think "I do not know exactly where I am headed, but heaven will help me!" No—heaven won't help. An adult walks only because he stumbled for many months when a little child. We are on earth to develop all terrestrial possibilities, not merely celestial possibilities—as to the latter, it is heaven that develops them within us; as to the former, it is up to us to cultivate them.

We must educate ourselves, whatever our profession. See the facts as they are and not as we imagine or wish them to be. There is a laziness of the body as well as a laziness of the mind and of the will. Shake yourself up! Were God to give you everything because your intentions are good, he would be doing you a disservice: your spiritual future would be lost. Before God grants us the impossible, we must have tried all of our possibles. Who among us can truly say: "I have done everything I could?"

Simultaneously, keep this precious simplicity—this inestimable gift of heaven—and after having laid the groundwork, studied all facets of your enterprise, weighed the pros and cons, evaluated the competition, calculated the profits, start your endeavor wholeheartedly and put yourself in God's hands—that is simplicity. When clever competitors assail you, set traps, and baffle you with their discursive discussions, give them only the essentials—that is simplicity.

THE KINGDOM OF GOD

Keep your equanimity lucid, realistic—that is simplicity. Not to lie is simplicity. And to gather all arrogances into one sheaf of obedience and confidence in God is supreme simplicity.

Grandeur, force, nobility are simple. Vanity is simple. Beauty is but a subtle simplification, rich in heterogeneous elements. Simplicity differs in essence from ignorance, stupidity. or coarseness. Because it is a slow process of a thousand diverse forces, simplicity demands a very great deal of internal work along with numerous daily and experimental notions—the process of which is regulated, and the results coordinated, by prudence. Prudence governs your external acts; simplicity governs you internally. You can show your prudence; but, if your adversaries realize that you are simple, they will attack you increased cynicism.

Wisdom is the realistic and practical conciliation of all the couples of opposite faculties and opposite virtues. Consult the gospel in that spirit, and you will see your incertitudes disappear: the whole secret is to will adequately.

Spiritual simplicity is a rectitude of judgment that abolishes having useless qualms of conscience regarding our selves or our acts. We can be sincere without being simple; we might not lie, yet worry unnecessarily of being mistaken. Whoever is scrupulous is not simple, is not at ease, nor puts others at ease either; rather, he is either lured by the external or worried and absorbed by his interior being.

The disciple who aims at simplicity begins by ridding himself or detaching himself from external objects so as to apply his time towards self-amelioration. Then he begins to be concerned about God, to fear him; he worries about not fearing him enough—a concern that is quite useful and teaches him to know himself better. But as soon as God

Apostolate

allows him peace, he must grab it and try to preserve it; he must lean towards being less self-absorbed and more absorbed in God. Then God makes him progressively aware of his faculties. When the disciple stops composing an artificial personage, he liberates himself, shunning both fear and presumption.

The principal effort demanded of us is our willingness to totally abandon any personal interest and be convinced that all that happens is just what is needed for our advancement. Acquiescence procures simplicity.

First and foremost, we must not try to be simple, or speak of ourselves with affected modesty, self-depreciation, or complacency. Humble words often conceal vanity. We must work with courage, live with optimism, and trust in God. During periods of indifference, depression, aridity, languor, distractions, we gather the best fruit, because in spite of these obstacles we still fulfill our duties. In short, simplicity is a fruit of abandonment.

Everything is connected: acceptance of sufferings, renunciation, confidence, obedience, prayer, simplicity, perseverance depend upon and engender one another as we march toward God. Our greatest obstacles come from within: if we are not attentive, we risk dissipation; if we are too careful, too scrupulous, too uptight, we bring on melancholy.

Dissipation is not cured by restraint or forceful meditations, for we are by nature incurably dissipated. Thus, God alone, and not nature, can administer the remedy.

During these periods, first of all let us turn toward God, accept our limitations, endure mental infirmities to the bitter end. We obtain fixity of heart only after having endured its agitation. We must concentrate our energies upon the task at hand—the hour following will take care of the next problem. It matters not if our imagination errs on a thousand ideas, provided that the bottom of our heart remains focused upon God. Let your distraction fall by the wayside, just as you would ignore the bark of a snarling dog. Each time your mind drifts, drawn away by something, close your eyes, shut your ears, and call upon God. You will not find peaceful contemplation by yourself; it will only come from God. Otherwise, you will become constrained, melancholic, and refractory.

When the Word withdraws the sensation of his presence, do not be concerned; it is time to put your faith to work. What we must guard against is to create artificially by dint of reasoning and auto-suggestion an image of the divine presence within us. During the course of the day, amid the details of your occupations, be content to aim a glance and a thought peacefully toward God. One becomes distracted by fearing distractions and regretting having had them. When a traveler sets out in the morning, he first checks out the various items he thinks he will need; he does not stop thereafter at every other step to check if he will pursue his trip. Do not look back. If you fall a hundred times, get up a hundred times. Do everything with God in mind. Love of God is our fundamental strength.

If this seems too simplistic, it because the self loves complications. It fancies that to advance it must fuss and struggle. How wrong that is! God takes care of our advance; all we have to do is follow his impelling force. However numerous our professional charges may be, we must first meet them, but do so for God's sake, in view of God; in this way, they will they serve us for spiritual advancement. We are mistaken when we think that prayer is invalid unless supported with transports of delight. To the con-

Apostolate

trary, the arid and painful prayer goes further. Do not confuse the ardor of imagination or psychic sensitivity with that total offering of oneself that alone constitutes prayer. Any spiritual gratification is a gratuitous, unmerited gift to which we have no right. Love thrives way beyond this—love feeds upon privations.

Were we to utilize fully all the good thoughts that swarm spontaneously in our minds, our carelessness and blunders would diminish, and the Father would give us more. We resemble the spoiled brats who soon tire of their latest toy and immediately wish for another, which they will just as quickly discard. Also, we must never allow ourselves to be crestfallen; we must live in the absolute. Religion as a whole consists in relinquishing our personal limitations so as to enter into God, in extracting the "I" from the self, so that God can be installed in its place.

Naturally, these desires of heaven must be corroborated through acts. And should we falter, let us feel humiliated, but not discouraged. To bring our heart back to God when we feel our attention diverted from him, to stop doing wrong as soon as we notice our error, to proceed on our forward march regardless of fatigue, to deny ourselves selfish satisfactions—these are the remedies for lukewarmness.

I recognize that among all inner states the most painful is that of plain naked faith: although neither perceptible nor gratifying, yet it is the most fecund and trustworthy. It is a healthier penance than sought-after austerities would be. It is when God seems to abandon us that we must abandon ourselves to him. This is the only means to overcome sadness and disheartenment.

We would doubtless like to observe our progress; our pride takes offense at setbacks during the struggles against our faults; we are cross, mad at ourselves, and it progresses to our surroundings. We must realize that the work of God is not carried out in agony of mind. It demands peace interiorly, meaning trust, which means in turn love and total renunciation of everything not related to it. A single day spent doing the will of God brings possible and important results. It suffices it to renew the effort each morning. Believing the worst of yourself, throwing yourself into the arms of the Father, suppressing worries and febrile agitations—this brings about the annihilation of conceit, of self-centeredness. Our heart feels relieved, assuaged, is set free. We are surprised at seeing everything become easy and simple, when we had believed it to be complicated and arduous; we become aware that little has to be done for things to work out; we regret our faults naturally, but without bitterness, impatience, or resentment; we invite God to all our decisions, thanking him and rendering him homage. Being in accord with ourselves and in accord with God, we desire nothing that we do not possess; we do not want to be rid of anything from which we suffer, because it is up to him to remove the cross he shouldered us with. In the midst of tribulations, we keep our equanimity and dwell in joy—most intimate, purest, profound joy.

Worldly people suffer in the midst of pleasures because they always want something other than what they possess. Disciples are content and accept everything, so their heart is at ease in the expansion of peace, and their faces light up from the joyful luminosity of the spirit. There is, however, still one precaution to take regarding the experiences you will face and pursue during that period.

Whatever be the load of your numerous occupations, always keep some time to commune with God, morning

Apostolate

and night. During the day, when fatigue overtakes you, take a few minutes to reinstate yourself in God. These minutes will even serve your temporal affairs, refreshing your mind, strengthening your attention, procuring new vistas to your work. God hides behind inopportune and troublesome visitors, since they are being used to discipline our will and to disgust us with life.

In the beginning, do not prolong your prayers beyond your needs; do not tire your intellect; rather direct your heart slowly towards God. Do not let go of a pious sentiment without having exhausted its potency. Speak to God rather than reflect upon him. Do not fret about distractions; but than again, do not wander into vain reveries. Do not analyze yourself unnecessarily; veer towards God, sparing no effort to be content at suppressing your worries.

During the day while you attend to your business quietly, try to remain as if you were in a state of prayers. What is paramount is to love God and our fellowmen up to and in spite of our misfortunes and ordeals. This way, loving God does not mean having ecstasies, but feeling united with him in all occasions, with felicity.

An imperfect prayer is still useful; the unanswered prayer is not lost. We must pray unto death, trying to do better next time, keeping humbly to a simple prayer with undiluted faith. We are useless servants; we must always remain satisfied with whatever God grants us. Let us amalgamate patience in accepting our faults with vigilance in correcting them—a difficult task, but one towards which each person must assiduously strive. Never become impatient, never become discouraged. That can be attained by meditating upon the love God has for us, on his patience, upon the satisfaction he feels when he views our efforts—this is the very activity of hope. Let us ally ardor to work and abandonment to God—this is another psychological antinomy resolved through a clear distinction between worry and zeal. Worry shows lack of confidence; one needs robust, healthy zeal, incessant and tranquil, with people in sight, and not ourselves. Thus a taste for prayer is born, and our requests spring spontaneously from our hearts, alive, simple, at ease, and fruitful.

For our prayers to be worthy, let us suppress our tendency of blaming others for their faults; we are not here to correct them. Let us attempt, when possible, to attenuate the consequences and let us never criticize the perpetrators of these faults. The more perfect we are, the less imperfections irk us. That is why Christ exhorts us to ask the Father to treat us as we treat others. Only though experience do we learn our lessons.

The Harvester's Toil

THE EARTH LOVES the plants it has nurtured; it reluctantly parts with them. In the same way nature, which has provided man with his physical and mental powers, does everything it can to ensure that they return to it. Heaven's workers therefore inevitably come up against all kinds of family and social animosities, as they uproot human plants from their native soil and place them back in the celestial soil, removing them from the heat of the created suns to expose them to the light of the uncreated sun.

These workers, while refusing to fear for their own sake, must guard themselves because they are the instruments of divine action. They must never furnish temporal powers the least pretext for attack. They scrupulously obey laws

Apostolate

and customs unless they are contrary to the precepts of the Master.

Setting a good example for men means implicitly blaming them for their common conduct, thereby ill-disposing them against us. It means doing good in a salutary manner following in the steps of Christ, and in so doing advancing faster by taking a shorter road. This adds up to gaining time and cannot be achieved without repaying our balance-due in a shorter span of time than what might have otherwise required several incarnations.

The workers of God have much to suffer inwardly to become capable of doing their work; they also assume the tasks inherent to their mission, besides which they also take upon themselves to pay off the debts of another.

There are limits to our endurance to suffer, in body as well as in spirit. These voluntary victims consequently receive help from heaven enabling them to bear the pain. Among the few who are leaders in this work, their physical and psychic organs are pure enough for the light to dwell in them permanently. Among the others, this special influx occurs only in the faculties capable of receiving them; or else exceptionally, as in the case cited in the gospel of an appearance before a tribunal.

To sum up, the work of the apostle consists in his progressive identification with his Master. Just as he will conduct himself toward all beings as Jesus did, so will beings conduct themselves toward him as they do toward Jesus. The length of time this work takes does not matter, as the disciple having nothing but God in mind lives in the eternal.

To tell the truth, the relation of grandeur between the servant and Master is as zero is to the infinite; and the power of the former has a similar rapport with the latter. But speaking plainly, which means in the relative, the Master renews the incomprehensible miracle of the limits of this infinite towards to disciple: the servant whose life dwells in the relative, conditioned, temporary, local, is saturated with absolute, free, eternal, and universal existence. Our intellect cannot conceive this arcanum, but the heart feels it with certitude.

All that Jesus has endured, suffered, and experienced, just so will his friends endure and suffer. I do not mean to say they will experience similar forms of pain, but that the same tormenting angels will come to visit them.

Courage

THE APOSTLE must possess all phases of courage especially the courage of his opinions. Creatures, men or elementary spirits, gods or devils, are the only ones who make use of hiding places, who erect mausoleums, who manufacture safes, who hide the truth in hieroglyphics. Avarice, which heaven has put in the heart of beings, incites them to keep everything to themselves, while all they should withhold are the formulas of evil and the telling of evil deeds.

Hence, we have no right to withhold scientific documents, to keep our inventions to ourselves, to hold silence regarding what we know. Everything should belong to everyone, and if heaven reveals something to us rather than to our neighbor, it is because within us or around us are more facilities for comprehension and publication of this secret.

Were we to recall how sad is the life of inventors, filled with disappointments and jeering, how much more must

Apostolate

the torchbearers of the divine flame suffer—those whose thoughts are wholly set toward heaven, whose words are brimming with love, whose acts are made of sacrifices, who seek the poor, the afflicted, the forsaken, the simple-minded, the unbelievers, the depraved, in order to succor, heal, teach, and draw them back upon the right path!

But, whence does cowardice spring? From fear of suffering bodily or in the soul. Yet the servant of God is meant to suffer; hence he performs his task fearlessly without bravado, setting a good example to men, demons, gods, and all other creatures.

We have already learned, in the *Magnificat*, how the descent of the Word had caused (among other outcomes) the overthrow of natural hierarchies. In the worldly sphere, if perchance a new divine force penetrates fluids flowing right to left, they form a whirlpool revolving left to right. If this force enters the astral spheres all at once, what was below will rise up, what was black will pass into white, what was hidden will be made manifest. Moreover, it is within the smallest centers of this force that the action of the disciples brings the work of the Word to fruition.

Those upheavals take place everywhere and in all places where Jesus presents himself. This explains the inner sufferings of mysticism and well as the social convulsions and cataclysms that foretell the end of races.

It is essential that we banish fear from our hearts. Our material enemies can only deprive us of our material life; the demons of the air can only take away our etheric life; the demons of the mental world can only shatter our intellectual life. Whatever tests we endure, whether poverty, illness, temptation or despair, if we resist them with courage, they can not reach anything but the natural essence within us. As to our supernatural essence, through each pain endured the pure inner light remains tangible, intrepid, and shines more brilliantly.

But remember well that to obtain this result we must strive forward, fight unto agony, remain steady to our last drop of blood; for otherwise the enemy of men may drain some of our spiritual life.

Let us understand that when we live in this manner, we have very little merit, though it remains true that everything has been written ahead of time. And because every hair on our heads has been counted and not one falls without God's permission, we do not have the right to pluck out a white hair any more than to flee at the approach of the battle.

As regards our Master, as we deal or conduct ourselves with our fellowmen, so will he deal towards us before his Father. Hence the law that our pride regards as strict justice is in truth proof of a great indulgence on his part, because (as must repeat) in reality we have no merit: God does not need us. And yet, we should work as if our cooperation were indispensable to him.

Our spiritual eyes myopically perceive a great many contributions and antinomies in the decrees of providence. The Lord however, and he alone, sees everything at a glance, assigning to each existence its rightful direction and ordering the paths of all beings towards a goal that, according to our expectations, is inaccessible. This is why he brings peace to the world only mediately, successively, after the various milieus that make it up have passed through the wars of ethnographic, political, religious, psychic, scientific, physical, or cosmogonic separations.

Every corporeal organism, our body as well as our coun-

Apostolate

try, our planet, our universe, is a dwelling; a mineral molecule, a comet, a practical science, an art, a machine, are also dwellings wherein invisible forces live. Were we to liken the five persons Matthew speaks of to the five physical senses, to the five principles of Valentinus,[2] to the soul faculties (self, will, intellect, imagination, feeling) to the elements of Hermeticism, to the ethers or fluids of astral light, it would still be truth.

Gospel Hatreds

CHRIST BRINGS PEACE to the kernels, but he kindles wars in the husks. The zodiacal cities, the people of the empyrean, the nations on earth, our families, households, and persons are pyres he sets on fire at intervals when corruption has reached a peak without remedy—after which harmony reigns supreme in our heart and in the essential soul of any living form.

So, Matthew names the four persons we must "hate" in order to become a disciple; Luke speaks of seven. Let us try to understand this "hatred." It has already been said that if in the interval of centuries one man is born whose body, magnetism, and thought have not been formed or fashioned by nature, on the other hand his brothers are linked to matter by all the fibers of their being.

Paternal love as well as filial love are often based on selfish passions. When probing sequences of lives, they are the effect of positions relative to a certain group of individuals. All human loves may be selfish, cruel, and detrimental. It is our self that we love in our parents, in our children, in our

---

[2] Valentinus (c. AD 100–180) Christian Gnostic theologian.

mate. To love these beings with whom we have ties of flesh and blood should mean to be totally unselfish, to forget our self. This, however, is difficult and rare.

What Christ demands is that we love our family according to the spirit by providing for their physical, moral, and intellectual needs. We must honor our parents and set a good example to our children. We must bear the hardships they cause us, but at the same time prevent by all means possible (excepting violence) that their faults increase. Each time a small child receives from his parents an example of prayer and piety, heaven gives them credit.

This is how we attach ourselves to God and not to created beings, even the closest ones.

A being who is advanced spiritually is seldom born in a family as evolved as he. This is because the light is more fertile in darkness and enables latecomers to receive encouragement. It is not without good grounds that custom attributes to the eldest child charges similar to that of the head of the family. The fiercest battle, however, is the one the disciple must fight with himself. Man is his own greatest enemy. The combat may last centuries, because evil keeps being reborn within for the sole reason that we are mortals. We continuously commit new sins. We ought not believe what esoteric religions and schools teach: that we can attain total perfection. Theologians and adepts may make this claim, but the saints have the immense advantage over them of remaining humble and striving for something better. Perfection in the terrestrial human composite is a small part of the total *Great Work*.

To hate one's life, Jesus explains with lowered voice, is to renounce the self, to carry our cross, and to follow him.

Our parents are as well the invisible powers that have

Apostolate

fashioned our personality; our wife represents the subjective and objective powers through which we fulfill our desires; our children are the works of our self. All of which makes up our selves. These are the roots, branches, flowers, and fruits of our own will. They are the smiths of our strongest chains; they are our greediest creditors.

This is why, if one wants to follow Jesus, it is necessary that we engage in the struggle against our most puerile, most stringent, forms of selfishness as well as against the most superficial and deeply-rooted ones.

In the second place, we must bear the portion of sufferings each day brings us, so as to liquidate our debts of old.

Finally, following Jesus means living a life analogous to his; giving of ourselves, of our money, of our time, of our rest, of our intelligence, and of our hearts to all who ask, to all who seem to need us, without asking anything in return, neither gratefulness, nor help, nor affection. We must keep check over ourselves, because sensual desires always lie in wait hoping to satisfying themselves under the pretext of the noblest of pretexts.

On the other hand, the soldier of heaven need have no fear. He must not economize his forces: what he spends in the service of his Master on earth will be repaid a hundred fold. Danger is inconsequential to him. But he must not so expose himself for self-benefit or for vain satisfaction of overcoming it, or use it as a ladder to attain perfection. When we act out of a motive of self-interest, we inevitably succumb, no matter how sublime that motive may seem.

Therefore it is only when done unselfishly and free from any improper motives that the luminous value of our effort counts. The fulcrum of our will must be higher than the highest peaks of nature—it must be in the Absolute. This is the sole method that can unite us practically and substantially with the Word. For if our dealings with anyone are on par with the dignity we attribute to them, our recompense will be in proportion to this attribution. As Matthew states, if we receive a just man because he is a just man, it will be the god or the angel of good people who will reimburse us; but if we help a man because he is a disciple, the Master himself will recompense us.

In other words, the true families of created beings are those of their wills and of the different ideals they serve. But to help others because Christ has helped them, it will be Christ himself on the plane of essential reality that you will be helping; and as he embraces the Father within himself, your act will be transmitted directly, immediately, to the feet of the Father.

Hence, those who strive to obey the gospel precepts notice that all the substances of their being, from the physical to the spiritual, are undergoing a mysterious transmutation that renovates, regenerates, and recreates them. They become so similar to the Word that they appear as identical manifestations.

Such is the immense and supernatural force of real love. Love unifies all the beings it sets ablaze, from the least to the supreme, on up to the unknowable Father.

CHAPTER III

Spiritual Nourishment

ESUS THEN REBUKED the cities in which he had performed most of his miracles because they showed no signs of repenting.

"Woe to you, Chorazin! Woe to you, Bethsaida! Because if the miracles which have been performed among you had been effected at Tyre and Sidon, they would have repented, clothed in sackcloth, seated upon ashes, a long time ago. That is why, let me tell you, that on judgment day, it will be easier for Tyre and Sidon than for you.

"As for you, Capharnaum, which had been elevated in the eyes of heaven, you will be brought low to the sojourn of the dead, because, had the miracles which have been performed among you, taken place in Sodom, the city would still be there today. That is why, I declare that the land of Sodom, on the day of judgment, will be dealt with less rigorously than you!"

⊕

It was about this time that Herod, the tetrarch of Galilee, heard Jesus spoken about. "That man," he said to his courtesans, "is John the Baptist! He has come back from the dead! Because of this, miraculous powers are manifested in him!" Herod thus sought to meet him.

It was Herod who had John arrested, had him garroted and thrown into prison. He had done this because of Herodias, the wife of his brother Phillip, whom he had married, and because John had said to him: "It is not lawful for you to be married to this woman." Herodias really wanted to have John put to death; however, Herod feared John, knowing him to be a just and holy man. He was also afraid of public opinion, which regarded John as a prophet. He therefore kept him prisoner. Because of things that John had expressed which perplexed him, he took his advice on a number of matters. Upon his birthday, Herod gave a feast for his notables, his military commanders, and for the principal dignitaries of Galilee. The daughter of Herodias, so pleased the tetrarch when she danced in the banquet hall, that he swore on an oath that he would grant her anything she would ask, were it to comprise half of his kingdom. At the instigation of her mother, she told him: "Give me, right now, here on a platter, the head of John the Baptist." This saddened the king. Nevertheless, because of his oath, and also because of his guests, he commanded that it be given to her. A guard went and decapitated John in his prison. He brought John's head on a platter and gave it to the young girl, who handed it to her mother. John's disciples came and took his body and buried it. Then they went and told Jesus what had happened.

Having learned of John's death, Jesus left the locality by boat in order to withdraw to a place of solitude. However, the crowd, having heard of it, left the towns and followed him on foot. As he disembarked, seeing such an immense crowd, he had compassion for them and healed their sick.

As the sun began to set, the Twelve approached Jesus, entreating him: "Dismiss the crowd so that they can go

Spiritual Nourishment

to the nearby towns in the region to find lodging and something to eat. Here there is nothing but desert! And it is getting late."

Jesus replied: "The crowd does not need to leave! You yourselves are going to give them something to eat."

Then, surveying the crowd which had assembled about him, he said to Philip: "Where will we buy bread to nourish all these people?" He posed this question in order to test him, because, for his own part, Jesus knew full well what he was going to do. "Were each person to receive only a small ration," replied Philip, "two hundred deniers worth of bread would be insufficient!" Jesus continued: "How many loaves of bread do you have? Go and see." One of the disciples, Andrew, the brother of Simon Peter, said to Jesus: "There is a small boy here who has five barley loaves and two fish. But of what use is this for such a large crowd?" "Bring them here to me," said Jesus, "and have these people sit down in groups on the grass."

The grass was green and abundant where the crowd had assembled, and they sat in rows of one hundred and of fifty.

Jesus, taking the five loaves and the two fish, raised his eyes to heaven; he pronounced the blessing, broke the loaves, and gave them to the disciples to distribute to the crowd. He also distributed the two fish among them. They all had as much as they wanted. Everybody ate, and they were all satiated. Jesus then said to his disciples: "Collect the morsels which remain, so that nothing is lost." They therefore collected what was left over, and with the remains of the five barley loaves and the two fish they filled twelve baskets, which were carried away. About five thousand persons were fed.

The crowd, having witnessed the miracle that Jesus had performed, said: "This man is surely the prophet that the world is awaiting!"

Knowing that they wanted to prevail upon him by force to make him king, Jesus compelled his disciples to return to the boat, to precede him to the opposite shore, while he remained to dismiss the crowd.

As soon as he had sent the people away, he climbed the mountain and withdrew in order to pray in solitude.

Night fell. Jesus remained there, alone.

⊕

Meanwhile, the boat, by now out in the middle of the sea, was being battered by the waves, for the headwind was against it. At the fourth watch of the night (about 3 o'clock in the morning), Jesus came to them walking on the water. When the disciples saw him walking across the sea, they were upset, exclaiming in terror: "It is a phantom!" Jesus immediately spoke to them, saying: "Be at peace, it is I, do not be afraid." Peter then addressed him: "If it is you, Lord, command that I might walk towards you on the waves." "Come," said Jesus. Getting out of the boat, Peter walked upon the billows towards Jesus; however, when he felt the violence of the wind, he became afraid and began to sink. So he cried out: "Lord, save me." Jesus stretched out his hand, and taking hold of him said: "Man of little

Spiritual Nourishment

faith, why did you doubt?" They boarded the boat and the wind dropped. Then those who were present prostrated themselves before him, saying: "You are truly the Son of God."

Having crossed the lake, they came to the region of Genesareth. The people of the locality, having recognized him, alerted the entire neighborhood and they brought him their sick, begging him to allow them to just touch the fringe of his cloak. All those who touched it were healed.

⊕

Then scribes and Pharisees came to Jesus from Jerusalem and said: "Why do your disciples transgress the traditions of the elders? For they do not wash their hands when they eat." He answered them, "And why do transgress, the commandment of God for the sake of your tradition? For God commanded, 'Honor your father and your mother,' and 'He who speaks evil of father or mother, let him surely die.' But you say, 'if any one tells his father or his mother, What you have gained from me is given to God, he need not honor his father. So, for the sake of your tradition, you have made void the word of God. You hypocrites! Well did Isaiah prophesy of you, when he said:

'This people honors me with their lips,
but their heart, is far from me;
in vain do they worship me;
teaching as doctrines the precepts of men.'

THE KINGDOM OF GOD

Summoning the attention of the multitude, he said to them: "Listen and understand: what renders man impure is not what enters his mouth; what renders man impure is what comes out of his mouth." The disciples approached him and asked: "Do you know that the Pharisees, upon hearing these words, have been scandalized?" He replied: "Any plant that has not been planted by my heavenly Father will be pulled up by the roots. When a blind man leads another blind man, both will fall into a ditch." Peter, continuing, asked him: "Explain the parable to us." And he answered: "And you, are you too, still without comprehension? Do you not understand that everything which enters the mouth goes to the stomach and from there is rejected into a sewer? But what comes out of the mouth comes from the heart; this is what renders the heart of man impure! Evil thinking, homicide, adultery, fornication, theft, false witness and calumny come in fact from the heart; yes, this is what renders man impure! Eating without having washed one's hands has nothing to do with contracting moral impurity."

⊕

Jesus left the locality and withdrew to the coast near Tyre and Sidon. However, it was impossible for him to remain undiscovered. Shortly thereafter a Canaanite woman from the region came, beseeching him: "Lord, son of David, have pity on me, my daughter is cruelly tormented by a demon." Jesus did not utter a word. His disciples, intervening, asked him to send the woman away, saying: "She hounds us with her demands." Then Jesus spoke: "I have been sent only

Spiritual Nourishment

for the lost sheep of the house of Israel." But the woman prostrated herself before him saying: "Lord, help me." He then replied: "It is not right to take bread from children and to throw it to the puppies." She retorted: "Without doubt, Lord, but puppies eat the crumbs that the children let fall under the table of their masters." Jesus continued: "Oh woman! How strong your faith is! Let it be done according to your wish." And at that very moment her daughter was healed.

⊕

Leaving the region, Jesus traveled along the shore of the sea of Galilee. Then he climbed the mountain and remained there. Large groups of people arrived, bringing with them some paralytics, some blind, some deaf and dumb, some cripples, and many others, whom they deposited at his feet. He healed them all.

⊕

They brought to him a deaf person who had a speech impediment, begging him to lay his hands upon him.

Taking him aside from the crowd, he put his fingers into the man's ears and, with some saliva, touched his tongue; then, raising his eyes to heaven, sighing, he said: "Ephphata!" That is to say: "Be opened!" The ears of the deaf person opened, and his paralyzed tongue loosened immediately; he began to speak clearly.

Jesus commanded those present not to tell anyone. However, the more he admonished them, the more they broadcast what had happened, to such an extent that the crowd was filled with admiration to see that the dumb could speak, that the cripples were healed, the hunchbacks could walk upright, and the blind could see. "Everything that he does is perfect!" they exclaimed. And everybody glorified the God of Israel.

⊕

It happened once again that the crowd of people having gathered was quite large and had nothing to eat; Jesus called his disciples and said to them: "My heart goes out to this multitude. For three days they have not left me and they have nothing to eat. I do not want to send them away hungry, for fear that they might faint on the way, because some of them have come from a great distance." The disciples questioned him: "Where, in such an isolated place, might we find enough bread to nourish such a crowd?" "How many loaves of bread do you have?" Jesus asked them. "Seven," they replied, "and several fish." He ordered the crowd to be seated on the ground. Then he took the seven loaves and the fish and, giving thanks, broke them, gave them to the disciples, who in turn gave them to the crowd. Everybody ate his fill and the pieces that remained filled seven baskets. Four thousand men were thus fed, not counting the women and the children. When he had dismissed the multitude, he got back into the boat and went to the region of Magdala.

The following day, the crowd that had stayed on the other side of the sea saw that there had been only one boat there. They also saw that Jesus had not got into the boat with his disciples, but that his disciples had gone away alone.

Spiritual Nourishment

Meanwhile, other boats arrived from Tiberias near the place where the Lord had given thanks, following which he had fed the multitude.

The crowd, realizing that neither Jesus nor his disciples were there, embarked on these boats in order to look for him at Capharnaum. Finding him on the other shore, they asked him: "Master, when did you arrive here?" Jesus answered them: "Verily, you are not looking for me because of the miracles that you have witnessed, but because of the bread that you have eaten and that sated your hunger. Work not to acquire nourishment that perishes, but rather the nutriment that subsists for eternal life, that the Son of Man gives you, the Son whom God the Father has marked with his seal." They asked him: "What must we do in order to do the works of God?" Jesus answered them: "The work of God is to have faith in him whom he has sent." Then they asked him: "Explain to us the miracle which you perform, so that we might understand and that we might believe in you. What is the mission you are accomplishing? Our forefathers ate manna in the desert, as was written: 'He gave them to eat a bread that came from heaven.' Jesus answered them: "Truly, truly, Moses did not give you the bread that comes from heaven, but it is my Father who gives you bread that comes from heaven, the true bread of life, because the bread of God is he who descends from heaven and who gives life to the world." They asked him: "Lord, give us of this bread always."

Jesus continued: "It is I who am the bread of life. He who comes to me will never be hungry; he who believes in me will never thirst. But as I have said to you: 'Though you have seen me, you do not believe. All that my Father has given me belongs to me, and I will not thrust aside those who come to me, because I did not descend from heaven to do my will, but the will of he who sent me. Now, the will of him who sent me is that I lose nothing which he has given me, but that I resurrect everyone to life on the last day. Yes, the will of my Father, is that whoever gazes upon the Son and believes in him will have eternal life, and that I, personally, will raise him on the last day.'"

Nevertheless, the Jews took issue with what Jesus had said, which was: "It is I who am the bread which has come down from heaven." They were saying: "Is this not Jesus, the son of Joseph, Jesus, whose mother and father we know? How can this man say: 'I have come down from heaven?'" Jesus answered them: "Do not murmur among yourselves; no one can come to me without being drawn by the Father who sent me, and it is I who will raise him up on the last day. It was written by the prophets: 'They will all be taught by God.' Whoever has heard the Father and has understood, comes to me. Though no one has seen the Father, except he who comes on behalf of God; he, he has seen the Father. Verily, let me tell you that he who believes has eternal life. I am the bread of life. Your fathers ate the manna in the desert; then they died. Here is the bread which has come down from heaven in order that, in partaking of it, one will not die at all. I am the living bread descended from heaven. If anyone eats of this bread, he will live eternally. And the bread that I will give for the life of the world, is my flesh."

Spiritual Nourishment

A debate ensued among the Jews. They were saying: "How can this man give us his flesh to eat?" Jesus replied: "Verily, let me tell you that if you do not eat the flesh of the Son of Man and if you do not drink his blood, you do not have life in you. Whoever eats my flesh and drinks my blood has eternal life, and I will raise him up on the last day. Because my flesh is veritable nutriment, and my blood is a veritable beverage. Whosoever eats my flesh and drinks my blood lives in me, and I in him. Just as the Father who lives sent me and I live through the Father, so too he who draws his nourishment from me will live through me. Such is the bread descended from heaven. It is not as it was with the manna on which your fathers sustained themselves, and who later on died. Whosoever nourishes himself from this bread will live eternally."

Such was the sermon that Jesus delivered in the synagogue at Capharnaum. Having heard it, many of his disciples said: "This lesson is indeed demanding; who can heed it?"

Being aware of the murmuring of the disciples on this matter, Jesus said to them: "Does this shock you? And what if you were to see the Son of Man ascending to where he had been formerly! It is the Spirit that gives life; the flesh is of no consequence. The words that I have just used are spirit and are life. However, there are some among you who do not believe!" (Indeed, Jesus had known from the outset those among them who were totally incredulous, and who was the man who would betray him) "That is why," he added, "I told you that no one can come to me unless it be granted to him by the Father."

It was then that many of his disciples left; no longer followers of the crowd that walked with him. Whereupon Jesus said to the twelve: "And you, do you, too, wish to leave?" Simon Peter answered him: "Lord, to whom would we go? You have the message of eternal life, and we, we have believed and we have recognized that you are the anointed one of God." Jesus continued: "Was it not I who chose you, all twelve of you? Well, one of you is a demon!" He was speaking of Judas, the son of Simon, the Iscariot, because it was he who would betray him, he, one of the twelve.[1]

The Miracle

WHEN A MAN IS BORN, on whatever plane it be, everything needed for his sustenance is already there: his family, his country, his teachers, his profession, his religion. When we add to this the inner lights of the conscience, one would see that man always receives what is necessary for his life and for the work he must accomplish. And were we giving it due consideration, we would not, in order to progress, need anything but to accomplish our daily tasks and follow the indications of our moral inner voice.

But the desire for personal pleasures blinds us and often leads us into a ditch. Assistance both visible and invisible comes to our rescue under the guise of parents, educators,

---

[1] Matt. 11:20–24; Luke 10:13–15; Matt. 14:1–12; Mark 6:14–29; Luke 3:19–20; 9:7–9; Matt. 14:13–21; Mark 6:30–44; Luke 9:10–17; John 6:1–15; Matt. 14:22–36; Mark 6:45–56; John 6:16–21; Matt. 15:1–20; Mark 7:1–23; Luke 6:39; Matt. 15:21–28; Mark 7:24–30; Mark 7:31–37; Matt. 15:29–39; Mark 8:1–10; Matt. 16:1–4; 12:38–42; Mark 8:11–13; Luke 11:16, 29–32; 12:54–56. Matt. 16:5–12; Mark 8:14–21; Luke 12:1; John 6:26–65.

Spiritual Nourishment

friends, books, flashes of intuition, and tests. And if in spite of all this we obstinately go toward evil, heaven realizes the impossible to revive our vacillating inner light—hence the miracle intervenes.

There are several kinds of miracles. Some, called *geburoth* in Hebrew, *dynameis* in Greek, *virtutes* in Latin result in the employing of unknown natural forces, such as for example the telephone would be to a primitive tribe.

Others, called *aothoth*, *semeia*, or *signa* are produced outside of the human will, by supra-physical powers; thus do catastrophic events presage so-called divine anger to the intuitive eyes of the people.

The third kind, *nephiloth*, *terata*, or *thaumasia*, *prodigia* or *mirabilis*, are the results of divine forces that descend following the appeal of prayers—such are the miracles operated by saints.

Lastly come the works, *erga* or *opera*, of a man, having attained the plenitude of his power, at the ultimate development of his stature—such are the acts of Christ and those of the free missioners.

Man, the being, can accept the miracle and benefit from its blessings by opening the eyes of his spirit through faith. But he can also refuse it. That is why Jesus anathematizes cities that have seen him yet persisted in their errors.

When the miracle is not utilized, when the witnesses do not want to make the effort of simply accepting its consequences, they call death upon themselves; they kill something vital within, and this inner mystical assassination brings to them the cliché[2] of suicide in the very near future.

---

[2] A cliché is an invisible yet tangible form of some thought that passes by, and that we either can pick up or refuse.

There are witnesses to our actions. The higher position we occupy socially, the more witnesses there are. Whenever Christ acts, all creatures witness his work to give testimony. The spirits of the stones, plants, fields, and mountains have derived profits from his passage; and because of their close relationship with men, the spirits of hamlets, cities, and edifices have often misunderstood the divine voyager.

This is how the personal figures of speech addressed to certain townships of Israel can be explained.

The Martyr

JOHN THE BAPTIST'S asceticism comes to an end with the sacrifice of his life; he is the first man who died for the gospel: there too he was a precursor who hewed, who carved a path.

The web of our existence is but an uninterrupted series of holocausts that we offer our God; therefore he recompenses our devotions by admitting us sometimes, even while on earth, to his domain, by permitting us to participate in his own mode of life.

The Egyptian, Hindu, Persian, or Greek gods have not disappeared; they have only shed some of their mystery. Today we call them money, fame, prestige, sciences, don Juanism, delegation, etc. Their ever fervent and numerous faithful are less informed: they believe they work by and for themselves. The ancients were well aware that the immortals kept tight accounts of their servants.

But whether we serve these princes or the One, the master of them all, the same law governs homage, whether self interest prescribes it or love inspires it. The greater the effort on the part of the faithful, the more certain is the

Spiritual Nourishment

result; the more material the effort, the stronger will the existence of the god affirm itself. Hence nothing equals the propaganda of martyrdom. By shedding blood for an idea, it really does make its way to this material earth, and it will not only take shape in the minds of men, take on an active life in their hearts, but will come to fruition in social institutions, in building, in machines, one way or another.

Because the destiny of the invisible world as a whole is to become materialized, just as the fate of everything visible in the world today is to be assumed up someday to the etheric heavens of the universe.

The incessant oscillation of the armies composed of created beings from one end of nature to the other causes the Baptist to see his action diminishing from his imprisonment to his death, while that of his Master increases from day to day until such time as the earth, panting from having borne this splendor, will refuse the glory, still too heavy for it, of harboring its king any longer.

The Miracles of Bread

THE FIRST OF THESE miracles is related by the four evangelists: with five loaves of bread and two fish, Jesus fed five thousand men and twelve baskets-full remained over. The second of these miracles is related only by Mark and Matthew: with seven loaves and a few fish, Jesus fed four thousand persons, who had not eaten anything for "three" days, and seven baskets remained over.

Let us analyze the material aspect of these miracles.

It is not unusual in the East to see one hundred or two hundred persons, under the suggestive spell of the will of a fakir or the spirits of at a magician's command, convinced

THE KINGDOM OF GOD

of some thaumaturgical phenomenon or other. But divine law forbids such hypnotic suggestion because it infringes on our free will. Jesus never used it.

Another possible procedure would be through the absorption of astral foods. Physical man physically feeds unconsciously on magneto-telluric fluids, while astral man ingests astro-telluric substances during sleep. An adept can make this last mode of nourishment take place during wakefulness, through a momentary transposition, a kind of ecstasy of the subject's consciousness. It would be very difficult to achieve this effect several thousand people at once.

There is a third method. Any form on the physical plane is but the opaque envelope of the *essential* "type" of this form. Everything has its double. I employ the word "double" here because it is known, but it is not quite right. Material beings are *duplicata*, whereas their *types* or *genus* are *primata*, because the existence of the visible is subordinate to that of the invisible.

However, not all of these doubles materialize at the same time; there are store-houses where minerals, plants, animals, objects and limbs are kept in reserve, whose time of incarnation has not yet come. If, therefore, a miracle-worker were to find his way into these invisible granaries of Mother Nature, all he had to do was withdraw from them the arm, for instance, that a one-armed man lacks, the cog that will perfect a machine, the food by such and such a wreck—in three days, the double brought to the physical plane will have been clothed with all the matter needed.

But Christ did not employ such a slow procedure. When reviewing his life-story, we must recall that he is the Master (never will we recall this sufficiently). All he need do is give an order to the spirit of the bread and to that of the fish

Spiritual Nourishment

(everything is alive and has its own genus). Heaven needs neither time nor space to realize its decisions. We find ourselves in the supernatural here, in the true miracle; whereas the aforementioned three methods were merely set going by unknown natural laws, by means of science, or by the will.

What lessons can we draw from these wonders?

It is commonly thought that because we work, all that is necessary for us to do so—forces and food—is our due. But this is a mere presumption, for what is more difficult, to handle tools or put into the grain of wheat its force of growth, into the soil its nutritive power, into our body its capability of assimilation? An individual's effort is compensated by a far greater number of external efforts; and, by using our muscles, our senses, and our brains, we are only doing our duty, we deserve no reward.

This is why Jesus thanks the Father before distributing the pieces of bread. Moreover, each of our meals, while providing advancement to the food cells, it brings them suffering. The vegetable suffers less than the animal's flesh, and among all animals, the fish has less feeling. So the hunt is crueler than fishing. In any case, we should consider sparing the animal we sacrifice from pain. That is why the ancients, instead of slaughtering the cattle as we do (barbarians that we are), made them participants to their sacrifices, so that under the influence of perfumes, prayers, and incantations, the spirit of the creature passed, without being aware, into the *egregore* of the god of which it was the symbol. Lastly, that is why, extricated from polytheism by Jesus, we ask God, directly, to bless our food.

If we knew the true meaning of numbers, other mysteries would be unveiled in the telling of these two Christic works. But we have already seen that for our actual state of being, seeking to understand these arcana is in vain. We can, however, well enough conceive that the crowd Jesus fed was a universe at a certain degree of its evolution represented by the number five thousand. Two kinds of forces are being distributed to it: the first is basic, natural; the second is specific. It is thus that everyone possesses five senses through which the self is fed, but only a few possess the two other internal senses that put us in connection, on the one hand, with invisible nature, and on the other, with God. These are represented by the two fish, symbols of Christ.

On another level, this same universe, represented now by the number four thousand, has already passed through a process of selection; hence, the connections of its inhabitants with their surroundings are almost perfect: they have seven physical senses (the seven breads) and several spiritual senses (the fish). The beings on this second level or degree are more attentive, more conscientious; they leave only seven baskets instead of twelve.

To come back to a less imaginative order of ideas, let us remember that heaven never gives parsimoniously. It always sends us more than we can utilize; so that, if here and there beings are searching in vain for what they lack, it is not that God refuses it to them, it is because they squandered the share that was theirs, or let it go to waste; in this way, their minds developed accuracy, diligence, and economy.

When people teach children to respect bread, not to waste it, and to push aside the pieces of bread that fell on the sidewalk, they are obeying a true intuition. This also involves taking care of everything else as well. Nothing has been placed in our hands without a reason, and our smallest gesture, when inspired by our will to obey God, will be counted and rewarded.

Spiritual Nourishment

You remember when we mentioned a while back that if the operations of creatures are finite, those of the Absolute are universal. This is biologically true also. Hence, when the Son of God has nourished his own body as well as large crowds with bread and fish, at the same time he has endowed the wheat species and that flesh species with all the properties useful to the complete nourishment of the human organism. This may seem impossible if we are looking at nothing but the chemical laws of matter, and perhaps our faith, through which we could conceive the omnipotence of the will upon the psychological regimen, flinches.

Still, I repeat that our inner attitude changes the face of the world. He who serves heaven with all his might enters into the ever-present sphere where Christ lived; he immediately receives the radiating emanations and feeds upon them. And during their passage through this central plane the created forms that come to him undergo, upon the analogies of these forms such as they existed at that time, the modifications defined two thousand years ago through certain gestures, a certain word, or a certain act of Jesus.

This omnipotence of our will upon matter is not direct; our habitual, profound yearning evokes our ideals and brings it closer; this particular ideal, when combined with terrestrial life, modifies it.

The Sustenance of the Will

HAVING PRAYED during the first three hours of the night, Jesus walks upon the waters to rejoin the fishing boat in which his disciples were sailing, and Peter goes to meet him, but is afraid and sinks.

The noble simplicity of this gospel story thrills us. Sometimes there are words, songs, and lines that tear apart the veil of dreams before our eyes, allowing us to see the living splendor of their deeper meaning.

The story of Jesus is the manual of the impossible, the *vade mecum* of the unparalleled, the guide into the unknowable. All its episodes, when considered with the care they deserve (that is, with enthusiastic attention, devotional veneration, and ingenuous simplicity) must propel us beyond the self toward the marvelous region of the *ideal*; otherwise, we have merely tasted the outer skin, but have not bitten into the juicy pulp of this divine fruit.

Very few laypersons have referred to, or spoken of, the gospels. Fewer still have perceived anything therein beyond religious morality. But a day will soon come when a stronger breath from the spirit of intelligence will raise up one man to bring awareness to the correspondences of the Book, with all of the preoccupations of science, art, philosophy, and sociology; with all divisions within matter, with all the nuances of the heart's embers, with all the arcana of thought. May our efforts and wishes hasten the certain coming of this herald!

Our muscular force comes from "animal" electricity. Magnetic force comes from the vital telluric currents. Astral force comes to us through the refraction of planetary currents. The force of feeling comes from the fiery region of desire. Intellectual force comes from the cold region of the consciousness. Intuitive force is born out of our pains. But the force of the will feeds upon venomous substances, and its corruption vitiates the entire organism.

As you know, man is a universal being. He is the crossroads where all paths of all creatures cross one another. He wears on his bosom the coat-of-arms of the Father—free

Spiritual Nourishment

will. But, being placed at equal distance from the fruits of nature and the fruits of heaven, he too often forgets that, since the root of his soul is divine, it is from divine food that he should partake, and that any other food is unwholesome. If the lamp's flame is brilliant, the whole room will be lit up; if the will is pure, all of our powers will be pure.

By definition, the will is free. If it can be stopped by an obstacle, it is not a will anymore: it is a tendency. We possess will power only in the measure wherein we affirm it, live it, and realize it. The deed is indispensable to our psychic equilibrium.

We meditate logically, then contemplate feelingly; but these are only schools for the cultivation of the will—the force, the caliber, of our will is the measure of the individual. As the essence of this flame is liberty, its origin springs from a plane where there are no more conditions: no space, time, or matter. This is the Absolute, heaven, the sojourn of divinity. Hence, in order to grow, the will must feed solely from divine substances.

One has an inkling of the nature of these substances: they are known by their effects, which one calls harmony, concord, and love. When the will purges itself of its past intoxications, it is called repentance; when it hungers enough to let the objects of its desires pass from essence into existence, it is called faith; when satiated, it radiates wholesomely, and is called love.

One of the goals of Jesus's lessons is to tend the inner growth of these supernatural powers. Evolution *per se* takes place only through the synchronous involution of a superior power. Christ brought us the supreme light, but it can only be integrated if men provide the means to do so.

The portion of our will of which we are conscious may

act according to two modes. One is rational, calm, systematic, cold: its dynamism is measurable and mathematical; it grows by having recourse to rites, training, and to all that magic and formal religion comprises. The other is full of feeling, enthusiastic, measureless: its flame consumes everything, its impulse overturns all; it is as unaware of danger as it is of the impossible; it believes everything to be permissible; it is the *conflagration of love* wherein all our powers are consumed; it is the creative force that annihilates all the powers of the world and reduces them to ashes; it is this fulgurant lightning flash that Jesus ceaselessly refers to, whose explosion volatilizes all prejudices, all dross and slag, all the ashes of our past that sadden our heart.

To acquire this force demands superhuman effort. To feed upon divine essence requires that we fast from any created food. A few are aware of this, but to accomplish this task one must overcome all terrors. The dread of the flesh trembling before death is nothing compared to facing the trepidation of the intellect grappling with the shadows of primordial ignorance, when facing the agony of the soul that renounces itself while watching its life ebbing away one drop at a time. Such is to school of faith, such should be the daily repasts of our will.

As to the process Jesus used to remain above the waters, it was neither that of mediums nor of Simon the magician, whom invisible agents endowed with weightlessness. Nor was it that of the yogis, whose special mental tension overturns the direction of electromagnetic currents. The body of Christ was, in fact, created out of pure molecules, from earth as well as from beyond earth. Although his material appearance remained perceptively the same, the visible form of Jesus was extremely mobile, for what is pure is

Spiritual Nourishment

freed from conditions. While seemingly attached to the world here below, not only did he multiply his simultaneous presence on various planes, but he also brought into contact with this earth such and such regions as he had had dealings. He had not expressly wanted the aforementioned marvel. It was merely the result of one of the multiple voyages required by his mission; and coming back from a sphere less dense than ours, the body he had used there had remained for some few hours in the circumference of his physical body (if I may express it so) before being reabsorbed under the veil of his earthly body of flesh.

The Bread of Heaven

CHRIST REPROACHES his audiences of seeking him solely for his miracles and not for the spirit of which they were the signs. Perishable food is not limited to that of the stomach, but it comprises sensations, ideas, sentiments, sciences, aesthetic emotions—in short, everything procured for us by created beings. The food "which remains unto eternal life" is the light, it is our communion with the Word.

Do not misunderstand and think we must shun science, art, or ideas; on the contrary. But it is also true that our search for them is usually due to a more or less selfish cause, and that whatever we covet for our personal advantage in reality estranges us from God and draws us closer to hell. All men, inventors, artists, and philosophers, have the duty to cultivate the aptitudes that were given them in order to serve God, and to contribute to man's general advancement, that is, not merely to make money or derive honors and pleasures from them.

Everything comes to an end. If a science or art are born, it means they will die. They might last thousands of years; they might visit a great many races and several planetary orbs; but they will one day end their adventurous journey with a transformative fusion into the being of some god.

⊕

Although these foods and many others I am not mentioning here may be provisional, although we may not be able to assimilate them completely, although their reception is only a school without absolute value, it is necessary that we welcome them. They too are creatures of God. They have a right to our charity. They need us as much as we need them. Through them we develop tact, taste, sensitivity, judgment, intelligence, love, will, and all the subtle organs by means of which we will one day experience the modes of beatitude.

However, let us remember the provisional stamp of the seal all created things bear; let us not be attached to them; let us cultivate, love, and use them as tools for the work we are entrusted to do during a certain period of time, tools that we must return in a better condition and more apt to serve our successors than they were when we received them.

One being only in this vast universe bears the seal of the eternal—the Word. Each thing bears an inscription indicating, to whoever knows how to decipher it, its nature and its properties. What Hermeticism calls astrological signatures and correspondences are only the enfeebled radiation of the letters of this inscription. Only the child of God, however, may read the seal of the eternal; it remains not only hieroglyphic, but invisible, to the highest adepts: they travel in the lands of shadows, perceiving nothing but shadows; what is real and true remain hidden even from them.

And yet the real and the true are the only food and only

Spiritual Nourishment

drink worthy of the excellence of a human soul. "The work of God, is in fact, to believe in the One whom he has sent." This herald of God is the Word; let us seek him, find him, recognize him by his deeds.

For that, we must be constantly and intelligently attentive, as divine action may assume the earthiest forms. To know or recognize something implies a preliminary study. So, for instance, only after long practice does the eye of a painter discern the elegance of a contour or the charm of a tint. In like fashion, our heart will come to distinguish the spiritual qualities of the nourishing messages it receives only in consequence of the constancy and energy deployed during its practice of purification.

This is why the mystery of the incarnate Word remains mute to many intelligent people, while simple people have grasped it. Abstraction and meditation are not goals, they are but the means impelling us to action.

Can you imagine the highest among creatures, the princes of nebulas, coming and bringing to our spirits their rarest treasures (as sometimes happens)? These ideas, these feelings, these forces are, however, not perfect: whatever be their sublimity, their effect can only be temporary, since all nature must come to an end. The whole content of this vast world is only provisional. We must not abase what is eternal within of us by some kind of bond even to the most precious type of creaturely life.

A substance cannot give more than that of which it consists: since the manna with which Moses sustained his people in the desert came from Jehovah, it could only replenish what in the human organism belonged to that god.

Jesus declares that he himself is the celestial food, dispenser of absolute life.

THE KINGDOM OF GOD

As Jacob Boehme says, each creature feeds upon what is similar to it: the physical body feeds on matter, the astral body on fluids, the psychic body on feelings, intelligence, ideas, etc. Hence, what is eternal in us can desire only the eternal. That is why the food of our soul is God himself, who makes himself comprehensible by taking on a body in the person of the Word—his Son.

When Christ descended from heaven, he put on a veil appropriate to each plane's mode of existence, so that the sick of that plane could assimilate the omnipotent remedy that is he himself.

On the other hand, the soul is originally no more than a spark, whose fire grows as it consumes the different world substances it passes through, and with which it communicates by means of the visible and invisible organisms that make up our personalities, our spirit.

Insofar as we overcome the selfish tendencies of our natural energies, we exalt them toward the light of the soul, which in turn feeds upon it and grows—hence, suffering is its bread. And the great Martyr, the Angel of dolor, Jesus Christ, at each effort of the disciple celebrates the essential communion that transmutes into absolute life all particles of relative life which the ordeal has just purified.

Pay as close attention to the messages of the senses as to the fugitive contacts of intuition. Though imperceptible at first, if your psyche is at peace, little by little these intuitional flashes will become more explicit, and in time acquire the essential clarity our culture demands.

Spiritual Nourishment

The Spiritual Repast

BECAUSE IT DOES NOT contain absolute life, whatever creation has to offer cannot satisfy man. So, we experience disillusionments. Moralists have sufficiently discoursed upon the vanity of power, wealth, glory and earthly loves. No genius can give us real knowledge, since none possesses it; none can make us feel pure beauty, since there is ugliness within each being; none can invest us with boundless powers, since they are limited in their actions.

God alone fulfills man's desires; our most vertiginous strivings reach their goal in the person of the Word who lives among us. Heed his slightest words in their plenitude. When he promises the perfect food to whoever "comes" to him, you become aware that going to Jesus does not mean reading holy books when seated in an armchair by the fireplace. It means obeying his law, in spite of ordeals, mockeries, cabals, and desertions on the part of our family, friends, and the public. It means bearing all anguish, uncertainties, attacks. It means daring to be audacious for the sake of serving heaven.

To believe in God is not merely an intellectual or sentimental adherence. Faith is alive only when it digs its roots into the loam of sufferings. He whose serenity is untouched by pain, whose energy is exalted by boundless love, and who never trembles before terror, is in only in state of soul conducive to the descent of this virtue.

Just as food and drink are paired in the physiological world, so do action and faith complete each other to operate the aggregation and organization of supernatural substances that embody the divine stature of the Word in our innermost center.

THE KINGDOM OF GOD

This mystical alchemy develops its phases within those to whom the Father has given sufficient strength. It is they whom he entrusts to his Son; it is they over whom Jesus watches, despite their apparent distress and solitude; it is for them that he takes any suffering upon himself—even had they erred to the bottom of the deepest hell.

As Rulman Merswin explained it about seven hundred years ago, these friends do not stand out in a crowd. They live as anyone else. So it was that the Jews did not see Jesus as anyone other than the son of the carpenter. But whoever looks at these friends attentively will notice that they are the torch-bearers of an all-powerful light. Have forgotten hatred, their words are benedictions. Being beyond curiosity-seeking, their intelligence sees the truth within any creature. Have lost their self-assertiveness, their prayer wards off disease and catastrophes. Here on earth, *incognito*, they already enjoy some of the prerogatives that will be awarded them when the Master will have resurrected them.

Man is bound to time and space. A wealthy man or a prince suffer less from this dependency than does the poor man. The work of a genius makes child's play of these limitations because of the influence it exerts afar, upon future generations. Passion and will can momentarily project a being way beyond its material prison, such as we see in telepathy. Certain adepts have been able to dominate natural laws so as to extend the limits of their physical existence. But all such were in the wrong, for none of these accidents is comparable to the resurrection found in the bible.

Each time a man does good within the conditions prescribed by heaven (which means in humility and anonymity), the cells he made use of for the act are exalted even to the realm of his soul, for which they increase the reserve of

Spiritual Nourishment

light. This treasure accrues from life to life and, when the work of this man is at an end, all etheric-fluidic and physical matter that has been purified becomes his, and is his to use, by means of the secret that heaven imparts to him so that he may constitute for himself instantaneously the body he needs, here or there.

That body is not subject to any condition of relativity anymore, save when its possessor finds it useful. The promise of the Son is thus realized, crowning a long series of lives vivified by faith.

But to understand these things, hoist your self above the mental plane, above philosophies and esotericisms. The work of Christ is to open a direct path between men and the Father; at least we must be willing to set forth upon it. The unknown is not frightening: faith exerts itself in material struggles, in moral purification, in intellectual strivings. Let us not became attached to old habits, old opinions, old ideas. Let us not scorn them either. Yes, they are frail, decrepit servants, but they were precious servants. Everything in us moves, swarms, and lives; everything is provisional; everything is on the march.

If, while working with our muscles, with our minds, with our hearts, with all our energy, we keep in mind that, on our own, we will only achieve minimal results, it will be less difficult for us, when we are out of breath, to plunge into the maternal and regenerating night of faith in the midst of which the word of the Father resounds.

Because this word is life, ever-new, inexhaustible, indefatigable, this Word is the Son himself, Jesus, who beneath one or another of his aspects, vouches for the veracity of the One who sends him.

THE KINGDOM OF GOD

Eternal Life

ETERNAL LIFE does not mean a world everlasting, or an indefinite succession of lives. It is being. It is the day that has no more nights; the permanence of an immutability whose refractions alone vary in the prisms of the cosmos; omniscience without inquiry; effortless all-power; the individual who finds his triumph in total abandonment of self; union; harmony. always the same and always new; a beautiful enchantment that multiplies ceaselessly through the sacred contagion of all other beatitudes; the regime of admiration ever novel; the attitude of prayer into which the adorer sinks and remains silent; the perpetual impetus which had no beginning and will not end; the surge of love—supreme, distraught, extravagant love—knowing nothing, yet capable of everything; it is the Word.

When a farmer is sowing, he sees nothing but earth and seeds. But had he clear vision, he would perceive the whole ensemble of dynamic phenomena that unfold between the collective spirit of the vegetable species, the individual spirit of the seeds, and the spirit of the earth that receives them. And by influencing each of these invisible entities, he could completely change the physical appearance of the plant he is growing.

This perhaps gives us an idea of the method by which Moses materialized the substance of the manna that fed his people.

Broaden this process way beyond the limits of nature and you will have an idea of the incarnation of the Word. Were a cultivated, refined man imbued with all sensitivities to go and live among barbarous tribes in order to raise them up, everything in his apostolate would be painful to him, from

Spiritual Nourishment

the food up to the activates of his intelligence. But each of the efforts he put forth in this coarse atmosphere would prove itself in end by the birth of improvements.

How much more unutterable must be the tortures of the infinite! The tortures of the all-purity; in short, the tortures of the total being squeezed and limited within the ever-constricted, denser and coarser organisms! These are the dolors endured during the interminable voyage from heaven to the hells that form the human nature of Jesus. Each cell of his very chaste body, each spark of his invincible magnetism, each expression of his compassion, each diamond of his thought wears the crown of martyrdom. All these little beings were the first of the chosen, the most fervent of friends, the bravest of servants; so that, every time one of us stragglers desperately clings to the dazzling robe of the Word, the strength, the courage, the idea, the smile he receives are truly the spiritual flesh of the One who gives himself, to put us in confidence, the humble nickname Eldest Brother of men.

Whatever adepts may tell you, do not believe that one partakes of this divine food through ecstasies, no matter how lofty they may be. Only one's acts are viable and salutary. An ecstasy is nothing but a presentiment of what we will be living someday. It is a hope, not an actuality. Enduring ordeals of all kinds with patience, because it relieves us of the loads of our past, opens our eyes to temporal delusions, assuages our grief, strengthens our courage, becomes the flesh of the Word for us. And the precious blood, the organizing fluid, the artist of the glorious body, the factor of beauty, is love for our fellow man.

Indeed, loving others as oneself stops all toxic ferments, including those in the body; it universalizes the being; it transforms an educated man into an intelligent one; it overthrows the barriers of our thoughts; preconceived opinions crumble; narrow vistas broaden; our spirit advances further and deeper into the magnificent landscape of the invisible. Veritable charity is the most fruitful training of our energies because one cannot live it, one cannot experience it, without waging constant warfare against our love of comfort. Through it, the spirit learns, becomes refined and malleable; artificial proprieties dissolve; it exalts the possible to the beyond; it is the all-powerful force of love.

Thus, to eat the body of Christ means to accept suffering for others; to drink his blood means to love all of nature: one being after another, one fraction of a minute after another. We all bruise ourselves when we come into contact with those around us who are only slightly inferior to us. As we give of ourselves to our brothers and sisters, our being is nourished by the flesh and blood of the Word, and eventually, at the end of our cosmic journey, there is identification between our spiritual being and the spiritual being of Christ, and this identification is realized through our body of glory.

Wherever the corporal presence of Christ is, implies and necessitates a previous descent, but this descent is tantamount to a second creation. Thus the Father gives his Son three times—when he raises a particle of nothingness into being, when he saves it, finally, when he grants it beatitude.

An athlete follows a rigorous diet because the quality of his food affects his vigor. How much more active must the influence of spiritual foods be? And when we are able to assimilate one little crumb of the force of forces, the total transubstantiation of our being must follow. He who takes communion with the Word becomes an integral part of

Spiritual Nourishment

him; just as a viscera, just as the smallest cell of a body, follows its general state of being and cooperates with it, yet maintaining its initiative, its free will, so does, physiological well-being result from these harmonious collaborations of goodwill. Just as the spirit of the disciple is an organ of the cosmic body of the Word, so are the personal beatitude of man and total harmony the results of the plenitude with which he dedicates his energies to the fulfillment of the law.

These phenomena occur everywhere, because the Spirit, or life, are everywhere. Each being has influence in proportion to the quantity of spirit that dynamizes it; and each being receives truth, or verity, in proportion to what he labored hard to obtain. Matter is of no account by itself; its force and beauty are the radiations of the life saturating it. And men can understand the words of Jesus only in proportion to the tears, blood, and sweat that, to begin with, they had offered to the living Spirit whom we set apart from the Father and the Son only because of our intellectual powerlessness. Nothing has any value save through the Spirit—neither forms, nor colors, nor sounds, nor forces, nor multitudes, nor magics, nor sacraments have any virtue in themselves unless they are animated by the divine ray. Without God nothing can exist; but he needs no one, though his tenderness solicits us as if we were necessary to his happiness.

The immensity of the Most High blinds us. The harmonious symphony of his acts is so simple and vast that we detect dissonances only because our ear grasps but a few notes of the immense chord resounding from nadir to zenith. God's justice and kindness seem to be in conflict; so do his prescience and our liberty. From the beginning, he sees the possible as a whole, since it is he who has elaborated the various combinations. But the roads he has chosen for his creatures to walk are not geometrical lines; they have breadth; one can go from one side to the other, stretch out into a cool ditch, flounder in puddles, or remain in the middle of the embankment; one may pick the apples from adjoining gardens, or purchase them; one can take shelter during a storm or continue walking in spite of it; or push chariot wheels out of the mud, or spread bits of broken glass on the bicycles right-of-way.

It is within such a restricted sphere that our liberty is exercised. These are the commonplace practices that will provide it the force to exert influence upon entire races someday: all things start from humble beginnings.

Thus God himself chooses those who will return to him at stated times. It is not man who has the merit of conversion, for usually, through his own fault, too heavy a load crushes him. His despair, efforts, and repentance can only send forth a cry for help to be heard in the kingdom of the Word. And he cannot put his feet upon this land of the living unless the Lord has already washed them.

Understand, then, how true it is that no one can come to God unless "it has been given him"; how this saying determines the defection of many: and why, after having provoked the free suffrage of the Twelve by a direct question, Jesus reminds them that they know him only because he has willed it.

CHAPTER IV

Physical Alchemy

MONG THE PHARISEES there was a man named Nicodemus who was one of the rulers of the Jews. He came to Jesus by night and asked him: "Master, we know that you are a teacher come from God, because no one can perform the miracles that you do unless God is with him." Jesus answered him; "Verily, verily, let me tell you that if a man is not born again he cannot see the kingdom of God." Nicodemus replied: "How can a man be born again when he is old? Can he return to his mother's womb and be born over again?" Jesus replied: "Verily, verily, believe me when I say that if a man is not born of water and of spirit, he cannot enter the kingdom of God. That which is born of the flesh is flesh, and that which is born of the spirit is spirit. Do not be surprised when I tell you that you must be born again. The wind blows where it will and you hear the sound it makes; but you do not know whence it comes nor where it goes. So it is with everyone who is born of the spirit."

Nicodemus then asked him again: "How can these things be?" Jesus answered him: "You hold the office of a teacher of Israel, and yet you do not understand these things! I solemnly assure you that what we are talking about is known, and we testify to what we have seen; but you do not accept our testimony. If you do not believe me when I tell you about earthly things, how are you going to believe me when I talk to you about heavenly things? Nobody has gone up to heaven except for One who came down from heaven, the Son of Man who dwells in heaven. Just as Moses lifted up the serpent in the desert, so too must the Son of Man be lifted up so that all who believe in him may not perish, but have eternal life.

"For God did not send his Son into the world in order to judge the world, but that the world would be saved through him. Whosoever believes in him is not judged, but whosoever does not believe is already judged, because he did not believe in the name of the only Son of God. And the judgment is this: light came to the world, and men preferred darkness to light, because their deeds were evil. For anybody who practices evil hates the light, and does not come to the light for fear that his deeds be exposed. But he who acts in truth, comes to the truth to make clear that his deeds are done in God."

When Jesus went to the neighborhood of Caesarea Philippi, he queried his disciples: "Who do people say is the Son of Man?" They replied: "Some say it is John the Baptist, others say it is Elijah; still others say Jeremiah, or one of the prophets." He continued: "And you, who do you say I am?" Simon Peter answered: "You are Christ, the Son of the Living God."

Then Jesus told him: "Blessed are you, Simon son of Jonah, because it is neither flesh nor the blood that has revealed this to you, but my Father who is in heaven. I, for my part, declare that henceforth you shall be called "Rock," and on this rock I will build my Church, and the gates of the realm-of-death shall not prevail against it. I will entrust to you the keys to the kingdom of heaven, and whatsoever you bind on earth shall be

Physical Alchemy

bound in heaven; whatsoever you loose of earth shall be loosed in heaven." At the same time, he ordered his disciples strictly to not tell anyone that he was the Christ.

Then Jesus began to explain to his disciples that he would have to go to Jerusalem and would have to suffer greatly there at the hands of the elders, the chief priests, and the scribes; and be put to death; and rise again on the third day. At this, Peter took him aside and began to remonstrate with him. "May God have pity on you, Lord. Nothing like that will happen to you." Jesus turned on Peter and said to him: "Get thee hence! Get out of my sight, Satan! You seek to have me falter in my purpose. Your thoughts are not the thoughts of God but the thoughts of men."

Jesus then said to his disciples: "If anyone wishes to follow me, he must deny his very self, take up his cross, and follow me. Whosoever wants to save his life, will lose it; and whosoever loses his life because of me will find it. What would it profit a man if he were to gain the whole world and destroy his soul in the process? What can a man offer in exchange for his very life? The Son of Man will come in his Father's glory, accompanied by his angels, and when he does, he will reward each man according to his merits. I assure you, among those standing here there are some who will not experience death before they see the Son of Man coming into his kingdom."

Six days later, Jesus took Peter, James, and his brother John, and led them up onto a high mountain so they could be alone. He was transfigured before their eyes. His face became as dazzling as the sun, and his clothes became as radiant as light. Suddenly, Moses and Elijah appeared to them, conversing with him about his death and what he was to accomplish in Jerusalem. Then Peter said to Jesus, "Lord, it is good that we are here! With your permission I will erect three tents, one for you, one for Moses, and one for Elijah." He was still speaking when suddenly a bright cloud enveloped them. Out of the cloud came a voice that said, "This is My beloved Son upon whom My favor rests. Listen to him." When they heard this, the disciples fell face forward on the ground, overcome with fear. Jesus came toward them and, laying his hands on them, said, "Arise! Do not be afraid." When they looked up they saw no one but Jesus.

As they were coming down the mountainside, Jesus commanded them, "Do not tell anyone of this vision until the Son of Man rises from the dead." The disciples then asked him: "Why do the scribes claim that Elijah must come first?" He replied: "Elijah is indeed coming, and he will restore everything. I assure you, however, that Elijah has already come, but they did not recognize him and they did as they pleased with him. The Son of Man will suffer at their hands in the same way." The disciples then realized that he had been speaking to them about John the Baptist.

⊕

When they had rejoined the multitude, a man advanced towards him and, throwing himself on his

Physical Alchemy

knees, said to him: "Lord, have pity on my son; he is a lunatic, and he suffers greatly, because it often happens to him that he falls into the fire, and often also into the water. I have brought him to your disciples, but they have been unable to heal him." Jesus answered, "O incredulous and perverse generation, for how long will I stay with you, for how long will I have to put up with you? Bring the child to me here." As soon as the child set his eyes upon Jesus, the spirit agitated him violently. And Jesus asked of his father: "How long is it that this has been happening to him?" "Since his childhood," he replied; and he added, "If you can do something, help us, have pity on us." Jesus said to him: "Everything is possible for he who believes." Then the father of the child cried out: "I believe, come to the rescue of my unbelief." And Jesus reproached the demon who then left the child.

Later, the disciples, approaching Jesus privately, asked him: "Why was it that we were unable to cast out this demon?" He replied, "It was because of your lack of faith, because, let me assure you, if your faith were as large as a mustard seed, you could say to this mountain: 'From this place remove yourself yonder,' and it would remove itself yonder; nothing would be impossible for you. This type of demon can only be cast out through prayer and fasting."

⊕

When they arrived at Capernaum, the tax collectors who were collecting the didrachmes (the annual taxes to cover the expenses of the temple) spoke with Peter,

THE KINGDOM OF GOD

asking him: "Does not your master pay the taxes?" "He pays them," he replied. And when he entered the house, Jesus, reading his thoughts, said to him: "What is your opinion, Simon? From whom do the kings of the earth levy taxes or rents? From their sons or from strangers?" Peter replied: "From strangers." "Therefore," Jesus continued, "the sons are free; nevertheless: in order not to shock or offend them, go to the sea and throw in a fishing line. Take the first fish caught out of the water, open its mouth, and there you will find a large silver coin. Take this and give it to them for you and me."

⊕

This episode was followed by a Jewish feast day, and Jesus went up to Jerusalem. Near the sheep-gate there was a bathing pool (the word in Hebrew is Bethesda); it had five porticos, under which a multitude of sick were sprawled out: blind, crippled, paralyzed people. Among them was a man whose sickness had lasted for thirty-eight years. Seeing him lying down, and knowing that he had been there for a long time, Jesus said to him: "Do you wish to be healed?" The sick man answered him: "Lord, I have no one to lower me in the bathing pool when the waters are stirred. As I make my way there, another plunges in before me." Jesus said to him: "Get up, take your litter, and walk." This man was immediately healed; he took up his litter; he walked. This took place on a sabbath day. Then the Jews addressed the man who had been healed: "This is the sabbath day; you are not permitted to carry your litter." He answered them: "This very person who

Physical Alchemy

healed me told me: 'Pick up your litter and walk.' Then they asked him: "Who is this man who told you to pick it up and to walk?" But the man who had been cured knew not who it was. Meanwhile, Jesus had withdrawn because of the crowd that was there. Sometime later, Jesus met this man in the temple and said to him: "Now that you are healed, sin no more, lest something worse happen to you." This man went to tell the Jews that it was Jesus who had healed him. It was because Jesus did such things on a sabbath day, and for this particular reason that the Jews hounded him. But he said to them: "Right up to the very present my Father has been at work, and I too am at work." On account of this the Jews sought all the more to kill him, not only because he set aside the sabbath observances, but also because he said that God was his own Father, making himself equal to God.

Jesus then addressed them as follows: "Verily, verily, let me tell you, the Son can do nothing of his own accord; he does only what he sees his Father do. As a matter of fact, everything that the Father does, the Son likewise does; because the Father loves the Son and shows him everything that he does; and he shows him works that are much greater than these, in order that you might be captured with admiration. The same way, as a matter of fact, that the Father raises the dead, bringing them back to life, so too the Son revivifies whom he will. Because the Father judges no one, whoever he might be; but he has placed all judgment in the hands of the Son, so that all will honor the Son as they honor the Father. He who does not honor the Son does not honor the Father who sent him.

THE KINGDOM OF GOD

"Verily, verily, let me tell you, whosoever heeds my words and believes in him who sent me, possesses eternal life and will never appear in judgment: from death, he will have crossed into life. Verily, verily, let me tell you, a time is coming, and it has already come, wherein the dead will hear the voice of the Son of God, and those who would have listened to him will live. Because, as the Father is life itself, so too he has given it to the Son to have life in himself, and he has given him the power to exercise a judgment, because he is the Son of Man. Do not be astonished at this; because an hour is coming when all those who lie in the sepulcher will hear his voice and will come out; those who have done good will be raised to life in order that they might live, and those who have done evil will be brought back from the dead to be judged. Of myself, I can do nothing; as I hear, so I judge, and my judgment is just, because I do not seek my own will, but the will of he who sent me.

"If it is I who bear witness to myself, my testimony lacks veracity. It is another who renders me such testimony, and I know that the testimony he renders me is true. You went to talk with John, and he testified to the truth. As for me, it is not the testimony which comes from a man that I accept, but I speak of it so that you might be saved. It was he who was the torch that burned and that shone; you bathed in that illumination and for a moment you were delighted. As for me, I have a testimony greater than that of John; because I have works which the Father has given me to accomplish. The works I perform are the very things

Physical Alchemy

that bear witness to myself and attest that the Father sent me. Furthermore, the Father who sent me, he too has rendered witness to me. You have never heard his voice nor gazed upon his face; and as for his message, you do not have it in you, because you do not believe in him whom he has sent. You probe the Scriptures, because you think you will find eternal life there, yet it is they that bear me witness. Yet, you do not want to come to me to have life!

"The glory that comes from men, I do not accept; but I know that you do not have the love of God in you: I, who have come in the name of my Father, you do not accept! If another presents himself in his own name, you will accept him! How could you possibly believe, you who receive your glory from one another when you do not seek the glory that comes from God alone? Do not think that it will be I who accuse you before my Father. Your accuser is Moses, in whom you put your hope. Because, were you to believe in Moses, you would believe in me; as a matter of fact, it is I about whom his writings speak; but, if you do not believe in what he wrote, how can you believe in my message?[1]

---

[1] John 3:1–21; Matt. 16:13–20; Mark 8:27–30; Luke 9:18; Matt. 16:21–28; Mark 8:31; 9:1; Luke 9:22–27; Matt. 17:1–13; Mark 9:2–13; Luke 9:28–36; Matt. 17:14–23; Mark 9:14–32; Luke 9:37–45; 9:6; Matt. 17:24–27; John 5:1–9; John 5:10–47.

THE KINGDOM OF GOD

The Mystics' Task

THE WORK OF the Father is Jesus Christ. The responsibility of Jesus Christ is the assembly of his true, faithful disciples. The work of the Spirit is found within the achievements of this fraternal assembly. And the work of the Virgin is the substance itself out of which this triple operation will be embodied on the last day.

At such an altitude everything becomes one: the three works are unified into one, which is "sacrifice"; and the workers, the true disciples, must be real, active, live disciples, because truth, reality, and life are one and the same thing in God.

There are other saints on earth besides those found in the religious calendar. They are all united, incorporated, enfolded, amalgamated into one another as the inseparable particles of a spiritual diamond. What one accomplishes is done by all in the measure wherein his own will is identified with the will of the Father; and the plenary union becomes the strength of this elusive cohort.

Other men besides these pure servants of the God made flesh have attempted to reach similar unity—Merswin, Ruysbroeck, Rosenkreutz, Eckartshausen, and Lapoukine were the known protagonists of a few of these attempts. There were others who lived in France but who remained unknown. I will not reveal their obligatory incognito providentially decreed. But the genius of any man is incapable of realizing this marvellous feat alone. It is God who daily enumerates his elect, who teaches them, who trains them, who aggregates them to one another, who entrusts some tasks to them, and who sustains them when they falter. The various forms of these tasks are as varied as life, but it

Physical Alchemy

entails the same work—sacrifice. Jesus Christ is the incarnation of that sacrifice because he unites in his incomprehensible dual personality the god and the supplicant, the priest and the victim, the fire of the holocaust and the altar. He is the perfected sacrifice because of his absolute innocence. He is the all-powerfulness of sacrifice because of his incommensurable self-abasement.

From the divine point of view, sin engenders evil and individual sins engender individual ills. To swim upstream of the descending course of consequences there had to be an all-compassionate God, a voluntary penitent upon whom the innumerable guilty beings would model themselves, a sufficiently superhuman priest to dare introduce the sinner and disarm the judge, a pure victim, an unextinguishable fire, a universal altar. Christ alone fulfills all these conditions—he, the sacrificial Lamb immolated since the origin of the world.

Another key point: Jesus Christ is a priest after the order of Melchizedek, and not after the order of Moses. He does not fill the canonical conditions of the legal Jewish priest. Humanly, he comes (as it is announced) from a mysterious priest of a cult without rites that does not sacrifice any victims, who shows himself but once, and then disappears. Melchizedek, the king of peace, has neither father nor mother, nor descendants. The Scriptures mention neither his birth nor his death. He is alone. Jesus too is alone and his cult is that of the spirit. He appears only once during the course of centuries, then disappears.

In the outer order, a great many priests succeed one another at the altar. In the central order, one priest alone, the Word, perpetually celebrates his own sacrifice—who is Jesus. He obtains ceaselessly the salvation of men—that salvation being Christ. One is not surprised to learn that the priest according to the order of Melchizedek has been immolated in his own city by the temporal priest of the tribe of Levi. This immolation was preceded locally by innumerable analogous immolations; and in the centuries that followed, in the evolving worlds that are the steps of the ascension of the Word, other innumerable inconceivable immolations are still going on. The Word incarnates everywhere for the salvation of each humanity. Following his sacrifice, his servants everywhere, who belong to his spiritual substance, reproduce this sacrifice in the measure of their innocence and humility.

The only sacrifice we can make that is worthy of God consists in offering our free will (a total offering is understood), which extends to the material fact of each particular renunciation. Each time we practice self-abnegation may be an act of adoration, of thankfulness, an expiation, or a prayer. Jesus Christ deposited a seed of salvation in each kind of evil. Each suffering of his body, each horror imposed upon his feeling, each bitterness impregnating his heart, each error thwarting his intelligence—in short, all the ordeals he endured—became a light that penetrated to the essential core of each type of brutality, perversity, hardheartedness, ignorance, pride, and inertia. In turn, through each of their meager renunciations, his servants rejoin each of his perfect renunciations and reawaken the rays of salvation that come from the pure seeds sown by Christ. This is the manner in which universal redemption is disseminated gradually from one to another. This is the true hidden work that the veritable mystics accomplish.

Physical Alchemy

⊕

The framework of modern society and its occupations accommodate very well the needs of practical mysticism. No matter what the age, sex, nationality, profession, social standing, or culture of a disciple may be, whether he is a laborer or a statesman, it is always possible for him to sacrifice himself.

Sacrifice entails the consecration of the victim. It means offering himself, his immolation, his consummation, or communion to the God of the faithful. The disciple being consecrated to God renews this consecration daily. Each morning he attempts to offer God a purer heart; each morning God refines his clearness; hence each morning he breaks away from profane motives. Secondly, whenever the occasion arises to deprive himself of something or other, the disciple offers the privation to God. Then he splits in two, so to speak: he becomes a sacrificer and immolates the small part of his self that suffers from this privation. Later the courage deployed in accomplishing this deprivation joins the energy liberated by this renunciation, which then God uses as he pleases, either for the purposes the disciple has in view, or for the benefit of the disciple.

Christ has promised that whoever suffers for him will be recompensed doubly, on earth and in the future; but in order to earn it, one must first have forgotten it. It is through such exigencies that our Master cultivates within us this free, simple and limpid, direct and tireless behavior of true love. It is through such profound discipline that he enables us to penetrate the symbols that were the object of ancient studies, so as to traverse these images that at first confounded the generality Christians, in order to attain the realities at last.

THE KINGDOM OF GOD

As an example, the majority of the faithful come close to Christ only through the consumption of the eucharistic bread and wine. A few reach him through total forgiveness of their enemies. But there is scarcely one disciple per century who is capable of actually subsisting upon the body and blood of the Word.

We must never forget that the inner acts of our spirit are only fully fruitful when they are expressed in outer acts of our body. But our physical acts alone are far less operative than our mental acts alone. I must insist upon these common sense ideas so that you will comprehend how healthy, equilibrated, and harmonious must the mystic be. His personal unity, his unity within body, soul, and spirit engenders the collective unity of the archetypal church wherein all are brothers because of their identical desires, through their community of ideals, through their concordance of means. In short, anyone born in a hovel who obeys God with his whole being becomes in essence the brother of the one who, born in a palace, serves God with all his might. Moreover, these two men, vastly different, living apart, who will never meet, belong to a suprahuman, enduring brotherhood, because Jesus has said, "he who does the will of God is my brother."

Therefore, our modern mentality is not an obstacle to the mystic's awareness. To the contrary, this century offers them greater fields of endeavor, and because the eternal light never shines brighter than when it finds itself compressed beneath the great weight of darkness, we perceive that amid social discords, political upheavals, family squabbles, and individual wantonness, the misunderstood and scorned charity of a few scattered disciples, living in antithesis to contemporary customs, is preparing along with the

Physical Alchemy

salvation of the lost sheep, the remedy to collective crises and universal peacekeeping: the hungrily desired objective of all human kind.

Formalism

THE PREVAILING regulations regarding clothing, attitudes, domestic cleanliness, hygiene, and behavior that we find in such great number among all religious codes were originally meant to enable the faithful to profit from the best physical and etheric or fluid conditions. The ancients had knowledge of the laws concerning the secondary atmosphere. They knew what we have rediscovered under the name of magnetism and electricity. Their hygiene took care not only of the body's health, but also to the cleanliness of the double. From that were derived so many prescriptions relating to the cleansing of objects, to the attitude to be taken for eating, sleep, study, and work. Education was thus based on a body scientific facts, while the faith of the faithful directed the forces deployed in the observance of the rites toward the celestial center of their form of religiosity. A religion is the result of the visit of a god: or of God. The men for whom it is destined seek to cross the gates of the kingdom of that god. To achieve this end, they must slough off that portion of their clothing that is not in tune with that world, to get others, such as: intrinsic or organic qualities, moral virtues, intellectual ideas. The former can be obtained by obedience through canonic forms, the second through ethical rules, and the latter through comprehension of diverse theologies. But ethics, morals, is the password, the indispensable sign of acknowledgement, the only key to the paradises, because it is geared to the psychic center, to the will.

THE KINGDOM OF GOD

Formalism and worship, like knowledge, lose all value if they are enlivened by the purification of feeling. It is from this that the eternal value of the act, word, and idea derives. It is feeling or sentiment that, depending on the degree of altruism it harbors, swallows up or exalts the heroic and the vulgar, the petty and the sublime. That is why a man who, by refusing help from a church, still adheres to the simple practice of his inner religion, can with certainty expect the divine presence.

In this domain, therefore, as well as elsewhere, diplomacy is of no use. One must either find one's *egregores*, or remain alone. To choose among various systems of observances that one which "suits us" only brings about a loss of forces and obliges us to retrace our steps. We always forget that "emptiness," the space where passions, forces and ideas dwell and swirl, is filled with inhabitants. A people, a race, united by the same ideal is only the rear-guard or sentinel of the veritable army that battles for this supra-earthly being. The Eastern religions taught this fact explicitly; Catholicism has retained its most salient character when it calls to mind its doctrine of the communion of the three churches: the suffering, the militant, and the triumphant.

All these invisible, very active servants of the circuit that unites the god with his terrestrial worshippers perceive the latter's gestures and, being less indulgent than their master, are inclined to punish with rigor, to curb with violence the inconstancies of men. If you want to be in league with them, you have to give yourself completely; if you don't, you have to stay outside their sphere; they will not bother with the ones who want to be left alone.

In short, religions have both advantages and disadvantages. They are a great help to the will, the intelligence, and

Physical Alchemy

the sensibility. I will not repeat all that has been said about the enthusiasm that architecture, music, fragrances, and eloquence can arouse in the faithful, about the invisible help provided by the sacraments, about the noble contemplations to which theology can elevate us.

The danger of religious forms is to divert us eventually away from God on behalf of one of his aspects. But those who might have to fear that risk are rare and chosen beings indeed! There is a closer and more pressing danger: that by focusing our attention on following ceremonies and prescribed canons, we tend to accord them undue importance: preachers arise to proclaim the power of the rite to produce the virtue it symbolizes, so that little by little the sign takes the place of reality, and religion as a whole ends up wallowing in superstition.

This is what happened to Brahmanism, Taoism, Judaism: and Catholicism almost suffered the same fate.

We must not be frightened by the temporary character of everything in nature. The earth is an organism; it partakes from other planets and also sends forces to them. All the regions of its individuality are being ceaselessly modified. Because its spirit works, because it is progressing, it is sensible to influences without. All creatures, especially men, may through their will modify the life of this planet, especially if they unite in view of achieving the same goal, as one finds in states and religions. The representative of Lucifer also acts and weighs heavily upon the free-will of the earth. The representative of God also exerts his influence in various ways, but especially through the organization of religious *egregores*. Elective affinities also exist upon the invisible planes.

Each one receives truth the best he can. A simple person

THE KINGDOM OF GOD

assimilates it simply, which means purely. The intellectual dissects it so as to extract a skeleton, which he calls metaphysics or theology. The ambitious man forge chains out of it so as to subjugate his subordinates. The moralist extracts from it some casuistry. The occultist draws some magic out of it. The philosopher finds some symbols therein.

The light-bearing Angel knows the fate awaiting him when once he contacts the secondary atmosphere of this planet. All of these obscurations and dismemberings are expected. Indeed, the spirit uses them to penetrate the darkest of shadowy corners, employing to this purpose the forms comprehensible to each creature who receives him, in proportion to the empty place he prepared within himself to receive the expected Visitor.

Because in actuality nothing unforeseen ever happens to us. Something always heralds our visitors. The quivering of a muscle, a passing intuition, a meeting, a dream, a presentiment, would warn us, were we sufficiently attentive. Meditation alone would suffice, since nothing comes our way unless we have called it. The Word is the only one who can come to us without our being aware of the hour or place of his dawning, since he is the only free being.

Our reflections and passions prepare our acts. Our acts entrust the seeds of our feelings and of our future thoughts to the fields-of-becoming. Everything has roots within and outside of us. Everything labors to produce flowers and fruits. Everything is important when once we learn how to base it on an awareness that only a sense of the divine gives it. Thus it is that man finds his true place again, for through his heart he is the center of the universe.

When a physician dresses a wound and finds himself splattered with sanitizers, he certainly has not soiled his soul. Similarly, if an Israelite eats pork, a Hindu eats a dog, or a Catholic eats meat on Fridays—while yet knowing how to share their repast, their clothing, and their habitation with the poor—you may be certain that God will welcome them nonetheless. As you can readily feel, a calumniator, an avaricious boss, a debauchee, no matter how many indulgences they may accumulate and donate grandly to Peter's pence, if they do not mend their ways, the light they had within will give way to darkness.

We cannot work without becoming soiled. The workbench, the office, the workshop, the pulpit, the street, the field, housework—they all tire the body out, bring perspiration, dirty hands, and shapeless, worn-out clothing. But the heart aflame for an ideal transforms all filthy rubbish into lights. The god transfigures the offering.

Defilement

MAN'S ROLE is threefold: to receive, to transform, to distribute. He is not responsible for what nature brings him unless he has asked for it. No matter how vile or perverse these things might be, they cannot confound his spirit. But his personal work (therefore his responsibility) starts with the transformations he brings about through the various alembics he possesses (his stomach, lungs, sensorium, mentality, cerebellum, etc.) to the substances of all kinds that his milieu sends him.

He is also held fully accountable for the quality of the forces, feelings, and ideas he radiates. And if these works are evil, they will rebound and reenter him under another guise to corrupt him further.

The temptation we resist does not stain, but purifies us.

THE KINGDOM OF GOD

Any traveler must be welcomed; but still, the host must know how to keep his house in order.

Prudence recommends chasing all impure desires away as soon as they come. But it is preferable, if one has the necessary strength, to talk to them, to reason with them as one would with an indocile child, so as to convert them into energies for good. Saint-Martin states: "Man is a thought of God; he is regenerated successively in his thoughts, in his words, and lastly in his action." For purification to be durable, it must start from the inside; the value of yogas, fasting, receiving sacraments, and magical training are only worthwhile in the Absolute because of the heart-feeling that vitalizes them.

The powers sown in us as seeds by men or by their gods are not viable. It is the Father who oversees everything, and what he has not ordained does not last. A self-made adept may hold on to the privileges he has conquered or purchased for fifty years, for a few centuries even, but the day comes when he must give them back. No matter *how* gigantic a will may be, it governs only a small corner of the universe; no matter how vast an intellect, it reflects only a part of the whole. Someone who would become, on his own authority, the self-appointed director of his neighbor, is a blind man leading another, whereas those offices that destiny distributes, in all hierarchies, are accompanied by a special help that enables the holder of that office, despite his possible incapacity, to fulfill his function adequately all the same.

The critics of morality point out its variability, for which they blame God, although man is the author of these divergences. The synthetic formula of our conduct is that we must not do harm to any being, even to those who, for the moment, constitute our personality.

Physical Alchemy

Matthew enumerates seven kinds of evil; Mark thirteen. But whatever their number, any vice vitiates because it is the result of the collaboration of our will with a tenebrous power; it also corrupts the life within one of our organs. A bad or evil thought leads to an evil act; it destroys mental equilibrium. Adultery is a broken promise, a theft; it disorganizes the harmony of births.

Fornication squanders the forces that nature entrusts to us so as to offer the possibility of a life on earth to a greater number of souls; besides which, it feeds certain classes of unclean invisibles and occasionally facilitates grave disorders on the planes of incarnation. Murder removes a great number of souls from the advantages of advancement this life offers, and to which they have a right.

Cruelty and spitefulness draw to us the very torments it inflicts upon others. We are held accountable for the least misdemeanor we enable others to commit. Slander isolates us from providential protections and turns our spirit away from the straight and narrow road. Envy provokes discord and brings us to the attention of beings stronger than we are. There is no call to covet anything, because even the least among creatures possesses something no other possesses. Moreover, we always have just what we deserve.

Pride immobilizes and blinds us.

Blasphemy evokes despair; although it does not reach God, it sets off fearsome explosions in the invisible.

Finally, madness renders our presence on this earth largely useless: being the result of desires that are too violent, it disaligns the organs within us and hinders our work.

All forms of evil are closely interconnected; they engender and destroy each other in turn, only to be reborn all the more venomous. They are more or less active in us accord-

THE KINGDOM OF GOD

ing to the collaboration they receive from us. But heaven awaits our request to lessen and to transform them into good. How often does heaven put us to the test, only to force our call of distress to gush forth—as Jesus points out in his reply to the Grecian woman when she asked him for the salvation of her daughter.

On the other hand, we have no right to challenge heaven. Those who do so, prove their ill-will and how adulterated is their spirit. From a certain standpoint, the result of our acts is a union with the ideal we serve. Moreover, our spirit has a spiritual bridegroom, who is the Lord of the religion into which we were born. This is indicated in the legend of Krishna and the female cowherds or gopis, and in the infidelity of the Israelites, who forsook the *shekinah* for idols. The true God does not punish the fickle; he awaits their return in order to retrieve them, to take those who repent back with him. That is what, after having conquered death, Jesus does: as he ascends into heaven, he draws in his wake all who converted. As to the others, such as the prophet Jonas, between two existences they are submitted, over the course of three days, to the replay of their errors and crimes.

Jesus is very forgiving; he excuses our mistakes, because evil swarms within us with intense life. The seeds of all kinds of spiritual forces that are put in us from the beginning grow and bear fruit in proportion as we advance from life to life. And when they have undergone a special preparation, they serve to nourish many creatures surrounding us. This preparation is done by a leaven, and this leaven is what is found in the bottom of our heart. If it is sincerity, the fruits of our works will be wholesome despite our inadequacies, our errors. If it be a falsehood, these fruits will be venomous despite our knowledge and know-how.

Physical Alchemy

Thus does Christ put his disciples on guard against hypocrisy, knowing they have to deal with an inconstant deceitful crowd.

To give oneself airs of authority or of virtue, to satisfy our personal desires, brings forth illusions within us. The evil we commit in darkness (its natural habitat) multiplies rapidly. We profane deeds of light by putting them in service of darkness. When the shame of hypocrisy is revealed, men and invisible assistants will be scandalized; forces are wasted emitting into the secondary atmosphere vain forms: vampireish centers as to the individual and, as to the milieu, deceptions in subsequent existences. It is the devil who invented cunning and deviousness. Heaven wants everything to take place in the broad daylight of its sun.

Christ and his friends are the only ones we cannot dupe, because they are the only ones in whom dwells the truth.

In short, let us remember that everything lives; that we ourselves choose our society of invisibles, that any debt must be paid where it was contracted; that if we shy away from duty, nature—being just—burdens us with enduring the suffering caused by our laziness, and that seven incarnations will not pass before we are brought back to the same place, in similar circumstances and among the same people, to make the effort we refused to make long ago.

Remember that nothing grows without work; bad inner propensities and outer oppositions are resistances useful to the training of the spirit's forces. "Expend your life if you want to receive life," says Saint-Martin. Stagnation is forbidden. Whoever does not advance takes a step back; whoever does not develop, withers. "One is a saint," Ruysbroeck answered to a vacillating person, "in the measure wherein one wants to become one."

The will is truly powerful; we must use it, and learn by experience to see its perfection in its most intimate conformity with the law of the Father.

The Beloved

MOST OF JESUS'S acts clashed with the prejudices of the doctors of the law and of the officials. Scandal is a spiritual indigestion; just as the stomach rejects non-assimilable foods, so does our spirit revolt before what it does not comprehend. Sometimes this repugnance comes from the fact that the food is in fact unhealthy. Sometimes we stubbornly cling to prejudices, in which case scandal is the shock necessary to broaden our inner horizon. It is good not to barricade yourself to much, to keep your judgment free enough to welcome the new after an impartial examination. What is impossible and unbelievable today frequently becomes the ordinary fare of tomorrow. Each act is a seed sown in the field of the future. The contemporaries of Christ did not understand the constant innovation of things. Brought up on the letter of the Mosaic law, they believed their law to be eternal and immutable, and their obstinacy is one of the most frequent forms of intolerance.

Yet the Savior never misses an occasion of demonstrating the original characteristics of his work. When he unties the tongue of the mute, when he opens the eyes of the blind, when he restores the paralytic's limbs, an impartial witness cannot help but see the sovereign power of the Therapeut free from any formalism, disengaged from any tradition, commanding effortlessly, using any kind of method. Yet, this serene invincibility never operates without the expressed permission of the Father. This indomitable courage

Physical Alchemy

never falls into bravado; it dares defend itself; it dares flee when it judges it useful; as much as possible it operates on the physical plane using physical means. This Wisdom brings everything back to unity, designating sin as the only cause of suffering, indicating struggle as the only means of evolution, precognizing faith as the universal remedy and charity as the perfect rule of any life.

Christ always keeps in the background. He wants us to see him merely as the envoy of the Father.

The goal the ancient sages offered their disciples was the progressive exaltation of the individual. They gave them to understand that the best way to acquire happiness seemed to be to discern the providential plan of creation and to conform one's life to it. Christ on the other hand offers us, not the law of the land as model, but the legislator: practice is placed above theory, the act above science. The Son imitates the Father, man imitates the Son through a centralized effort rather than a circumferential effort as found in polytheisms.

Were the Son to do something on his own, he would not be the Son anymore. He is the Father materialized. He is the act of the Father. He is the form of the Father. Thus, in the absolute sense, he realizes the ancient adage: a healthy soul in a healthy body.

Moreover, the disciple who does something of his own accord is not a disciple anymore. Man is of the earth. The Son is the tree in whom the mineral evolves. As to the Father, in this case, as in everything else, he is the Creator.

The world is the materialization of the Word, and Jesus is the heart of the world, which is why the Father loves the Son. Discard all esoteric grounds that pretend to reveal three, five, or seven Logoi. Metaphysics only stimulates. It is only designed to move certain wills that lack the energy of love and action. The excursions it offers us, however attractive, lack the living value of effort. In order to understand Jesus even a little bit, just listen to the simple anecdotes he relates about himself.

"The Father loves the Son." Doesn't this phrase resonate in our hearts as the ancient words that send the bespectacled scholar back to the happy century when he remembers wandering free and happy in the hospitable forest? Men dare speak of love; their ignorance excuses them. Who knows how to love here on earth? Among the three million inhabitants of this city, among the thirty persons present here, united as we are by heaven to recall him, is there one heart that has lived ten minutes of absolute love?

When the Father projects his thought of the world into nothingness, the Son is born: he is the Alpha. Among the millions upon millions of seeds cast upon this soil, there has to be but one among them that will work perfectly, so that with the help of time this perfection will propagate everywhere: this again is the Son, scribe of the living Book. The Father cares for, nurtures, and cherishes this seed more than all others put together, because it works exclusively for him. And when the time of universal harvest draws near, which of the ears of corn appears last, the strongest, the most beautiful, because it has been buried the longest, the most loved because it has chosen the most obscure work? It is again the Son, now under his aspect of Omega.

Before the dawn, you were there. You will be there in the depths of night. You are the Word with wide open eyes, Servant of the servants, Unknown among unknowns, indefatigable Martyr through innumerable agonies, Healer of the world, the only one worthy of being loved by our Father.

Physical Alchemy

It is his Son whom the Father cherishes, in the cosmos as within each creature. But he, the object of universal adoration, considers himself as such a cipher that he does not dare speak of the infinite love which unites him to his Father. As the reciprocal delights of each other, they separate only to spread, to deepen, to exalt, love within their organs. It is we who are the bodies of the Word and the temples of God. Therefore, within each created being one finds at least one cell wherein heaven dwells.

This spark of the Father, yet distinct from him, is ceaselessly immersed in him, blended with him.

It is no longer a question of personality, free will, demiurges, or psychic powers; it is an organ obeying the Will that has been working on it all along, non-stop, with perfect patience, meticulousness, and power.

If the universe is the body of the Word, man is the heart of the spiritual and material world; and Christ is the archetype of ideal humanity. Nature finds its heaven in the spirit of man, and man finds his beatitude by becoming a cell of the glorious body of Jesus—so that unity is realized step by step through harmony.

All of this is the external point of view of the relationship between the Father and the Son wherein we perceive the three persons in God. The Trinity is an approximative formula, and yet our finest thinkers have broken their wings trying to approach that sun. We common mortals can, however, make a profitable study of the explanations of the divine ternary that abound in the books of the Doctors of the Church. Let me steer you to them. But I warn you that the Catholic Trinity is an original concept, not to be mistaken or assimilated to the Hindu *Trimurti*, or to the different ternaries of the Taoists, Buddhists, Mazdeists, Druids, or Hermeticists. By wanting everything to concur, one falsifies the whole.

As seen from the divine plane, the relationship between the Father and the Son—which is known as the Spirit—remains incomprehensible to us. The distance between our actual state of being and the perfect human nature of Christ is enormous. No matter. Progress is unending. After certain periods, the length of which disconcerts our imagination, the progress accomplished will be but the preparation for other climactic stages. There is no need of ever stopping. The greatest known marvels are seedlings of still loftier marvels. And the power that conquers the impossible in that manner is faith.

The Ideal

HEAVEN REALLY IS, as the liturgy celebrates, a virgin that is constantly violated by the desperate desires of the human soul; every stupor it undergoes engenders a new form of the Word; and the impossible becomes virgin again, offering itself once more to all the daring of faith.

All that Christ teaches is to starve our faith, so that we may understand—by living them—more and more vast aspects of this mystery (in itself bottomless) that we call God. Ever since the coming of our Lord, the world possesses, outside of its inborn force, a new force that it can extract from the infinite treasure of divine light, if it wants to. Without limits, nothing can become perfectible.

Nowadays, everything within us is enchained by time and space. Even our highest aspirations are prisoners. Were they free, would we not follow several at the same time? It is through matter that we suffer this shame, but God

Physical Alchemy

watches over us. He liberates us from it little by little, thanks to the infusion of eternal life, of his Son within us. Jesus is master of the world. He fulfills his duty as King by giving himself to all, but he chooses the hour for that gift.

In this case, says the pseudo-mystic, why should we bother to labor if the testing-time is immutably fixed? Only a corrupt servant reasons in this manner, however, not a devoted one. And were we in the least conscious of the inestimable treasure Jesus brings us, no agony would be too costly to hasten, were it but for one second, the moment of his coming.

This marvelous result demands no regimen, no training or abstruse sciences. It suffices that our will, or better still our love, be heaven-bent. By displacing the center of gravity of an object, you displace the whole mass. By uprooting the vine from our spirit and replanting it into the earth of the living, the vine will be renewed. There is no need to change our life outwardly. Let us simply change the goal of our daily tasks. This suffices to let us enter upon one of the numerous paths Christ cleared over two thousand years ago: short cuts to the divine homeland.

Only the intention that, from the depths of the heart, enlivens our actions, is valid in the eternal, and undergoes judgment. As we know nothing at all, it would not be just that we be held responsible for evil we commit thinking we were doing right, or that we be recompensed for good that might come out of the evil we wanted to do.

It is wise that only the possessor of light dispenses the recompense. Christ gives it to whomever he chooses, which means to those whom the Father designates. The meat that nourishes a man can kill an infant. Hence, were those who desire the light able to obtain it suddenly, they would endure atrocious sufferings. Eternal life is frightfully corrosive to all forms of natural life. How many people have I heard ask, beg, for spiritual progress, who were surprised, despairingly shouting invectives, when poverty, illness, or disease struck them the very next month! The more active is the medicine, the more violent its effect.

Moreover, who knows us inside out? Who has witnessed our countless births and deaths? Who has repeatedly held back our criminal arm? Who has sustained us in our weariness? The very One, our Friend, to whom it is right to leave the care of our advancement. Everything lives. Spiritual progress is expressed, in the heart of the world, by a complete drama. You cannot enjoy the benefits of a social group without giving that collective something in return. In order for our ego to be allowed to cross the border into a more beautiful country, the guards demand that it take off its travel-soiled clothes, and prove its usefulness. On the earthly plane this cleansing and proof translate into suffering. But we need to have the stamina to carry out these tasks!

There is only one who knows the history of each of us; only one who has observed all the cells of our body and all the powers of our psyche from their genesis; only one who knows their future; only one who can test the flexion point of what the will is capable of: it is he, the Friend, who never abandons us.

A judgment requires the appearance of the accused. As no creature could withstand being before the Father, it is essential that the Son be our judge, because he is the angel of compassion. Having endured all of our ordeals, he can appraise them.

On the other hand, justice demands that a thief make

Physical Alchemy

restitution; therefore, we must make compensation for our misdeeds where we committed them. What about God's goodness, will you say? It works in this way: Having found a nest of blackbirds, an urchin amuses himself pulling out their feathers. You, the outraged passerby, give him a talking to. He does not understand, and says, "They are just birds!" Were you to draw him across your knees and pull out *his* hair, he would immediately understand the birds' suffering. But he would still not be reformed, because you will not be there at his next act of cruelty.

Thus man unknowingly does evil, just for the pleasure, we being somewhat stupid brutes! We think we are the only ones who live and feel and suffer. As for the others, they do not matter! So nature steps in to show us, through experience, that they matter. And as nature has a vigilant police force, each of our misdeeds inevitably becomes the theme of a corrective redress. Yet, heaven's indulgence always minimizes the penalty, and so never, never, do we endure the equivalent of what we caused others to suffer. According to the liturgical formula, the "difference" has been covered by the merits of our Lord Jesus Christ.

We have already talked enough about faith for it to be worth repeating the imperviousness that its possession confers. He in whom this flame burns is above the ocean of destiny; he has passed the dead point on which the universes pivot. The eternal life in which he dwells immunizes him; he is above the law, since he is part of the very Being of the Lawgiver. What's more, he becomes the living embodiment of this law wherever it pleases the Father that he re-descend.

THE KINGDOM OF GOD

The Witnesses of Jesus Christ

PRIMARILY they are those he saved, those he healed, those he judged. It seems as though the Father in his love were consulting us in administering our destiny. A throng extending its supplicating arms toward the ideal struggles in the spirit of man; we desire to possess all powers, all truthfulness, all beauties. We yearn to possess knowledge, we long for harmony and love. Our anguish can only be assuaged in the person of the Son. Therefore it is we who give him the right of judging us.

That is why he has descended into all the domains of death, bringing life to all who are willing to accept it. These beings are chosen by him in advance, at each of his visits, in full foreknowledge of the facts. It is from him that they receive the faculty of listening profoundly, ceaselessly, totally attentive. It is he who expands his light in them, to the very limits of their selves, to their actions.

This life that he dispenses to the dying, both material and spiritual, is the comprehensible aspect of the Father, corresponding to humanity's ideal. That is why Jesus calls himself Son of Man and why he is the canon by which we are appraised and judged. When we consider the role of the Word in the universe, he is its law; consequently he regulates the advance of all creatures. When we consider his individuality, he is its perfection, hence all progress accomplished is measured from him.

The gospel verses we study are not allegorical. They recall real phenomena. This is how simple faith understands them, and how the seer verifies them. Each word of the Word is an act; each of his acts is a word.

To listen is more than an auditory sensation; the word

Physical Alchemy

heard must be incorporated into our spirit as a piece of bread transforms itself into organic cells. For that to be, it is necessary to have perfect mastery of self, because everything around us speaks and everything within us has ears.

If the sound of the elements sometimes moves the traveler to the point of unveiling his deepest intimacies, how much more can Jesus's voice, made of all harmonies, redolent with all pains, ringing with all audacities, not spark the flame that was smoldering, almost extinguished, under the ashes of our old idolatries?

And twenty centuries ago, this voice, still relevant today, called out to us.

No one today merits the title of a living being. Our life is made up of a thousand deaths, and we can do nothing about it—other than open ourselves to healing. The body dies and is reborn without cease, until such time as it reaches the long night from which it returns to wherever its Judge has given the order to resume its work. Every disappointment is the death of one of our feelings, until our heart, having exhausted the cults of the gods, finally surrenders to the light yoke of its true master. Our intelligence only grows through countless deaths. In books, there is the writer's own error of conception, the treachery of the pen that almost never expresses the right thought, the students' incomprehension that daily mixes his personal equation with the author's opinion. Any knowledge acquired cerebrally remains provisional until such time as we are able to face the sun of truth—the august stature of Jesus. To attain this stage, we need to become accustomed to the air of that country, whether by feeling with sincerity or acting in verity. Errors and illusions then vanish of their own accord, like swamp vapors at dawn.

THE KINGDOM OF GOD

What we call evil is still a creature of the Father. Who are the truly dead, who are the dwellers in darkness if not sinners and devils? It is for them especially that Christ has come. They are beings consumed by a devouring ardor. They are greedy for everything, and their violence clothes them with such brightness that it overshadows the virtues of honest men, which pale in comparison. Whoever masters his fear of heights over the abysses can face the vertigo of the stars. Whoever plunges deeply into evil will be able to rise very high into good.

With soulful eyes, Christ goes towards these very beings. And so they mob him, clothe themselves with his vestments, wrest away his knowledge and snatch his charm, drag him so as to inspire terror all around them. And he, accepting the laissez-faire policy, knows that the drops of his blood that are shed for these revolted ones will act unbeknownst to them. He knows that little by little the perfume of his vestments will mollify their anger. Eternity is on his side. Thus does the voice of the Word resuscitate the dead.

As to our will, whatsoever is not a source of agony for it, impairs it. For example, by winning a lucrative job by pull, and becoming too attached to it, we become its slave, while if we spurn that job on account of a higher ambition, we remain a slave, merely changing masters. Consequently, the triumph over the will is solemnized through total renunciation: then it is not anymore the being who wills, it is God acting through it.

These are, in outline, some of the ways in which the Word gives royal life to his tenants. Each of them receives it in full, according to the full capacity of his spirit and even of his body. Nothing heaven does is truncated. Its favors always end up on the physical plane. And there really will be

Physical Alchemy

a resurrection of the dead, a raising of the dust, a reorganization of skeleton and of tissue. We know a little about the subject; that is why the apparent difficulty regarding it frightens us: the conversion of a heart is a much more complicated miracle, but it does not astonish us, because we know nothing of the spirit of man.

Remember that resurrection is promised everyone. The whole is everywhere. Hence, if the planes of nature, of the created, interpenetrate one another only within certain limits (about which the geometrical data of the n dimensions give us a symbol), the planes of the spirit, the states of the human heart, are imbued with a freedom to which there are no barriers, veils, or precipices. Hell is everywhere the self dominates. Heaven is everywhere sacrifice reigns.

After each judgment, beings are allocated according to their individual needs and according to the needs of the relevant milieu: within or beyond space; more or less elevated. But in the end, all creatures will be admitted into the palaces of the Father.

Everyone may become an auxiliary to the Word. The collaboration he solicits from us constitutes the essence of our work and carries its own recompense. Because Jesus is everywhere, he assumes all forms, and the modes of his activity multiply *ad infinitum*.

You must realize that the sublimest pages ever written, or that will ever be written, about Christ amount to vague approximations. Such efforts are rather like the search of the astronomer peering at a star through his telescope, but knowing nothing, really, about the being of that star. It is a simple enough matter to state that the Word came on earth to help his friends. But these words hardly represent the frightful operation entailed!

THE KINGDOM OF GOD

When an emperor decides to fulfill his duty to the utmost, it is impossible for him to examine everything personally. And yet Jesus does that. And he does so, not only towards a mere handful of men, but for the numberless peoples among created beings. To purify all forms of matter and place each in a better spot; to rectify the orb of planets, of comets, and of events; to distribute sciences, arts, and inventors; to open better communicating roads between the cosmic cities and villages; to heal, give hope, feed the god and the worm, restrain the demons or leave them free-rein, celebrate the zodiacal feasts that mark the periods of universal cycles; to determine births and deaths; to plan the sowings upon all earths within all ethers and all spirits—this is the work of Christ, which he alone can accomplish.

For, he does not work of his own accord. He duplicates within nature what he has seen the Father bring to pass in the Absolute. Consequently, he does not violate any liberty. He leaves beings free to act, even in error, satisfied with holding them back when they plummet down a hillside. his helping arm is called: the guardian angel.

As far as Christ is concerned, he does not want to have a will of his own; that is why everything obeys him. He is not curious: that is why the voice of all things must perforce tell him nothing but the truth. And he loves each creature with equal discerning and sapient tenderness. Consequently, he has the right to judge everything. He restores order in the universe without anger, without scorn or discouragement. Do please take notice once more of the radical opposition between the human and the divine procedures of behavior and of knowledge.

But who will prove the spiritual legality of Christ's mission? As a man, the divine missionary will suffer criticism

Physical Alchemy

and discussion; as God, his testimony would be irresistible; but his tenderness seals his lips so as not to crush the unbelievers. Jesus cites three witnesses.

The first testimony is that of the Precursor, whose declarations were sincere, seeing that he cemented them with his penance and blood. Moreover, they were veracious because although he met his Master but once in Israel, his spirit had accompanied him often during the course of his long and dolorous descent. The voice of the Baptist usually addressed itself to the masses.

The second testimony is that of the works Christ declares having received the power to accomplish from the Father. Whether he teaches, heals, or prophesies, he never forgets to render thanks to the Father—to begin with (because he is certain of his success) to set the example and to underscore the singular character of his action. But everyone cannot understand the character of sovereign mastery that the works of Jesus possess: he is king; he has but to command to be obeyed; all creatures serve him; any force is malleable in his hands. But the majority of men do not feel the power of his word. Only those in whom love has developed their second sight are aware of it.

The third testimony of the Son is the Father himself. Now, no one has ever heard the voice of the Father, or contemplated his face, for in each creature there is a tenebrous root that could never withstand absolute light. This is why Jesus invites his auditors to seek the testimony of his Father in the Scriptures, since they transmit messages received by a few privileged persons. This proof is addressed to the intellect. The ancients received hope from this proof, and when the inner flame vacillates, it is through this scriptural proof that the Spirit revivifies it with his breath.

THE KINGDOM OF GOD

It is not for his personal satisfaction that Christ is concerned about human suffrage. He knows that what we glorify in our great men is ourselves, without suspecting that those we triumph over will often become our accusers. He knows that if we do not come to him, it is out of incomprehension; the sense of the things of heaven only develops the mind, then in the etheric-fluidic, then in the physical, when the love of God already exists in the heart; and this last flame is only generated by a transformation of charity. These masterpieces of inner architecture are the crowning achievement of a very long labor. But this is nothing. What is essential is to open the door and render divine collaboration possible. You understand that a plant can live only if it has roots; that our faculties, powers, virtues, are seeds whose foster-mother or soil is our earthly life. So, you must force yourself to act. Don't let any thought, any impulse, die in reverie; give them substance, if not in action, at least in speech or in writing.

An ordinary religious initiator, such as a Krishna, a Lao-Tze, a Buddha, or a Moses, although far surpassing the common stature, nevertheless remains a created being, a circumscribed being. The treasure he brings is therefore limited, and demands effort on the part of his beneficiaries in return; in other words, a commercial transaction or contract, so to speak. If the faithful, who have received their share, fail to fulfill the duties implicit in this gift, they are liable to a penalty. On the other hand, the Word brings us a limitless treasure. This is the reason why, when he judges, he does not accuse; whereas, to the contrary, the other religious protagonists, who are merely men, accuse but cannot judge.

Illumination only seems to come suddenly. Look at the innumerable phenomena of nature one by one: they all are

Physical Alchemy

the results of a long, tedious, hidden work. A descent of the Word alone may sometimes come suddenly. But, had the whole of creation understood Christ instantaneously, how many beings would have died! This is why Jesus tells Peter it was not his natural faculties that permitted him to recognize him as the Christ, but that this capacity came through divine grace.

Meanwhile, Catholics were wrong to presume so early that the promise he made to the chief of the apostles on that occasion was meant for them. And the Protestants were equally wrong in rejecting it. Christ said: "I will give you the keys of the kingdom." Could he really entrust them to the man who, a few days later, was to deny him? The function and the power that he promised this man will surely devolve upon him—but later, when the materials of the veritable Church will have really been assembled. This archetypal Church does not yet exist. The sanctuaries of all confessions have served too many crimes for the Spirit to rest therein. And the interior Church, foreseen by certain Church Fathers, by the Rosicrucians, by Lopoukhin, Swedenborg, and Eckartshausen, is only the preparation for the Holy Assembly by which our earth will someday become a part of heaven.

Before the foundations of this ultimate temple could be dug, the very ground had to be washed with the innocent blood of the most-pure Prince, by the death of Jesus. Before a planet can be redeemed, it is indispensable that all beings who inhabit and constitute this planet, from its subterranean abysses up to its soul-heavens, receive the visit of the light; and the light cannot enter into the darkness without suffering; that is why the life of Jesus was nothing but a series of ordeals and painful experiences—far more numerous than those the four gospels relate. These ordeals were ultimately crowned through the martyrdom of the Passion.

Moreover, Peter is promised to be the base of this living edifice, and not the summit. The pediment is there for all to see; it stands there in the sunlight, exactly as the temporal successors of the humble Galilean fisherman will do. But as for the foundations, buried in the cold, dark earth, nobody cares about them, and yet they support the whole edifice. Would this not be the true work of this robust spirit, thanks to whose invisible dedication, for twenty centuries, all that is beautiful and great in Catholicism has been able to shine forth and spread, despite greedy clergy and proud prelatures?

I have often repeated that everything is alive, that what we call abstractions, ideas, psychism are really living persons par excellence. Any terrestrial form is the cloak of a genius; and the being of Christ himself welcomes all other beings. Hence, the end of his mission is not suffering per se. He suffered all agonies known and unknown, to teach us how to welcome them, so that the universal genius of dolor may also one day enter the Kingdom

Renunciation

THE OLDER THE SPIRIT, the broader its expanse; the more sensitive it is, the more it suffers; the closer it approaches its final purification, the more painful its inner struggle becomes, and action on the outside becomes harsher. Just as the cannon ball spins ever faster as it progresses through the length of the gun, so does man feel his inner resistances and energies exacerbated as he reaches the moment when, similarly to the projectile, he finds himself hurled from the

Physical Alchemy

obscure prisons of nature to the radiant landscapes of the divine.

When work intensifies, courage must rise to the occasion. To the man who yearns for heaven, an ordeal becomes a rejoicing of his intimate being, even when painful to his organs, because each pain is a step toward the ideal. That is why Jesus, whose heart burns, consumed by the passion of sacrifice, longs for the hour of martyrdom. In his eyes, physical death and the moral anguish that must accompany it are nothing more than passionately awaited visitors, providing him with the means to complete his redemptive work.

To Peter's expressed desire that these painful hours not take place, Christ replies as if Satan had spoken. The devil is indifferent to our sufferings; but in order to deplete our energy, he resorts to inserting false compassion. Someone whom we know to have been designated to fulfill a divine mission should not inspire our pity, but, on the contrary, our envy. Such a spectacle should rouse ardor, stir emulation, increase our enthusiasm. Because if the man's spirit, body, and intelligence have received the noble privilege of torture, you may be certain that his soul remains serene, that its flame radiates a warmth you can feel. It is written: Blessed are those who suffer!

In truth, beatitude is usually found in the midst of torments, because there is in man a part that is natural and another that is supernatural. Here, then, is a correct, meticulous, impeccable painting; the work of a talented man, from which a student may learn a great deal. But next to it you find a canvas with dabs of color and a few lines, no more than a rough sketch. Nothing holds it together and it was daubed in five minutes. Yet you feel something beautiful stirring within you. The being in man is similar to that.

THE KINGDOM OF GOD

He is made up of several cogwheels (some delicate, some highly efficient, functioning marvelously, interplaying without a hitch) that one can study, analyze, and sometimes reproduce: muscles, nerves, viscera, fluids, electric currents and sensations, ideas, memory, reasoning, desires, instincts, will—and still many other mechanisms, all of which turn, twirl, advance, shift into gear, from the small circle of ordinary life up to the cosmic presences dwelling in the stars. All of these, on their way to perfection, become subject to pain and agony.

But let a breath of the Spirit waft by, and the interplay of this wonderful machinery will seem only a game. Suffering will shed its anguish, despair its harrowing, because a tiny, pale, formless glimmer will have appeared, one with no apparent glory, but through which one may perceive the vibrant halo of the radiant, unfathomable abyss of the uncreated.

Be conscious of the inestimable jewel that rests in the core of our self. What matters ignorance, penury, persecution, since the veritable self is worth infinitely more than the treasures of the princes of the cosmos. Understand how science, talent, juggling occult sciences, and all other prerogatives are nothing in comparison to our soul. Everything in nature can be bought; the most narrow-minded man of today may be, a few million years hence, or tomorrow, the regent of a planetary cohort. The soul alone is free, unconditioned, inexpressible, priceless, imperceptible, incommensurable.

Fainthearted children, why do you fear death? Try to be men who can gauge things at their true measure; or else become infants again, who fear nothing because they know nothing.

It was with good reason that the Brahmans assigned the

role of great hierophant to one of the forms of Shiva the Destroyer, and that Matthew twice repeats the precept of renunciation. Death is the universal initiator. It is the fateful means of progress; and yet, despite this autocracy, the day will come when we too will conquer it. We must use discernment in this case. If you profess along with the old Lao-Tzu that to scorn a thing places man above that thing, that scorning personal efforts renders the will omnipotent, you are transplanting the precept of renunciation upon the plane of spiritual pride. Our psycho-physiologists of today have reached the stage.

Krishna furnishes a healthier axiom when he commands us to act without worrying about the fruits of our acts. This does diminish our pride, but we find that this kind of prudence is more concerned with guaranteeing a trouble-free future than helping the unfortunate.

The counsel of Christ is threefold. It embraces the three periods of time, the three poles of any existence, the three modes of our human life: the inner adversaries, the external enemies, and the resistance of matter.

It is of prime importance to pull out the weeds. The devil attacks the elite only; the fewer venomous plants there are, the better chance good seeds have to grow in fine soil.

Meister Eckhart writes: "When man becomes a cipher to created beings and to himself, God flows therein."

To welcome the ordeals we brought upon ourselves through past misdeeds reestablishes our connections with all the beings we are linked to. This restores peace, which is the indispensable condition for productive work; it gives a solid foundation to the action (properly speaking) through which we may "follow" the Word.

The complexity of the human composite is such that its

perfection takes place by fits and starts. This time, one group of organs improves; the next existence will purify a second group. Man thus gradually becomes free in every sphere whose burdens he has borne; until the day when, clean of all defilement, rich in all experience, washed by all pain, he enters the realm of perfect autonomy.

We will never sufficiently comprehend that nothing in and of ourselves belongs to us. For months a man may pursue a particular faculty or strive to gain a certain advantage, but he possesses neither that power nor that supremacy. The thing we run after holds us in its grip and we become slaves of the gods whom we have succeeded to reach.

And, what is more, how can we be sure our prerogatives will last? He who is endowed by nature with a fine mind and the means to enrich it receives this privilege only for the progress of the collectivity, although he may also derive personal joy from it. But there is no guarantee that in his next incarnation this man will regain his past mentality. Directors of existences consider the whole; there is little favoritism in the administration of souls; wealth and psychic powers are placed in the hands of those who can spread their benefits to humanity. As far as the individual benefit to be expected from good management, the fruit of our labors is distributed to all of nature; to we ourselves, our soul, is attributed, in the Absolute, only the light it has generated by carrying out these labors with a pure will and a heart filled with abnegation.

The immortal psychic personality of a St Francis or of a Louis Pasteur is not enriched from the benefits that their virtue or science have determined for the future; all this is diffused and diluted in the collective mass beings. The spiritual body of such a hero is essentially increased only by the

Physical Alchemy

pure light kindled by his idealistic love and sustained by his his laborious sufferings.

Hence, let us abandon any possessive attitude whatever. The angel of faith must become our familiar host; nature's radiant magnificences are but a handful of mud compared to the least of the uncreated lights. Our soul is our sole veritable treasure.

Constant pride and perversity may depreciate it. This diminution is wrought by the Son of Man at the times, when, appearing in his glorious body, he is ashamed of those who denied him.

When he foretells that some of his auditors will see those days, this prediction, which has not yet been realized, is not (as a modern commentator claims) the effect of intellectual imperfection in his human nature. Neither is it, as rationalist theology interprets it, the announcement of the Ascension. It presages that our hope faces far greater perspectives. Yes, judgments do take place at prearranged dates, but we do not know them, nor do we know the places where they will occur. Therefore we, whose eyes are blinded before the invisible lights, do not know if a particular worldwide war, cataclysm, or epidemic are not the physical results of an occult work of spiritual and collective reorganization. Attila did not lay claim to the awesome title of being the "scourge of god" for nothing.

It is possible, it is certain, that a few men are still living today who saw Christ in Judea two thousand years ago. The genealogy of matter is unknown. We are ignorant of the true growth of physical cells; of the molecules of carbon, iron, hydrogen, etc., that are inside of us right now. We cannot deduce from what tree, animal, or rock they came. Only the child of God can see that at a glance. And if heaven has judged matter precious enough to descend into it, heaven will not abandon its education. Therefore, if once upon a time a certain portion of physical substance physically received the precious favor of divine contact, it is necessary for these organisms to remain as permanent witnesses for the sake of the beings that came after the ineffable miracle which took place in their presence long ago.

For in this way, the individuations of ponderable matter, with their perpetual renewals, continue to receive, through the centuries, in their living essence, the remedy that, in the time of Christ, cured some of them.

The men of whom I speak (there are perhaps only two or three) do not seem to have escaped death in the eyes of their successive contemporaries; but their spirit has never crossed the chasm separating our earth from that of the departed. They themselves (I mean their watchful conscience) do not suspect the miracle they are; if they did, they would be falsely proud themselves and thus weaken the effect of their role.[2]

The Transfiguration

THE LEARNED MONKS Sicard de Cremona (1155–1215) and Guillaume Durand de Mende (c. 1230–1296) have proven that this theophany took place on August 6th. Modern exegetes believe that, contrary to tradition, it did not take place on Mount Tabor, but on one of the summits of the great Mount Hermon. These facts would be important

---

[2] Here we can refer back to the well-known verse: "This generation will not have passed, before all this is accomplished." (Matt. 24:34)

Physical Alchemy

only if we wanted to establish, in the domain of occult sciences, the significance of this prodigy. All we need ascertain here is the logical place it occupies in the history of Christ.

Seven actors participated in this drama. Three are corporeal: Peter, James, and John. Three are spiritual: the Voice, Moses, and Elijah. The hero, Jesus, stands at the boundary of the two worlds. To understand the Transfiguration, one would have to understand time and space in their living essence. The one as well as the other are creatures; they are even the vastest of all beings, since all the others move and develop within them. When man believes he has escaped from their grasp through the application of science and will-power, all he really does is submit to another of their forms. We need only look around us to notice that we can only overcome the one by submitting to the other. To gain time, an express train needs distance; to increase in volume, any body needs time.

Imagine spaces that develop in other dimensions than our own. Imagine times that have a different rate of speed. Such spaces and times (an immense variety) exist in this creation. The organic and mental laws of the beings they contain are very different from our own. Bodies and minds function in inconceivable ways. And if one of these spheres were to touch our planet, spectators would either not notice anything, or if they did, everything in them would have to change momentarily: their consciousness, their sensorium, their very physical appearance.

Now, in the phenomenon with which we are concerned, a triple conjunction took place: this earth, the land of the prophets, and the kingdom of the Father were brought together by their summits. For the three apostles were the crown of humanity; Elijah and Moses were the two greatest heralds of the Word; and the voice of God himself was heard.

If Christ therefore changed physical form, this was necessary since, being the cause, the means, and the agent of the prodigy, he had to bring these three planes together in himself. And the apostles only lost consciousness because they were mere spectators; they were only sensitive to the atmosphere of the miracle; the fact itself overwhelmed them.

Moses and Elijah are the only personages in the sacred history of Judaism (for that matter, in the universal history of religions) whose bodies have not been reclaimed by the earth.[3] By this we must understand that it is not an acquired privilege but the result of the special nature of these bodies. The accounting between biological exchanges is subject to inviolable regulations; any organism must return to the mother who engendered it. Any body that comes from the earth is returned to the earth, but the earth cannot claim what it has not given! Hence, if a man is assumed into heaven, it is not thanks to any power he gained from the initiatory crypts. Neither is it conferred as a favor. It is because the spirit of his physical life comes from another planet than our own. And yet, neither the anatomist nor the chemist would ever find in his flesh elements different from those in any other cadaver.

This episode lasted but one instant, yet was sufficient for the world to receive a new grace: the inauguration of a road between heaven, this earth, and the land of the dead. Is not the Word the universal mediator? And had he not promised to a few that they would not die without having seen him again, in his glory?

---

[3] Enoch is an antediluvian patriarch.

Physical Alchemy

We will understand this better by probing within ourselves. Mount Tabor, says Ruysbroeck, is the nudity that the light reaches at the summit of our spirit. We must become Peter through the knowledge of truth—by *faith*; we must become James by supplanting the world—by *hope*; we must become John through the plenitude of grace—by *love*. It is up there that the men of God are buried. When the Word has taken on his full stature in us, there comes a visit from the Father, before whose brilliance our highest virtues vanish.

Man's goal is the realization of his innate freedom in nature. To achieve this goal, he possesses a physical element (his body) and a winged instrument (his self). Body, self, and freedom are in constant interplay.

Freedom acting with the self produces spiritual faculties; acting with the body, it gives conscious, sensory, or mental faculties.

The mind and the body in balance is wakefulness.

When the spirit descends into bodily life, by means of somnambulism for example, it produces presentiment, prevision, divination, forms of lethargy. When the body rises to spiritual life, dreaming, enthusiasm, rapture appear, forms of ecstasy.

Let us not proceed any further in these researches of Hoene-Wronski, who borrowed the plan from the layout of the Kabbalah. It is evident that the phenomenon of the transfiguration was for Christ an ecstasy, since he remained fully conscious, fully awake.

As far as one can define a phenomenon of which we do not understand the mechanism, ecstasy means that the personality has been transported to an extraordinary plane. It is an intensification of the nervous system that becomes capable of registering contacts of an entirely different kind than those of our waking state. In fact, any perception is always a contact.

In the terminology of the rationalist Brahmins, if mental conception is a focus; will, a line; meditation, a surface; action, a solid; then ecstasy belongs to the stellar realm.

But on all levels there are stars of darkness and stars of light. In certain Far Eastern paintings one notices that these people knew far better than we do the ecstasies of the lower world, those of the senses, of fright, and of cruelty. Whenever a god, seizing us by the hair, takes our corporeal life with him, there is an ecstasy.

When a man fully awake has reached the stage of realizing perfect double sight simultaneously with supernatural illumination, he is a thaumaturge. His work consists in constantly introducing sparks of the Spirit into matter. Christ is the archetype of this man.

Because of misunderstanding and scandal, these things must remain secret, until general evolution allows them to be declared without dazzling the intellect with too bright a glare, which would injure it instead of perfecting it.

CHAPTER V

The Disciple and Society

HEN IN the house, Jesus asked his disciples: "What were you discoursing about on the way?" They kept silent because as they were walking they were disputing among themselves as to which one among them was the greatest. Jesus told them: "If anyone wants to be the greatest, he must become the least of all, and the servant of all." Then he called a child, sat him in their midst and said: "I am telling you truly that if you do not change and become such as this child, you will not enter into the kingdom of God. Hence, he who will become as humble as a child, that one shall become the greatest in the kingdom of God, and whoever welcomes a child such as he, in my name, welcomes me."

John spoke up: "We have seen someone who casts out devils in your name, yet who does not belong to our group; so we forbade him to do so because he does not follow us. Jesus replied: "Do not forbid him, because no one who performs a miracle in my name will ever speak ill of me afterwards. Whoever is not against us is with us.

"And whoever shall give you a glass of water in my name, because you belong to Christ, I promise you, he shall not lose his reward. But he who shall have caused one of these little children who believe in me to fall, it would be better that a millstone be hung around his neck and that he be cast into the deep. Woe to the world to whoever causes scandals! Scandals do occur, but woe to the man through whom they come.

"If your hand and your foot are causing you to fall, cut them off and throw them afar; it is better for you to enter into life lame or cripple than to be thrown with both your hands or two feet into eternal fire. If your eye is for you the cause of your falling, tear it out and throw it away from you; it is better to enter into life with one eye than to be thrown with your eyes into Gehenna, where the worm never dies and the fire is never quenched.

"Beware of feeling contempt towards these little ones! Because I assure you, their angels who are in heaven ceaselessly see the face of my Father who is in heaven.

"If your brother has sinned against you, go to him, and when you are alone, tax him with it. If he is sorry, you will have won a brother. If he does not listen to you, bring one or two people, so that everything can be decided upon according to the advice of two or three witnesses. And if he refuses to heed them, then speak of it to the church. And if he refuses to listen to the church, then count him as one of the pagans and publicans. Truly, I tell you that whatever you will have bound on earth shall be bound in heaven; and everything you will have loosed on earth shall be loosed in heaven.

"Moreover, I am telling you that when two among you on earth agree to ask for something, they shall obtain it from my Father who is in heaven. Because there where two or three are gathered in my name, there am I in the midst of them."

The Disciple and Society

Then Peter approached him and asked: "Lord, if my brother does me wrong, how often should I forgive him? Seven times?" Jesus replied: "I did not tell you seven times, but seventy times seven. This story is similar to an image of the kingdom of heaven: there was a king who demanded his servants to render their accounts. While he began counting up, one presented him a debit for ten thousand talents. As he could not make payments, his master ordered him to be sold, he, his wife, children and all he possessed, to acquit his debt. This servant fell on his knees, begged him, saying: 'Be patient toward me, I shall refund it all to you.' The master took pity on his servant, let him go, and discharged him of the debt. On his way out, the servant met one of his fellow-servants who owed him one hundred pieces of silver; then, holding him with a stranglehold, he told him: 'Give me back what you owe me!' His fellow-servant fell to his knees, begging him: 'Be patient toward me, I shall refund it to you.' But he refused, and threw him into prison until his debt was paid. Witnessing what had occurred, the other servants, deeply distressed, came and told their master what they had seen. So the master summoned the one who had acted in this manner and said: 'You are a bad servant: I forgave you your entire debt because you had begged me. Should you not have had pity on your fellow-servant, as I had pity toward you?' So the master, irritated, delivered this man to the executioners until his debt was paid. Thus shall my celestial Father do unto you if you do not forgive your brother wholeheartedly."

THE KINGDOM OF GOD

⊕

However, the days when he was to be taken from the world were coming nigh; so he resolved to go to Jerusalem, sending messengers ahead of him. When they entered into a village of Samaria to prepare a lodging for him, they refused to receive him because he was headed toward Jerusalem. Two of his disciples, James and John, having found out about it asked him whether they should ask fire from heaven to descend upon these people and reduce them to ashes. Jesus turned toward them and reprimanded them—then, they went to another village.[1]

Cleansing

WHEN WE UNDERSTAND that in reality death transforms only the envelope of a being and that the soul escapes from its scythe, we must not to surprised to see Moses and Elijah appear by Jesus's side at the Transfiguration, even admitting that Elijah and the Baptist are but two aspects of the same spirit.

In fact, the land of the dead is separated from ours by a simple veil. If the new body of the departed is invisible to our eyes, so is ours imperceptible to theirs. But the fact that the lands of the external organisms differ does not prevent them from remaining compatriots, from remaining together, if their wills pursue the same goal, by the same

---

[1] Matt. 8:1–6; Mark 9:33–37; Luke 9:46–48; Mark 9:38–41; Luke 9:49–50; Matt. 18:7–10; Mark 9:42–48; Luke 17:1–2; Matt. 18:15–35; Luke 17:3–4; Luke 9:51–56.

The Disciple and Society

means. This is the fact that legitimizes the ecclesiastical dogma of the communion of the living and the dead. All spirits who serve the same ideal naturally come together; and, if their energy persists without faltering, they even manage to group together as far as their earthly lives are concerned.

Our dead, whom we loved in the divine sense of the word, and with whom we have pursued the same ideal, remain close to home. That is why spiritualist practices are useless; for the testimonies they provide are nothing if not confirmed by soul certainty. The deceased may have been given a body on a planet on the other end of the world; it is enough for him to have led a beneficial life for the survivors he loved to feel his comforting presence in them and sometimes around them.

The spaces in which bodies move and the one in which the self moves are very different. For those reasons and many others, the presence of the Lawgiver and of the Precursor at the side of Jesus are not extraordinary.

For planes of different quality to be simultaneously perceptible, all that is needed is for a strong enough hand to pull back the curtain that separates them, and for someone to pay the price for this spectacle.

Now, a leader likes to see his tired companions take their share when they return from their triumphal welcome; and he brings them with him into the palace of the King. This is what a man does for his bodily servants. So does the Word treat the best of his agents.

The work of Moses was colossal: to regiment the Hebrews, to conceive the frameworks of an organization that would foresee from the smallest details of ordinary life up to the vastest eventualities of psychurgy, to formulate a

THE KINGDOM OF GOD

philosophy, a symbolism, and a sociology that would be a sufficiently exact image of the universe, so that the great event of the coming of the Messiah would be the triple crowning of intellect, religion, and state: these are the broad outlines of his work.

As to the prophets, they were rectifiers, among whom the most powerful, the one who spoke the least but beneath whose steps miracles would emerge, was Elijah. He did not discourse on the future Christ, but he foreshadowed his works. Before putting oil in a lamp that is going out, someone has to cleanse it. This external cleansing was John the Baptist's function, just as the internal cleansing was the function of Jesus: Jesus is the illuminator, the Baptist is the penitent.

The Precursor repairs, tills, ploughs, and puts things in order. The Messiah regenerates, saves, sows, and completes. The former obeys completely the law as proclaimed by Moses, both on earth and in the invisible; the latter perfects this law by proclaiming the hitherto hidden life that underpins it. And both receive a similar welcome from men: persecution, mockery, death.

Being attached, as we are, to appearances, we can hardly conceive how the life of a hermit in the desert, such as the Baptist, could have as great an influence as Christ seems to tell us. Just as the most common plant often possesses the highest medicinal virtue, so in a humble, prosaic, anonymous life, do we find marvelous jewels hidden.

Natural energies act from the outer to the inner, whereas light shines from center to circumference. Any object that a pure-hearted man touches, any word he utters, any compassion he extends, any idea he meditates upon, are fertile seeds that he sows. They are regenerative ferments that

The Disciple and Society

spread like busy ants into the most hidden corners of the physical, fluidic, and mental spheres.

Human groups in the visible world should correspond with to groupings of souls in the invisible. Any discordance between these two hierarchies spring from our faults, which dismember the collective being. But a general law governs the reverse and obverse sides of the world: the younger the being, the larger his family; in proportion as he advances, he becomes isolated; and were we able to wander freely in the cosmic spheres, we would occasionally meet some solitary travelers. These are the great torchbearers, the pioneers, those who clear the virgin forests and fertilize the deserts. In their advance they pull along with them the sheep-like crowd with superhuman effort. They have to face hate, fear, and distress. No being understands them, and the love they kindle is but another source of pain and open wounds to them. And so they keep aiming for the heights. Passion for the eternal burns in them. Their arrival is a limpid dawn for the worlds they touch. Their departure, as splendid as the fires of sunset, instills in all men an unspeakable nostalgia for the ideal.

Our Jesus is the prince of this aristocracy of solitaries, and his friends, scattered far and wide, are its knights. Their outer life may seem insignificant and miserable, but their interior life is as a hearth whence, by the Spirit's breath, fly incessant showers of sparks.

This, our invisible society, becomes rarefied the closer one approaches the center; and as well, the soul's actions acquire a more powerful importance, since it is the hidden that moves the manifested, and the higher that leads the lower. Hence the voice of a Precursor effortlessly rouses multiple echoes because he stands upon the summits. It is this that explains the universal influence of the Baptist: we humans see him and understand him because he is of our own race, because he came out of the same quagmires in which we still wallow. This elder brother, having reached the zenith of his expansion, speaks in a tongue we understand because it vibrates with the same pains, because it quivers with the same hopes.

Purification

JOHN MAY SUMMON the light because he has it within. The physician is able to heal if he knows the laws of healing, which means that at least he understands health intellectually. This is why Christ's cures were perfect and those of the apostles failed occasionally, as happened in the case of the young lunatic.

We would find quite peculiar causes at the back of epilepsy, were we permitted to pry. But let us be satisfied with the triple key Christ gives to those who would heal others: faith, fasting, and prayer.

When we barricade ourselves into voluntary blindness regarding divine omnipotence, we enchain our energies. Everything is possible to him who believes. But this faith must be more than a purely intellectual or intuitive notion; it must be followed by actions that nourish this brightness; it must be organically enlarged by all the physical cells, all the fluidic waves, all the passionate fires, all the ideations that we think of as living according to God's law. When the abyss of despair suddenly opens at our feet, when the flames of suffering are licking at our clothing, do not fear to take one more step—an angel will extinguish the brazier and close up the precipice. Thus do the boundaries of the

The Disciple and Society

possible recede until, having reached the limit, all the walls of matter and of selfishness shatter under the formidable pressure of the irresistible explosive known as faith.

It is imperative to surmount fear, indecision, doubt. If our adversary seems a hundred times stronger than we, let us even so engage in the struggle: heaven has but to make a single gesture to award us victory. If we succumb, it will never be anything but another piece of clothing we have lost. The soul, being less entangled, sparkles more radiantly.

Man is organized in such a way that the overstressing of one of his centers causes all the others to fall asleep; this is what our psychologists call "mono-ideism." The scientist, the inventor, the artist, who work passionately in their laboratory or studio forget their body's needs, which is a kind of ecstasy. Our inner self can be enraptured in a supraconscious activity that abstracts it from any other part of the world. The intellect cannot elevate itself to such contemplation without an artificial support: opium and yoga are used for this purpose by Easterners. The animic person reaches this stage on his own, because the most powerful prime mover of attention is love.

But when neither the voluntary state nor the affective state are strong enough for our being to recover its spiritual unity for one moment, we must imitate the ancient sages who made use of a physical object to draw the corresponding hyper-physical state. A corporeal fast, since it weakens our physical life, leaves a free field to psychic life; and the higher is the organ that sustains the fast, the more powerful will be its effect internally. A moral fast, a fast from selfish individualism, will be the best springboard our faith can use to obtain the substance it desires from the secret light.

Whether we deprive ourselves of a food, of a vulgar satisfaction, or of a delicate pleasure, the mechanism of the fast remains the same. No physical or mental function is accomplished without an outlay of energy. Therefore, material or fluidic cells find their death in their devotion to the common cause. Indeed, this death is anticipated in their destiny and supplies fuel to the function where it takes place. So if the will deprives an organ of that fuel in order to continue growing, this organ calls upon cells of a higher order for help. Its normal auxiliaries are liberated, to be used elsewhere, and the essence of the sacrifice of its superior auxiliaries releases a more essential energy. Those are the two dynamisms generated by a fast that the purposeful desire of the ascetic animates toward the realization of his goal.

Thus, when we abstain from a meal, the pneumogastric calls upon the fatty cells; the neural force unused by the digestion returns to its center, the cerebellum and the brain; the magnetic and mental powers are increased. And if one repeats the fast, the plane of our conscience changes through a kind of cerebral fever that automatically inaugurates hyperphysical sensations such as telepathy, visions, etc. The energies released by these practices are led by the intentions to the goal designated by the will or desired by love.

The Ancients very cleverly multiplied their ritual fasts. A science of fasting should be instituted, because at whatever place in the body privation is felt, the released forces change their nature and effect. Christ indicates this specifically when he says: "This kind of demons is driven away only through fasting and prayer."

This is so, because although a being has relationships with the whole world, he is more closely bound to some forms of creatures than others. Thus it is that devils have an affinity with matter, and that some among them remain close to the corporeal man. As the remedy is always in the proximity of the disease, in this latter case it is our physical organism that can furnish the cure for epilepsy.

The action of heaven is hidden. The old Lao Tzu, echo of the ancient I Ching teachings, explains it in other terms. According to a certain plane of existence, the autochthonous forces deploy themselves visibly thereupon; and the forces foreign to it manifesting thereupon are far less perceptible because they come from still further away. The vision of the prophet Elijah explains the same mechanism. The absolute is somewhat foreign to nature, which though it feels its influence, is not able to understand it. The absolute transforms without fanfare, noiselessly. Rare are those who can diagnose its presence. For this reason, we must not fear to probe profoundly within ourselves, to burrow within our being, so that our desire will approach as close as can be to the little permanent, silent light in the abyss of our heart.

We must examine ourselves thoroughly. The roots of selfishness entangle our very core, and spiritual fasting must not fear reaching the venomous beasts lying in wait in the darkest caverns of the psychic organism. As for prayer—we have already spoken about it at length.

Civic Duty

IF WE ARE BEHOLDEN to society, it is because it furnishes us numerous advantages, and does so constantly. But we are still indebted to it for a quantity of forces, feelings, and ideas inherited from the efforts of our ancestors, to which we must add the esthetics of our country, thanks to which our whole personality, from ideation (its sheath) to its formation of ideas, takes on the very special coloring one calls nationality.

Patriotism is a healthy and real feeling. The duties it implies are truly ineluctable and real. The governing body regulating incarnations reserve penalties for those who try to shirk them. In short, had the genius of our people not accepted us, we would not have been able to incarnate. It is our natal soil that furnishes us our body. Our concepts and feeling reactions enter within us with the air we breathe. The souls of our ancestors overshadow us without our being aware—they lead us toward the course of life that characterizes the ethnic collectivity of which we are a cell.

One must not refuse the draft, or taxes, or gratuitous public functions, or any social responsibility. Refusing to fulfill one's engagements and duties (especially the first of these) brings us irresistibly back to earth once more, in order to repair the damage our desertion caused.

However, he whose entire personality possesses no substance from the planet where he finds himself has no debts toward his apparent country. Such was the case of Christ, such is that of his friends, the free-men who from time to time appear here and there for a mission. However, as an example in humility, these free-men do still assume some social functions. This is the reason Jesus enables Peter to find a piece of money in the mouth of a fish.

Since those in whom nothing is earth-bound nonetheless readily submit to the yoke they should not have to shoulder, there is all the more reason for the likes of us to obey. From the absolute standpoint, nothing is unjust. From the relative standpoint, there might be tyrannical and unjust

The Disciple and Society

laws. But we are subjected to them only with God's permission. Let us, then, bear them in this spirit.

It happens that we have been given latitude to work during the week; then to rest on Sundays, and take Mondays off. Then comes a decree setting an obligatory holiday—so we decry this arbitrary order to use all ruses imaginable to work even on that day.

It is wiser to do what we are ordered. The legislator is certain that his decrees are solely the result of his intelligence, although he has merely been the very modest collaborator to an invisible power, whether good or bad. If the law bothers us, we will have a strong propensity to have it declared anti-social and we will revolt. But one does not cure evil by evil. By accepting an iniquitous decree, we prevent tyranny from going elsewhere to oppress our brothers; and the suffering imposed upon us perhaps kindles within the invisible author of that law the first spark of an amelioration for the future.

Innocence

EVERYTHING CONCORDS to bring us to accept that the means for our rebirth in the eternal lies in our voluntary simplification. Man starts from zero. He agglomerates around him a more or less important mass of experiences and substances. Then he returns to his initial zero by abandoning the concept of possessiveness.

The gates of heaven open only to him who has become as the naked little child he was when he walked through them. This is the hidden mystery of the friends of God: possessors all treasures, they act as if they did not possess them; powerful with all powers, they have an innermost belief of their personal weakness and of their omnipotence in God.

THE KINGDOM OF GOD

Eternal life is the counterpart of our natural life; as the ancient Emerald Tablet promulgates: "that which is below is as what is above," but in the contrary direction. Since the summits in the absolute are abysses in the relative world, temporal power must decrease so that eternal life may increase within us. And as it is the notion of selfhood that shapes our psychic stature, if it diminishes on the plane of selfishness through a scrupulous struggle against all forms of antipathy, it will increase proportionately on the plane of altruism.

But to constantly take a back seat through calculation leads to the realm of spiritual pride, and not to the kingdom of God! Whoever humbles himself through an inner pact teaches self-sacrifice toward the public welfare. The more an individual stands in the shadows, the brighter shines the principle in honor of which he humiliated himself.

But what an arduous apprenticeship! It is not difficult to be kind to those we love; but to welcome the indifferent, the repugnant, the insulters, and the ungrateful—that is a most productive practice. In fact, a person seems congenial and likeable to us only because a prior encounter had already rubbed away both his rough corners and ours. To continue taking care solely of him is merely to redo a work almost finished. It is more profitable for us and for others to seek new fields and to polish our still rough surfaces.

"Antipathy is really nothing else but the confrontation of two equal states of egoism, of selfishness." Hence, the one who still has a small gleam of light within himself must draw aside; but a great many of these wounds, and all parts of his being, will have had to bleed, one after the other, before the divine flower of innocence whose perfume the child of heaven exudes may blossom.

The Disciple and Society

Besides, antipathy is not only felt toward our brothers; it also finds pretext for things, animals, opinions, ideas, and events. We must overcome them under each of these forms. For the morale of non-acceptance is anti-Christian; stressing personality means wearing a mask; the eternal *ipseity*, the real self, can only manifest itself in proportion as the mask falls in tatters. Morally, acceptance alone installs us in the role of being intermediaries, to welcome grown-ups as well as gather up the little ones, to elevate matter and humble the spirit, to finally establish universal free-trade.

By accepting everything with equanimity, we experience the vanity of worries, and the fragility of ivory towers; and, when we find out that having recourse to any kind of intermediary has become useless to our distress, from the bottom of this dismal darkness the light-beam will glow from our Friend's eyes. From then on, beauty will have lost its charm, all power its attraction; seeing heaven in each being and elevating them all to it, we will walk briskly along the broad highways as well as on the animals' paths, with the youthful smile of trust and an enthusiasm that sparkles upon the radiant countenance of children.

The totality of man's efforts to defend and better himself throughout the course of many lives results in constructing a secondary personality, morbid and artificial, that strangles the autochthonous self, just as ivy vampirizes the oak to which it clings. This is the parasite we must tear out by discarding selfish preoccupations, sufferings, and temporal goals. No matter how long or painful this pruning, man cannot do it by himself. It is the Spirit who will unearth the deep root of selfishness by means of the essential baptism.

The child Christ offers us as model is characterized by ever-renewed spontaneity, obliterating the past, and indifference to the future—just as the child of God lives in a perpetual present as if he were already in heaven, where neither the notion of time nor that of space exists anymore. We must forget our pains and ancient faults because repentance is not despair. And as to the future, trust in the love of God. Humility in the child is real because he sincerely believes others to be better than he; for our part, let us verify our progress by observing whether we suffer more or less from the attacks of things or men.

These are some of the reasons why it is written that heaven helps only the meek. He who believes himself strong arrests his development, though he would expand it. Whoever believes himself weak even as he does his utmost, leaves the doors open to supernatural succor: nothing fazes him, nothing hews him down, he fears nothing, since he relies totally upon God.

This immovable state of mind prevents his being scandalized. Christ refers to this state as a redoubtable contradiction. The soul that has no experience yet, that has lived but a few times, is innocent—accordingly any manifestation of evil scandalizes it, especially when it attacks divine truths. These brutal lessons are necessary because they awaken somnolent energies in the childlike soul; because without violence, kindness would not grow. The true knowledge or science that life teaches us—experiential science, that is—must become food for our organs, physical as well as magnetic, animic, and mental. The will, the self, must seek for another kind of nourishment, which is the will of the Father. By this method man, deeply within himself, remains a little child, and from his multiple outer faculties he brings out the powers wherein the seed is buried.

The Disciple and Society

To scandalize an innocent is to teach him evil; and one assumes responsibility for all the ruins that this malefic form will sow, up to the time it has exhausted its trajectory—all of which causes many lives of ordeals for the corrupter. It would have been better for him to kill himself before instilling his venom into a candid heart.

The dynamic mechanism of the world means that the repercussions of a movement propagate indefinitely, so that the murderer, for example, could never pay his debt. But the inertia of matter always dampens these waves, and divine indulgence stops them from time to time, when the exhausted sinner is about to be swallowed up in their whirlpools.

However, scandal sometimes comes from a truth that blooms too soon, so we need to be cautious as an initiator and free from prejudice as a listener.

When we reach a certain mystical level, we face a sort of duty to never be scandalized: Mark and John give us a clue in the anecdote of the unknown exorcist who was operating in the name of Christ, without being one among the disciples. The Master, solving this apparent antinomy simply, gives John to understand that it is in the region of principles that one must search for truth; the visible aspects have no value unless the spirit vitalizes them. The strength of an association does not lie in its temporal power, but in the unity of its ideal, and in the plenitude with which this ideal possesses its faithful.

On this account, when someone acts for the glory of Christ, it is not only Christ who is glorified, but the Father as well. And for the same reason, whoever wrongs a disciple maligns the Master as well and faces being severely penalized.

Man is never alone; he is surrounded by societies, each upon a special plane of life. When he is conscious of one, he is unconscious of the others, although they are there anyway—the course of the planets around the sun and the satellites around the planets offering an image of these movements. But within us a truly central sphere exists, dependent upon the invisible sun, at the door of which the guardian angel to whom the Father entrusts us stands ready to come to our help. This angelic being perceives under their essential form all of our actions through our words, our feelings, our thoughts; all of our visions, the genii, the devils, and external circumstances.

This celestial witness to our life is the spiritual form of the divine mercy that comes down to each of us personally. He accompanies and attempts to guide us. If we follow him, he leads us to God by the shortest route; if we do not listen to him, it is he who follows us in spite of our stubbornness. Moreover, this ineluctable presence increases our responsibility.

Violence

THE CLASSICAL TREATISES of the six systems of Hindu philosophy (and still better, their manuals upon union, which the *Song of the Blessed* sums up most clearly) all insist on the importance of conceiving the self to be distinct from the sensorial as well as from the mental organs. But nothing illustrates those theories more vigorously than the counsel of Christ: "If your hand leads you to sin, cut it off, because it is better that you should come into the world one-handed, rather than to live with two hands and to be thrown into the eternal fire."

The Disciple and Society

The ensemble of an individual self is like a people that the will governs more or less badly. No more than a king should capitulate to popular views should that will become captive to the designs of its organs. These latter are instruments or tools for the will, which has to supply sustenance to these auxiliaries of the work for which it is responsible. We are a kingdom through which pass an immense number of cells of all kinds during the total cycle of incarnations. The direction we instill in them either saves or destroys them. It is just, therefore, that they should follow in heaven or in gehenna (hell) the central agent that led them. The molecules of our bodies, the currents of our fluids, the spirits of our thoughts, all the organs a soul may receive (sometimes simultaneously upon the various planes of the world) have their own desires, which our will must know and rectify.

Let us consider terrestrial man only. We find the choleric type who has difficulty resisting the impulse of hitting his adversaries. The cells of his arm are intelligent; they enjoy the action of hitting, and they aim at renewing that pleasure, so that each time that man becomes angry it becomes more difficult for him to control himself. Remember that everything in nature circulates. The (material) corporeal life that is in his biceps today will perhaps a few years hence find itself in his brain. His brain power will then produce nothing but angry thoughts; and as he is the principal of the physiological machinery, the arm will not be able to resist the impulse—the cerebral order—and so that man will succumb to the temptation. As the gray cells are at the highest degree of physiological evolution, the evil their spirits can spread will swell from strength to strength, corrupting mineral, plant, and animal life, vitiating electro-telluric fluids, and perverting science, art, and society.

THE KINGDOM OF GOD

Though nothing within ourselves belongs to us; though we do not have the right to impose fatigues or deprive our body for a personal purpose, it would be far better to kill one of our organs than to wallow in evil just to satisfy it, dragging along with us in our fall a host of inferior lives entrusted to our care. Because the salvation of the cells in matter lies in their incorporation with the human spirit.

But make no mistake: such conduct is the epitome of heroism. The vast majority are only capable of letting themselves go, even if it means later undergoing the torture of the immortal worm (which is the vice vivified by our weaknesses) and fire (which is the purifying ordeal). In a single century we will hardly find one of these "violent" men whose titanic audacity takes heaven by storm.

We are not talking here of initiatory exercises, abstract thought, or inner impulses. The gospel teachings always envisage the objective reality of the plane whence they are promulgated. It is matter that our current consciousness moves, and it is through action that we must fight, even to shedding our blood.

Now, a desire is something that comes out of ourselves. In the universe, beings have their paths all mapped out ahead of time.

To understand this, let us imagine the forms of life as if they were individual creatures coming from infinitely diverse races that man would like to capture for his service. But he cannot do it. He can gather but a few soldiers, for instance from Plutus, from Ganesha, or from some of the thirty-three million gods strung out along the innumerable tiers of this universe. Our desire, still unsated, continues its quest, and each time it reaches some satisfaction, it is in fact a force of ourselves that, finding itself removed from its

The Disciple and Society

orbit, settles in an abode unassigned by the providential decrees.

Hence, the man who gives in to his personal tendencies advances more and more rapidly toward dismemberment and corruption. The salt mentioned in the gospel is the remedy that stalls disorganization; it is the fire of the test. And as the whole being, saturated with matter, feels drawn to this crumbling, everything—even the sacrifices offered to God—must be put into a crucible. Which is why it is almost impossible to act totally disinterestedly.

To give in to our covetousness brings about discord both within and without us; harmony, by contrast, consists of reciprocal understanding, mutual consent, freely accepted subordination by all the parts of the whole.

Any transgression of the law brings about a material displacement. The sinner grabs cells destined for others, and so there comes a time when he must refund, pay back. This restitution begins with remorse and is effected through illness or physical ordeals.

If the transgression occurred in either the sentimental or intellectual realms, the mode of payment remains psychic, although the outward reckoning may have to be undergone simultaneously. For instance, let us say a speculator ruins a family; if he caused the ruin without being aware of it, the poverty he will soon suffer will only affect his physical needs: he will experience little humiliations, worries, and anxieties. But if he was conscious of his misdeed he will later undergo, besides partial poverty, all sorts of mental anguish. Thus, physical suffering is the worm in the gospel, and psychic suffering is its fire.

The means of living in peace is to cultivate a taste for mortification.

THE KINGDOM OF GOD

Christian Fraternity

PEACEMAKING is the sign of a perfectly healthy state in the mutual relationships between beings; it is the splendor of the ontological processions whose regulator is the breath that circulates ceaselessly between the Father and the Son. The Spirit is the divine artist because he harmonizes, unifies, and refreshes. He exalts beings way above forms because he is the angel of beauty. He purifies because in his presence matter evaporates into senselessness. He is total gnosis because he penetrates everything. He is the consoler because he furnishes certitude. He is the pacifier because he volatilizes the diamond of selfishness that the ancient dragon holds in his jaw. He is the omnipotent because he deploys himself in the ineffable freedom of love.

However, on the rare occasions Jesus mentioned the Spirit, he remained mute regarding the means by which we could learn how to bring the Spirit closer to us. This is because, there where the Son is, so also are the other divine persons. And if we are permitted a mundane explanation to clarify this mystery: since the Spirit is the atmosphere binding the Father to the Son, he accompanies the living wills of the Father step-by-step; and circulates throughout all the places they pass, because Christ has promised the descent of the Consoler to follow his death.

Obedience to the Savior's teachings is therefore the only secret to the evocation of the Spirit, because the act in its pure essence is, microcosmically, an incarnation of the Word, and the presence of the latter always implies that of the other two divine Persons.

This synchronic plenitude of the gestures of the Absolute is the sole reason for their harmony. Our existence should

The Disciple and Society

reflect it, which is what the gospels tell us. They refer to a plane where the will, the act, and its inspiring angel concur; only when man sends him away does the angel abscond; and it often happens that the will desires one thing while the body wants another. What virtue can we then possess, since "any kingdom divided against itself shall perish"?

So, Jesus insists upon the importance of this total accord. He entrusts everything that is weak, small, pitiful to our care, since he himself gave himself to all the "lost" souls whom the world neglected.

Transposing these universal examples to our tiny sphere, you will see that it is preferable, in spite of scandal, to appear spineless rather than to start a lawsuit; to appear to be duped rather than be the duper. In spite of it all, the man who acts out of profound conviction always commands respect, no matter what form his actions may take. Our ideals always make up for the clumsiness of our undertakings.

Jesus then orders conciliation through individual initiative; two men who are conversing understand each other better than when facing an audience or a tribunal. The gospel reiterates constantly how to avoid all set forms, how to prepare a direct passage for the light to reach the little ones, how not to immobilize it at the natural or social hierarchies; and heaven accommodates itself to this rectilinear descent, since the spirit is always free.

The society Jesus wishes to establish really includes equality, fraternity and liberty; the nuts and bolts are thereby reduced to strict necessity. There are no penal codes, no legislation, no police. Everything is based upon one's given word; morality is the sole judge. There are no commercial or financial regulations since everyone must be the servant of all.

God is the sole ideal of these brothers. Consequently, they are individually and collectively in constant union with him. As they never do anything here on earth that does not conform to the will of the Father, what they bind or unbind on earth is, to the letter, bound or unbound in heaven.

These ideas will remain utopian for a long time to come. Let us remember that the true principle of association is spiritual, not material; that it is the quality and not the quantity of the elements that gives it strength, and that if the composites of a collectivity are faithless to its spirit, all the privileges it enjoyed will vanish. Whether Peter and his followers possessed special powers does not necessarily mean that all priests possess them, no matter what theology has to say; if perchance it happens that one of them does not follow the poor sacrificial life of the true disciple, the spirit will take wing from within him.

Because the sacrament is a sign instituted by our Lord Jesus Christ to enable grace to descend into our souls, its essential virtue is the light that heaven has put into the act by means of which the Savior instituted that sacrament. Besides, it also possesses a virtue that comes from the heart of the priest, from a force constituted through the aggregate of all the recipients and of all the priests who have received or conferred it; it is an aura radiating in its ritualistic form: words, gestures, and perfumes.

Its essential virtue lasts if the priest remains holy; otherwise it returns to the spirit. And often the last two virtues of the forces mentioned above are, alas, the only ones from which the faithful benefit.

In fact, Jesus's promises about asking questions together and his presence in an assembly are told to his disciples, to

The Disciple and Society

his truly faithful followers, and not to those merely "tagged" as his followers—because we know the majority prefer the wide thoroughfare, while the shortest, narrow path tempts only the courageous ones.

A disciple is a rare being. We ourselves are mere infants who can barely stand up alone. Saints and adepts are teenagers. But as for men! There are but few. No matter how far we are from true discipleship, we must attempt to attain it with all our heart, and at all times, because in that way we prepare something very worthwhile.

The place where two persons can be united most easily in the name of the Son is within the family. It goes without saying that this union must be both cordial and voluntary. If two beings living at opposite ends of the earth share the same ideal, they are more closely united than carnal lovers.

Two miserable souls praying together clumsily still make for an irresistible evocation of the Word, and Jesus feels obligated to come to them. Then he conveys their lamentation to the Father.

The family is the simplest among organic unities that man has to create. The divisions of country and of humanity follow. The *Grand Oeuvre* of Creation will be completed only when harmony exists among all cosmic races.

Finally, we have to build our own inner unity. There are also various people within us who are imprisoned in the flesh; it is a question of transforming this imposed incarceration into a free and desired union. For this to occur, our heart must obey God, our intelligence must obey the heart, and our body must obey reason. As we do not know the true nature of the heart, or that of the body, or that of the intellect, this harmonization operates beyond our control. For this or other results to occur, we must subjugate to obedience that part of ourselves of which we are conscious. But whatever may be the plane upon which this reunion takes place, Christ presides over it, since he is the principle and the goal of any harmonious organism.

Vengeance

MAN THWARTS the law ceaselessly, at times through ignorance, more often through deliberate design. If he is prudent, he will treat his brothers as he himself wants to be treated. Such is the human motive of forgiveness. Each one of us resembles the servant who obtains a postponement from his master to reimburse the millions he owes him, but who pitilessly pursues his less fortunate brother for a miserable one hundred dollars owing.

Truthfully, what do we not owe the Father? He has given us our being, our intelligence, sensitivity, strength, knowledge, parents, friends; a family, a country, a social position, nourishment on all planes, and servants visible and invisible. How many times a day do we prove ungrateful by betraying him? In spite of all, he shows himself to be long-suffering. He patiently adds lessons upon lessons, years upon years, lives after lives—in spite of our rejecting his help, laughing at his servants, killing his soldiers. Nevertheless, he comes to our aid, multiplies his solicitude. And when his ambassadors go back to him still bloodied from the wounds we inflicted upon them, he descends (might we say) personally into our midst under the form of his Son.

On the other hand, see how little we come to the aid of our brothers. Due to the fact that we exist, we naturally give something back to the milieu to which we belong; but we cannot help performing physical labor, intellectual or

The Disciple and Society

soul work. Justly speaking, we really do not have any right to claim anything.

When we give a little money, love, or knowledge to one of our brothers, what is that miserable alms compared to the largesse of the Father? Who dares pretend he gives without thinking of a return? The alms we give are nothing but loans.

The gift we give must be spontaneous, a natural outpouring; nothing from ourselves belongs to us; everything belongs to everyone.

On the other hand, nothing happens unless we have engendered it in the past. The dispensations we suffer at the hands of others should not affect us. There is no call to bear a grudge against anyone, since no one could attack us had we not earlier taken the offensive, whether one hour or one hundred years ago.

Resentment is an infernal seed; so is anger. Jesus has never borne any arms save those of indulgence and mercy. Even if, forgetting any personal vindictiveness, we still feel the insults to our ideal, we must not attempt to punish. Christ expressly taught that, when he chided some disciples for wanting to call down the fire of heaven upon an inhospitable town.

If an idea can defend itself, so much more so can the Father do it. But he is not concerned. He is too far above for any mud to splash him. Only our strayings afflict him. Never does he avenge himself, because he loves us too much to take offense from our revolts. Love, invincible love fears no torture. Love always hopes that the spectacle of its resignation will melt the heart of its executioners.

The rest of us, therefore, must forgive, since we only ever bear the backlash of our just enemies; and, when we have suffered them all, we will still have to forgive our unjust enemies, so that the light of mercy may descend upon them.

To enable us to understand something regarding providential decrees, we must remember that the Father did not give life to the world so as to take it away, but for it to increase. What fanatics refer to as divine vengeance are nothing but fortuitous redresses. The sword with which the Word fights the demons is gentility. So we must forgive ceaselessly. We must renew our efforts without lassitude; patience is the only virtue that conquers time. The disciple does not work merely for triumph. The athletes crowned at the cosmic judgments are but provisional triumphers.

As no enemy can ever touch our true Light, any suffering, even the one that seems to tear our soul, reaches but a shell.

In order to ameliorate our brother, we must make use of all means except harshness. We must reason with him, find in science, in philosophy and in art whatever may be useful to him; try to move him by sentiment, and then ask Heaven to grant intuition to our intelligence and persuasive charm to our speech.

CHAPTER VI

The Faithful Heart

HILE they were on the road, a scribe told him: "I shall follow you wherever you go." Jesus answered him: "The foxes have their lair and the birds of heaven have their nests; but the son of man has no place to lay his head." To another he said: "Follow me." This man answered: "Please let me go to bury my father first." But Jesus told him: "Leave the dead to bury the dead: as for you, go and announce the kingdom of the Father." Another also said: "I shall follow you, Lord, but first let me take leave of my family." To this man Jesus answered: "Whoever has put his hand to the plough and looks back is not ready to enter the kingdom of God."

⊕

Later the Lord appointed seventy-two disciples and gave them the mission to precede him, two by two in every city and every place he was to go. He told them: "Go! Take no purse, nor sack, nor shoes, and greet no one on the way. Remain wherever you have been made welcome, eat and drink whatever is there, because the servant is worthy of his hire. Do not go from one house to another. In whatever city you shall enter and where you will be made welcome, eat whatever is offered you; heal the sick who are in the city and tell them: The kingdom of God is nigh. But in whatever city you enter and are not made welcome, go to the public squares and tell them: 'We shake off the very dust of your city which is upon our shoes, so as to give it back to you; know this: the kingdom of God is at hand! I declare to you that it will go less hard for Gomorrah than for that city.' Whoever listens to you, listens to me; whoever despises you, despises me; and whoever despises us, despises he who sent me."

The seventy came back full of joy; they were saying, "Even the devils submit to us, in your name." He answered: "When Satan was cast out of heaven, I saw him fall as a lightning flash. Yes, I have given you the power to trample down the serpents, the scorpions, and all the forces of the enemy beneath your feet, and no evil will befall you. However, instead of rejoicing that the spirits yield and submit to you, you should rejoice that your names are inscribed in the heavens!"

⊕

At that same moment, he explained in a transport of joy that came from the Holy Spirit: "I bless you Father, Lord of heaven and earth, that you have hidden these things from the wise and the intellectuals, and that you have revealed them to the little children. Yes, Father, I thank you that such was your good pleasure." Then turning toward his disciples: "Everything has been entrusted me by my Father, and no one knows what the Son is except the Father, nor what the Father is, except the Son and he to whom it pleases the Son to reveal it."

Then in private he told them: "Happy are those who have eyes to see! Believe me, when I say that many prophets and kings have wanted to see what you see, and did not see it; to hear what you hear, but did not hear it. Come to me you who are fatigued and heavy-

The Faithful Heart

laden, I shall relieve you. Shoulder my yoke and learn from me, because I am kind and humble of heart and you will find repose for your souls; because my yoke is easy and my burden light."

⊕

A lawyer, wanting to test him stood up and said: "Master, what should I do to inherit eternal life?" Jesus asked him: "What has been written in the Law? What do you read therein?" The lawyer answered him: "You shall love the Lord thy God with all your heart, all your soul, with all your might, with all your mind, and your neighbor as yourself!" "You have answered well," said Jesus; do that and you shall live. But the lawyer, wanting to justify himself again asked Jesus: "Who is my neighbor?" Jesus continued: "A man was coming down from Jerusalem to Jericho; he fell into the hands of brigands who stripped him, leaving him full of wounds and half dead. A priest happened to come along the same road; he saw the man but went by. A Levite came, saw, and he too passed by the man. But a certain Samaritan who was traveling came by, and seeing the man, was filled with compassion; he approached him; after having poured oil and wine he bound his wounds, lifted him upon his own mount, brought him to an inn and took care of him. The next day he gave the innkeeper two denari, saying: 'Take care of this man; and whatever you spend beyond this, I shall reimburse you upon my return.' Which of these three seems to have been the neighbor to the man who had fallen in with robbers? The lawyer answered: 'He who was compassionate toward the man.'" Then Jesus told him: "Go and you too, do likewise."

⊕

Having heard that the Pharisees had heard said that he gathered more disciples and baptized more than John (though he himself did not baptize, but had his disciples perform the baptism), the Lord left Judea and went back to Galilee. He still had to cross Samaria.

Then he arrived at a city called Sychar, close to the land that Jacob had given to his son Joseph, There, he found Jacob's well. It was about the sixth hour (noon). A woman from Samaria came to draw water. Jesus asked her. "Draw me water" (his disciples had gone to the town to buy groceries); the Samaritan woman answered him: "How can you ask me to give you a drink as you are a Jew and I am a Samaritan?" (The Jews, as one knows, have no dealings with Samaritans.) Jesus then told her: "If you knew of the gift of God, and who is the one who asks you: 'give me a drink,' you yourself would make the same request of him and he would give you living water." The woman said: "Lord, you have nothing to draw water with, and the well is deep. Where do you get this living water? Are you greater than our father Jacob who gave us this well, and from which he, his sons, and sheep drank?" Jesus answered: "Whoever drinks from this water will still be thirsty; but he who shall drink the water that I shall give him will never thirst again; on the contrary, the water I shall give him will become within him a spring of water filled with eternal life." The woman continued, "Lord, give me of that water, to quench my

The Faithful Heart

thirst, so that I shall not have to come back to this well." Jesus told her: "Go and call your husband and come back here." The woman answered: "I do not have a husband." Jesus retorted: "You are right to say I have no husband, because you have had five husbands and the one you are with now is not your husband; so what you said is true." "Lord," the woman answered, "I see that you are a prophet. Our fathers used to worship on this mountain; and yet you say that Jerusalem is the place we should worship in." Jesus told her: "Woman, believe me, the time is coming when you will neither adore the Father upon this mountain nor in Jerusalem; you people adore that which you do not know; we, we adore that which we know because salvation is to come from the Jews. But the hour is at hand, in fact it has already come when the true worshippers will adore the Father in spirit and in truth; because this is the kind of worshippers that the Father wants. God is spirit and those who adore him must adore him in spirit and in truth." The woman retorted: "I know that a Messiah (the word means Christ) is coming. When he shall have come he shall teach us everything." Jesus told her: I am he, I who am speaking to you."

Thereupon the disciples arrived; they were surprised to see him talking to a woman, yet none of them asked him: what are you asking?" Nor, why are you talking to her? As for the woman, she put down the jug and left for the city to tell them one and all: "Come and see this man who has told me everything I have done; might he not be the Christ?" So they left the city and came to find Jesus.

THE KINGDOM OF GOD

Meanwhile, the disciples were insisting, urging him: "Master, eat." He answered: "The food which nourishes me is one you do not know." The disciples were asking each other: "Did someone bring him food?" Jesus continued: "My food is to do the will of the one who sent me, which is to accomplish the tasks he gave me. You are saying that there are four more months to go before the harvest. Well, I say: Raise your eyes and look at the fields, they are already ripe, ready for the harvest. The harvester is already receiving his due, gathering up the fruit for eternal life, so that the sower and reaper will rejoice together. Here, the proverb is being verified: the one sows and the other reaps. I have sent you to sow there where you had not worked. Others had worked and you, you have benefited from their work."

Many Samaritans from the city believed in him, because of the testimony brought by the woman: He told me all about what I have done! So, the Samaritans asked him to remain and dwell among them. Jesus spent two days there; and a far greater number after listening to him began to believe in him, so they told the woman: It is not the report you made which makes us believe, because now we have heard him ourselves and we know that he really is the Savior of the world.

⊕

There was a sick man called Lazarus, who was from Bethany, the village of Mary and of Martha, her sister. Mary (Magdalene) was the one who anointed the feet of the Lord with a perfumed precious oil and who wiped his feet with her hair; and it was her brother

The Faithful Heart

Lazarus who was ill. The two sisters sent word to Jesus saying: "Lord, the one you love is sick." Upon hearing it, Jesus said: "This sickness does not lead to death, but it is for the glory of God, so that the Son of God will be glorified because of it." Jesus loved Martha, her sister, and Lazarus. Yet, when he heard that the latter was sick, he still remained for two more days where he was.

After which, he told his disciples: "Let us return to Judea. The disciples said: "But Master, even yesterday the Jews were trying to stone you, and you want to return among them!" Jesus answered: "Are there not twelve hours in a day? If someone walks by day, he does not falter because he sees the light of the world. But if someone walks by night, he stumbles because he does not see the light." Thus he spake, then added: "My friend Lazarus has fallen asleep; but I am going to awaken him." His disciples said: "If he is asleep Lord, he shall be healed." But Jesus had made that comment regarding the death of Lazarus, while they had thought he was speaking of ordinary sleep. Jesus then openly told them: "Lazarus is dead; I rejoice for you that I was not there so that you will believe; let us go to him." Upon which, Thomas, called Didymus, told the other disciples: "Let us go also, to die along with him!"

Upon his arrival, Jesus found out that Lazarus was already in the tomb, having died four days previously. Now, Bethany was only about fifteen stades (three kilometers) distant from Jerusalem. Many Jews had come to Martha and Mary to console them of the death of their brother. When Martha heard that Jesus was approaching, she went to meet him, while Mary remained seated at home. Martha told Jesus: "Had you been here, Lord, my brother would not have died; but even now, I know that whatever you shall ask of God, God will grant you." Jesus told her: "Your brother shall be resurrected." Martha answered: "I know that he shall be resurrected at the Resurrection on the last day." Jesus told her: "I am the resurrection and the life, whoever believes in me, even were he dead, shall live. And whoever lives and believes in me shall live eternally. Do you believe this?" She answered him: "Yes, Lord, I believe you are Christ, the Son of God, the one who was to come into the world."

Having spoken thus, she left, called her sister Mary in secrecy and said: "The Lord is here and he calls for you." Upon hearing this, Mary promptly got up and went to him. But Jesus had not yet entered into the village; he was still at the same place where Martha had met him. When the Jews who were with Mary in the house, to console her, saw her get up and leave so promptly, they followed her, believing she was going to go and weep at the tomb. But Mary having reached the place where Jesus was, as soon as she saw him threw herself at his feet, saying: "Lord, had you been here, my brother would not have died." When Jesus saw her weeping, he was deeply moved and distressed. "Where have you buried him?" he asked her. They answered: "Lord, come and see." Then Jesus wept. The Jews remarked: "See how much he loved him!" So a few among them said: "He who has opened the eyes of the blind, could he not have done something for this man not to die?"

Jesus, quivering inwardly, came to the tomb. It was a grotto, at the entrance of which a stone had been

The Faithful Heart

placed. "Remove the stone," Jesus said. Martha, the dead man's sister answered: "Lord, he smells already, for he has been here four days." Jesus continued: "Have I not told you that if you believe you shall witness the glory of God?" So, they took the stone away. Jesus raised his eyes toward heaven and said: "Father, I thank Thee for having heard my prayer. I know that you always grant what I ask for, but I am speaking thus because of the crowd which surrounds me, that they will believe it is You who sent me." Having said this, he shouted loudly: "Lazarus, come forth!" The dead man came out; his feet and his hands were bound with linen strips, and his face swathed in a shroud. Jesus ordered: "Untie him and let him go free."

Many of the Jews who had come with Mary, upon seeing what Jesus had performed, believed in him. But a few went off to the Pharisees to report what Jesus had done.

⊕

Then the Pharisees and the chief priests (sacrificers) summoned the Sanhedrin and said: "What shall we do? Because this man performs many miracles, if we let him continue, everyone will believe in him and the Romans will come to destroy both this place and our nation?" But one of them, Caiaphas who was the high-priest that year, told them: "You do not understand what it means; you do not reflect that it is preferable for you that one man die for the people, so that the whole nation will not perish." He was not speaking for himself, but being the chief sacrificer that particular year, he prophesied that Jesus had to die for the sake of the nation; and not only for the nation's sake, but to bring together into one body all the children of God far and wide. From that day on, they plotted to put him to death.

That is why Jesus did not go openly among the Jews anymore. Instead he went in the region adjoining the desert, to a city called Ephraim, where he sojourned with his disciples. The Paschal feast of the Jews was close at hand and many of the country people were coming up to Jerusalem, before the Passover, to purify themselves.

They were searching for Jesus. As they stood in the temple they were asking each other: "What do you think? Will he not come to the feast?" Both the principal priests and the Pharisees had given the command that, if anyone knew where Jesus was, he must advise them, that they might seize him.[1]

Exile

EVERY LIVING CREATURE evolves in one direction or another. In the heart of the world, its progress and setbacks are expressed in steps and counter-steps; the structure of the language itself indicates these spiritual movements.

To move towards a goal, to go towards an ideal, to take a path, to follow a master, is not only to accomplish a certain systematic series of acts, feelings, and thoughts. This training of our earthly organisms is only possible, in fact, as

---

[1] Matt. 8:18–22; Luke 9:57–62; Luke 10:1–12, 16–20; Luke 10:21–24; Matt. 11:25–30; 13:16–17; Luke 10:25–37; John 4:1–42; John 11:1–46; John 11:47–57; Matt. 26:1–5; Mark 14:1–2; Luke 22:1–2.

The Faithful Heart

reactions, in the field of consciousness, of the intuitive and faithful advance that our principle of will, the individual heart, effects in the realm of the cosmic heart.

The scribe who under the most perceptive gaze of Jesus cries out enthusiastically, who engages himself to "follow him everywhere he goes," speaks from his spirit; meanwhile his reason does not apprehend the import of its promises.

This man has not seen the enormous cancer that gnaws creation. He has not understood that the gods (kings of existence) as well as the kings (gods of their nations) provide for and support only those who serve them. The princes of ruse and of murder provide lairs for their partisan functionaries. The genii of vanity, with their flashy look and mean calculations, give their flatterers the wherewithal to feather their nests. But where is the tyrant of the world who will protect the humanity of the One who comes to dislodge him from his throne?

Nowhere in this universe built with his hands does the Lord find a shelter for his body or a host to serve him. This solitude does not disconcert him, but ingratitude saddens him. As himself, he is impassible, immutable, and firm; but in his function as Savior he assumes all the responsibilities, worries, and delights of love.

In proportion as the disciple imitates him, his solitude increases. Around him, creatures shy away; so do the geniuses and the gods. They all attack him because his mere presence becomes a slashing reproach. Constancy then becomes more difficult. Even the Son of Man in the midst of one of these squalls asked that "this cup be taken away!"

The more advanced the soul, the fewer peers it has. Along the centuries there are a few who suffer and bleed in such deserts of the vast universe without even meeting a friend to comfort them. But if common wisdom cries out: *Vae Soli!* (Woe to the one who is alone!), the angel of supernatural love, whose glance suffices to set a heart afire, pours the strong wine of his blessings upon the foolhardy pioneer of the divine who fears no strangers.

Yet this intrepid voyager occasionally finds attentive ears and eyes expressing admiration; and the gems he extracts from the caverns of nothingness belong to him, so that he is neither completely denuded nor totally poor, nor absolutely alone.

The Son of Man endured this indescribable abandonment. That is why we must cherish him, become one with him with burning ardor, see everything through his eyes, exalt everything to his level, learn everything conformably to his crucifying method, extract all energy from his arm—in short, see him within all things.

Fatigue

HOW CAN WE make our visible and invisible bodies do a maximum measure of work with a minimum of wear and tear? How can we repair this wear and tear?

Get your doctor to explain to you what muscular fatigue consists of, and you will understand the mechanism of the various sorts of nervous, magnetic, mental, and psychic fatigues. Since our faculties are all fashioned out of material substances (although more or less subtle and more or less ponderable), everything in us is limited and conditioned. Everything needs nourishment and rest; everything wears out. Even the raiment of our soul is renewed after three or four centuries.

The Faithful Heart

Fatigue is an onslaught upon the organism from the residues of the live combustion that work represents. It disappears after the cleansings, which physiologically are both sleep and the afflux of arterial blood: the descent of a superior force and the nutrition of tissues. So then, physical, fluidic, and mental life are but the different dosages of universal life—from the life of the spirit. The Master of the spirit is the Word, who has stated "I am the life"; and also, "I shall be with you until the end of time." Therefore, call upon Jesus, the perpetual, universal renovator.

We must yearn and pine for him, for him to come to us. To become one with him we must evoke this objective union by realizing interior unity.

Call Jesus when you open your eyes in the morning. Call him before undertaking any work during the day. A second is all you need! After all, don't you work for him? Hence, he is ready to descend into each act of ours. Let all these acts, then, be in union with him—from simplest to noblest. In each put your whole strength, your whole heart—mind and soul. Do not work at one thing while thinking of another, since you want God to send his angel to that one. Thus your smallest undertakings will be total.

Since everything in us holds together, from the crest of our soul down to the marrow of our bones, it is impossible to section these innumerable cog-wheels. Do not think about other projects while putting on your shoes, because your meditation would be incomplete, your performance awkward, and the expenditure of your energies doubled or tripled.

We have two domains within: the supernatural (that of the soul), and the natural (which comprises the rest). In the latter, everything has limits: there are wears and tears and needs for rest. In the former, nothing wears out: it is divine Life. That is where our contact with Jesus is. You can feel and retain that contact when, once and for all, you have abandoned all that which is natural—which means that in the midst of tumults and upheavals you can maintain this union, this intimate, profound, peaceful union that remains almost imperceptible. This is true mysticism.

Your organs, bodies, and faculties will then work without yourself holding on to them in fear that they might be lost—for this is the great weakness of man. Thus does fatigue diminish. Try to walk five miles, willing that your muscles work voluntarily. Then forget your legs, and you will notice how much ground you cover without fatigue. That is what Jesus meant when he said that his "yoke is easy and his burden light." This is what the mystics express when saying that everything is easy in love. This is how in the midst of our most difficult ordeals we can show our brothers a smiling face and the cheerfulness that will attract them to our Master better than any discourse ever would.

Friendship

ANOTHER MISCONCEPTION of the gospel is that, because it demands renunciation, we think it forbids us any pleasure. We are mistaken. If nothing on earth is pure, it is our fault. Were something of perfect beauty offered us, we would not recognize its value. We push it away because we are impure and mean. And yet there stirs within us a memory and the hope of a country without frontiers that, way beyond the stars, develops its landscapes under ever-shining noonday suns. Up there, the bright colors never hide any tenebrous monster; the nobility of the forms do not result

The Faithful Heart

from the thousand muddied skirmishes, as do our flowers of our fields; its suave perfumes do not emanate out of pestilential manure; the delicacy of touch is not derived from fats and toxins; and the musical harmonies do not conceal feverish rivalries.

Our nostalgia is just and our hope legitimate. Let us be sensible and not impute our regrets to others rather than to ourselves. We are aware that a land of beatitude exists; we yearn to settle there; but our attempts are gauche and stiff. We attempt making gestures of love, but with the scowl of the recalcitrant miser doling out alms. We lift our surly faces to the limpid skies where smiling angels are soaring. Matter is so powerful within us that we are almost incapable of feeling spiritual bliss.

We must relax. God is not only in the infinite, he also traverses the finite; heaven does not exclude the earth. If we want to lead others, let us not hide that its air is pleasant and delightful to breathe. Yes, to wallow in the pleasures of this world is an error; but to curse its petty, almost wholesome pleasures, and its meager almost noble beauties that we can pluck in its pathways—is another error.

This comes from our incurable distrust. When we engaged ourself to walk the narrow path, either we gave ourselves to Jesus with reticence, or else we took a miserable letter of credit for the hereafter. Constrained, hunched up, expectant, how can we receive the free, expansive, fluidic, surging spontaneous joy of God?

Cheer up, open windows and doors; welcome any being and everything heartily. "Love ye one another" does not mean to put restraints on your actions or on theirs by imposing mutual fetters. Let your encounters be joyful occasions; be suns to one another; let your manners be affable. You may not be rich in goods, but let your heart be bountiful.

May your friendship find deeper roots into the ineffable beneath the invocation of the Master who transposes everything to the supernatural. Surpass yourselves. As much as the faith of the Christian mystic differs from the Stoic's impassibility, so much more so does Christian love excel the nobility of human friendships.

These friendships require esteem, trust, sincerity, an open-hearted soul, and sharing each others' good and bad luck. Friendships between Christians are all of that—but in addition, are superabundant, inexhaustible, gushing as if involuntary, and effortless. Of such qualities was the communication formerly shared jealously by some friends in antiquity. It is the schooling of the kingdom wherein each becomes the servant of all: servant but not slave, friend rather than servant. There, everyone is eager to help the passer-by; no mistrust closes the hearts; all approach each other in the joy of the peace, and take their leave only to serve other, new expansions.

As we are miserable hearts ossifying, we must stretch the tendinous membranes of selfishness so as to render them supple, because as lowly as we might be, yet we are the bearers of a marvel: a clear pure gleam that fears nothing, that does not mind foreseeing, that on the contrary is all impulse, an offering, a welcome. Look at that light: a particle of the splendor of Christ! It is a delegation from eternal wisdom; it is the ever virginal, future tabernacle wherein the Word will be born in you someday. Raise your consciousness to its level. Mold your character upon the august simplicity of its proportions. Make your limbs docile to its discreet orders. Take the habit to see and to will in this clarity. If you do, the universe will, little by little, take on a different aspect and meaning for you.

Instead of a rocky crag you will discover infinite horizons. There, where you had figured you had all your tasks, you will find greater works to be done. You will be made aware that you have not yet taken your definitive vow, neither effected your total gift of self, nor lit the lamp of love that never sleeps.

Aspire after these things; recall them during your solitary hours; ask to receive their live substance. How sweet will your life become, how filled with grace will its flowerets be! Your reunions will become feasts and your exchanges burn with divine ardor. You will have taken a step toward the world of eternal joy; and in return, its precious exhalations having descended upon you, will be inhaled, absorbed by whosoever approaches you.

Spiritualism

IT IS DIFFICULT to love our neighbor disinterestedly. As soon as the angel of compassion has finally anchored a foothold in our spirit, the wills of the flesh and of the blood attempt to grab for their benefit the light emanating from that angel. So that, after having given help to one of our brothers simply and spontaneously, without our being aware of it we begin to love that person because of the pleasure or advantage we derive from his acquaintance. And in consequence, the pure sentiment that at first animated us towards him becomes, through imperceptible deformations, a passion that occasionally degenerates into carnal aberrations.

THE KINGDOM OF GOD

It is to prevent such errors that Christ chooses filial love, the purest among earthly affections, when he gives the disciple who asks permission to go and bury his father this impassible answer: "Let the dead bury the dead, and follow me." This does not proscribe giving the last rites to the dead, nor put in question social mores or proprieties.

The worldly machinery is organized better than we think. Creatures change abodes only for a good cause. Death never is an unforeseen accident. It is an incident in the individual's life, a logical conclusion to one of the cycles in the long voyages he accomplishes throughout creation.

Had we complete trust in God, our mournings would not turn into lamentations. No one leaves this earth before his time; no one lives in a certain locality without having work to fulfill there. If our parents and friends depart, it means they have work to do elsewhere. Our immoderate regrets only serve to keep them earthbound in an abnormal way. And the prejudice is aggravated when we call them back through spiritualism.

This does not mean that spiritualism is altogether false. Its philosophical basis, reincarnation, conceived as one of the consequences of divine justice, is exact. But to attempt incursions into the land of the dead is reckless: we know nothing of that kingdom, of the road that leads there, or of its inhabitants. We are exposed to unforeseen dangers, to hazardous encounters, to errors and impostures.

Practicing spiritualism is an attack against the established order, no matter how good the intention of the practitioner. Each time we want to step into an apartment that we are not destined to enter, we must pay the guardian. That is why spiritualism and practicing occult arts usually bring about a streak of material ill-luck.

The Faithful Heart

If on the contrary from the bottom of our heart we fulfill the will of heaven, we draw harmony about us. The fences erected to prevent our straying fall, and in this case it may be that our departed ones will spontaneously manifest at the family hearth.

If this proof is given us, we must not take pride in it, or propagandize it. Everything comes at its hour.

The Will

WERE MAN REALLY aware of how important his conduct generally is, he would undertake his tasks more seriously. He cannot emit the least idea, the most hidden desire, or make the smallest gesture, without a considerable number of beings of all sorts being affected by this movement.

It follows that before learning anything we should carefully examine the project, be wary of our clairvoyance, and definitely solicit the source of all light to lead us by the hand according to his Will. But we must not expect to receive anything from visions, from psychic phenomena, from divinatory artifices. The web of ordinary events of our lives offers providence a sufficiently vast terrain to propagate its fires and erect its parapets.

Yet, a will fully secure in its motive, ready for action, determines the rotation of great numbers of orbs; its trajectory modifies the evolutive curve of the minerals, plants, animals, invisibles, and humans that constitute its spiritual family. This is why an act engenders such deep and varied repercussions.

Any ideal not based in God possesses some part of error; to follow it, leads us fatally astray. And when we have been made aware of our mistake, we must retrace our steps.

Solely our quest for heaven is sound, appeasing, true, since it is the supreme ideal.

The will is uplifted depending upon the goal aimed at; the higher it goes, the stronger the will becomes. If the goal is God, it communicates to the being who travails for it something of his all-powerfulness; but the servant, in his littleness, must reproduce the homogenous, impassive, unchanging unity of his Master.

Thereby the three requests and the three answers of Jesus correspond to the three great chains that bind us to this world—money, human affections, and our instinct for self-preservation. We must drag them along the whole length of our dolorous pilgrimage towards heaven; only one acid corrodes them—it is the water of the baptism of the Spirit when the trumpets of deliverance will resound at the solemn hour spoken about by the seer of Patmos. Then will man receive from the Trinity itself the triple and definitive purification that removes from his mind any memory of evil committed, and of any pains suffered.

Simplicity of Heart

WHY DOES THE beloved disciple relate the episode of the Samaritan woman in such detail? It is because many important lessons are to be learned from it.

Foremost, the practice of tolerance. The long-standing hatred between Jews and Samaritans remained violent and vitriolic. Religious wraths are the most nefarious because our sentiments have that much more influence upon the future, the loftier their objective is. By addressing a woman of the detested sect, Jesus exposed himself to all the vituperations on the part of the Israelites. No matter; as usual, he

The Faithful Heart

chose the most difficult task, the least prudent humanly speaking, the most hazardous risk for his endeavor and himself: he always played the difficult game with Satan; and it is always he who strikes the iron in the fight.

For instance, in that anecdote, it is Jesus who asks for a drink. It gives rise to a pretext of a teaching, specific to the woman, general for the sect, fortuitous for the disciples. In the eyes of the invisible suzerains of nature, our actions are worth only what they cost us in labor and what success they bring. But in the eyes of the Father, their value depends upon the innocence of the desire engendering them and the rectitude of our intention.

Without losing our way in the maze of scholarly esoteric research in the concerning Jacob's well and about this mysterious drink; without researching why the Church commemorates this conversion on a Friday, the 19th day of Lent (which is not so difficult to understand); without foraging into kabbalistic calculations upon the name of Photina attributed traditionally to the Samaritan woman, or upon the date of her feast day, the 20th of March, let us hold to a simplistic explanation—it will surely be the more true.

Everything within us is substantial. Our desires—sometimes known as appetites—are the hungers and thirsts of our hyperphysical organs. Just as there are no totally solid or totally liquid foods, our psychic faculties, and especially our spiritual heart, are searching for foods of an analogous order to theirs, some of which provide the substratum and the others providing strength. This is what the species of bread and wine signify in the real allegory of the religious sacrifice.

Water is the original mother; solid matter is merely an extract; and there are no terrestrial waters, organic liquids,

THE KINGDOM OF GOD

sidereal fluids, intelligibles, things firm or mental, except because there is on the divine plane the water of eternal life.

This beverage that the sacred hands of the Savior offer generously, profusely, does not merely produce the magnificent blossoming of the flowers of light within us; it is the universal medicine penetrating everywhere, restoring everything, even our physical body. No one can truly heal the sick unless he is able to give them a few drops of it. It possesses an intense force of cohesion; the least dewdrop one receives from it irresistibly brings abundance from the eternal spring. Such is the virtue of love.

Therefore, any desire is a fire; it ignites a fever, no matter what organism it devours. Jacob Boehme demonstrated this in depth by explaining the march of the seven wheels of nature.[2] When this desire has been consumed, has become exalted, has projected itself in all directions, the acquisition of its object extinguishes it, just as water extinguishes fire. But our natural desires, no matter how profound or sublime they be, always carry some mark of individualism that consequently consecrates them *a priori* to a more or less imminent corruption, to a more or less bitter disillusion, because their aims or objectives do not embody the essential reality.

Hence, nothing in this vast universe can satisfy man's desires. Nothing therein is stable, not even the inert tranquility of the stone. Nothing therein is permanent, not even the frightening vastness of a cosmic god.

No spring will ever quench the thirst that consumes us, because our heart can only be slaked from the absolute.

---

[2] The vortices of desire are what the theosophic shoemaker calls the three primary forms; the fire of desire is the fourth; its satisfaction is the fifth; its realization includes the last two forms.

The Faithful Heart

Nostalgia for its original birthplace is the mystical fire through which it learns to live, while learning how to die; hence it is this light that we must keep on feeding, meanwhile unifying all the others that are but sooty and vacillating flames.

Simplicity of Mind

SO JESUS, after having kindled a desire for this uncommon source, shows us the path; he does so by amalgamating our material affections as well as our spiritual affinities. Conjugal love synthesizes the first ones, divine love the second.

We have already looked into the grandeur of marriage, how it has to subsist through constant and reciprocal sacrifices on the part of each, how it is the "natural" school by which one can emerge gradually from the mire of the flesh. The union between a man and a woman is not only the rudiment of society that opens the door to souls in need of being reincarnated; it must also offer an exact image of this mutual, perfect gift that characterizes life in the kingdom of God. It presents this ideal first to mankind, but also to all kinds of visible and invisible creatures whose spirits throng around a truly pure hearth.

The seat of harmony is not located in the corporeal but in the spiritual, because the true, the good, and the beautiful inhabit the latter and not the former.

Just as true human love does not take account of any differences between social classes, or of dissimilarities in temperament, or of disparities in character, so also does divine love have no interest in time or set places. The Samaritan and Jewish disputes on the superiority of the mountains versus Jerusalem, monkish skirmishes, and sectarian rivalry

THE KINGDOM OF GOD

are all in vain. The Spirit of God is everywhere. Some societies among men are closer to the Father than others, but they all accord the same illusory importance to the conditions of cults, rites, formulas, and places.

Error impregnates matter; the Spirit possesses truth, verity. Hence, as soon as the Father decreed the birth of Jesus to take place among the Jews, they were given a comprehensiveness (of which the Samaritans were deprived) in order to "normalize" this event. Consequently, orthodox Israelites found themselves guided in their prayers and in their works, not through any merit on their part, but so as to furnish certain materials, and to prepare as best they could the channels for the incarnation of the Word.

Thus, Moses laid the first foundations for this "salvation by the Jews" on account of qualities germane to the Jews and to the perfection of Egyptian theosophy.

The originality of the evangelic religion lies in these two points:

(1) In worship of the Father: in suppression of polytheistic worship (even without idolatry); in direct recourse (no matter how small or great the request), direct homage, indirect thanksgiving.

(2) In spirit: in freedom, without rites, observances, or conditions; in truth: by means of the material realization of the true, through good deed, pure feeling, right thinking.

One must not fear to push these axioms to their ultimate consequences.

Nature is a field; man is its cultivator; God is its master. Now, it is not the foreman who feeds the worker, it is the boss; if the worker works at his whim, he will not be paid by the boss, but by those whom he has pleased; if the worker can eat at the canteen, it is because he did his work.

The Faithful Heart

The man who chases a fortune is fed by Mammon; the one who serves God is fed by God. The matter in foodstuffs, in clothing—in all of our physical needs—possesses only the value of the vital quality animating it, and this quality changes with the spiritual orientation of the consumer. Let me give you an example. In the same shop, a usurer buys a loaf of bread and a good man buys the one next to it; a chemist would find no distinction between the two loaves; yet the moment they are sold, they receive from the god of each of the purchasers an influx that, sacerdotally speaking, is called a consecration, by means of which they will furnish a fluidic contribution to the consumer and add a link to the chain that binds the latter to his god.

The god feeds the faithful; this food is not differentiated in its material substance, but in its spiritual essence. Everything furnished man by his milieu, from bread to his thoughts, is colored by the tints of the ideal this man adores in proportion to the plenitude with which he devotes himself to it, and to the elevation of the ideal he serves. He who serves God with all his might can truly believe that all his needs—both subsistent and superfluous—will be assured by the angels, the immediate servants of God. Fulfilling the will of the supreme Being, therefore, procures both temporal as well as eternal life.

However, such perfect obedience is met but rarely. From the beginning, the universe is a divine creation; but the garden of Eden became a garden of thorns. Workers who clear the field are rare; the sowers are chosen by heaven, as are the harvesters.

It follows that no matter whether it be a substance, a race, a civilization, a planet, a zodiac, a kingdom, or an individual, the workers of the Father, no matter what function has been entrusted to them, fulfill roles that are equally essential. Therefore they cannot be proud of the work they do, but must instead remain servants to one another, just as they were once upon a time in heaven. Just as, in the mechanical field of the world, the law of the transformation of forces rules, so in the spiritual field wherein these workers toil, whatever the task gains in duration, it loses in intensity, and vice versa—because, whether the day begins earlier or later, it ends at the same minute for all.

Lastly, let us note that these two essential truths—worship in the spirit and abnegation in the work—Jesus promulgated in Samaria, a country held as detestably heretical by orthodox Jews. Thus, man often misjudges the moral capacities of his fellow men; and so, the depth of the pit into which the individual or nation falls is a sure indication of a power not possessed by those who timidly stand halfway between right and wrong.

The Gentle Master

THIS PARADOX is explained in the parable of the workmen who came at various hours. St Augustine and St Gregory the Great see it as the resumé of the religious history of the white race. The vine represents the Church; the master is God; the first hour is Adam; the third is Noah; Abraham is the sixth; Moses is the ninth, and the Messiah the eleventh. It could symbolize the evolution of the cells in the lymphs, in the bone, muscular, blood, and nervous systems of the body; or it could represent the history of the self evolving throughout incarnations.

No matter on what level we judge or consider this parable, it teaches us that the cells, the souls, the individualities,

The Faithful Heart

and the nations that were the last to leave their respective original source will return first (their circuit is short), while those who left first will return last (their circuit is long). Providence follows a fixed program; all the paths that it traced at the origin of the world—each of which represents a very definite distinct work—must be trodden. The broadest, easiest, the most level, ones are also the longest and most frequented. The steeper the climb, the fewer voyagers one meets; but the journey is shorter.

Things are arranged so that each person is on the road that suits him best; hence, it is needless to worry about the kind of work we have to do. If our route does not lead us to our elected choice, it will certainly lead us to another. At each judgment, very few are chosen. But how many judgments will there be until the end of this universe! Let us rejoice, let us submit to the Father's decrees in perfect obedience.

The bandit may become a saint, but the mediocre crook will never become anything but an equally mediocre man. To the child of God all creatures seem worthy of receiving the same care; he judges them, not as we do, based upon physiognomy, clothing, idioms, or opinions, but according to the quality of life he finds in them. At the inception of a religion or a philosophical institution, adherence or rejection can well serve to classify men—because the spirit of the society is still bare—but when commentaries, formulas, and rites have clothed, petrified, and morseled it out, sects multiply according to the outer shoots and are subject to variant interpretations—and so one loses the faculty of evaluating men and things.

If we want to judge, let us first make a clean sweep, put aside all polemics and personal interests; all assets of tyranny, of politics, of materialistic science; all current opinions and the approbation and disapprobation of the masses; let us cast off the system, unveil the idea, lay our heart bare, and compare ourselves with the absolute yardstick that lies within us in the "middle chamber," in the tabernacle of our soul.

Be aware how difficult this is, because if years are barely sufficient to let us drop the habit of making reckless judgments, centuries will be needed to teach us to make salutary and impartial comparisons of men and of things.

Jesus sends his seventy disciples forth in pairs for a profoundly central reason. In fact, each of his acts is determined by an ideal motive that is the pivot or hub of a wheel, the multiple spokes of which are other, more comprehensible motives. In its lower echelon, the work of man is to bring the divine here-below. But, as everything in creation proceeds by pairs, nothing is generated in substance, nor in the flesh, nor in the psychic realm, unless two agents marry; and the ideal to which this union is dedicated confers upon the child that will be born from it the quality of its spiritual light. Thus it is that "two or three must be gathered together in the name of Jesus" for his presence to be manifested. To enable the spirit to walk between them was his reason for sending them on the road two by two, so that while one was speaking and healing the other continued his silent orison; and also, so that they would find comfort in one another, were their human nature to fail.

The sending-forth of the seventy disciples is nothing but the first fulfillment of a new providential disposition in the regency of the world. Nothing on earth occurs without visible or invisible preparations. Before Christ, cosmic life had sought to release the seeds it had held since the beginning.

The Faithful Heart

With Christ, cosmic life receives a new impulse: unknown seeds are to be entrusted to it; but first the ground must be tilled, and John the Baptist and the seventy are the ploughmen. From that time on, when a force descends here for the first time, two heralds precede it, find it a home, and will hew its path. This takes place whenever a new metal arrives from the sun to the earth, when a flora or fauna abandon their planet for ours, when the first couple of a new race springs up in an uninhabited region, when the conception of a new science, of an unknown art, germinates in a brain, or when an emissary of the spirit is going to don a body of flesh.

The apostle is the physical instrument of the Spirit; they need each other for their work to be good. The invisible harvester is able of do his work, but he needs a scythe; the scythe can do nothing without him; it has only to stand in perfect docility; without murmuring or defending itself against fatigue, wear, stones; for it is against it that the soil and the ears of corn will chafe, since it is it alone that they feel. The men of the devil attack and persecute the men of God because they are unable to reach the invisible that these men manifest.

For this task, the disciple must maintain all the physical, fluidic, and mental connections in constant rapport with his spiritual sun; it is from it that he derives everything—clothing, food and light—because the difficulty and delicacy of his work are such that an uninterrupted concentration is essential to ensure that no food, no perception, no idea can reach the disciple unless chosen and prepared by the Spirit.

These are the only conditions under which the disciple will be able to say without falsehood: Peace be upon this house, on this heart, on this body. Things and people will receive this peace insofar as they first desire it, through the almighty magic of the act of kind acts and pure feelings.

A city, a town, a territorial district, are organic entities—everything therein is born and develops according to the vital universal law. It is not only to prevent quarrels and jealousies that the Master orders his envoys not to have several domiciles. They bring a seed of light; and one cannot put two of them in the same organism because they would not find sufficient nourishment. Neither should we transplant a very young plant, because it would become feeble.

These seeds of light must be placed in the city as well as in the home, and in bodies as well as in souls. The disciple has no special precautions to take; it is his guide who puts him in touch with the spirits of the various material formations; he is simply the tool, the witness, the visible sign of the invisible Artisan; he warns the consciousness of the sick man and the material being, so that they lend themselves to the operation of the Spirit.

And if his voice is not accepted, he has the right to cut himself off from the being who refuses it. This latter draws reprobation upon himself because of the setback his refusal has caused, and because of the great many struggles, anguish, and illnesses that will ensue for himself and all other beings with whom he is connected. We must remember that adherence to divine law engenders health upon all planes, and that suffering—whether close or distant, insensible or superhuman—is always the result of disobedience.

When Jesus says: "I saw Satan falling from heaven like lightning," let us not attribute to his words a meaning he did not wish to confer. It is literally exact that before him the whole human race had become corrupt and had been

The Faithful Heart

led astray long enough for the adversary, little by little, to win the regency over the gods entrusted with the multiple directions of our planet. And if one of the results of the work of Jesus was to cause his downfall from this throne, the prince of this world, though dethroned, has not abated his activity. However, he exerts it ever since in the shade, as a conspirator.

Yet, his fall should not be a cause for rejoicing to man. The ones we call devils are useful, and from the point of view of the absolute they render us a great service. Neither their capture nor thaumaturgy give us the certainty of beatitude; only those among us whose names are written in the Book of Life are assured of it; and amid the mass of men, they are as rare as are the meek.

Among our brothers, those who occupy the highest echelons of knowledge and of intelligence are not ripe for heaven; hence this affirmation seems to be the ironical paradox of a capricious divinity. But try if you will to conceive what is heaven, the absolute, the being of omniscience and of omnipotence. Imagine an inconceivable grandeur. Build up a limitless world whose inhabitants are also measureless. You will see that nothing of this world of ours will be able to subsist before that world. Moreover, the more that thought and will are filled with measurable things, the less sensitive will they be to the Immeasurable. As in mathematics, infinite grandeurs are no more compatible with the finite, than what occurs in the kingdom of the Father is accessible to a mind filled solely with temporal perceptions.

Jesus adds: "It is thus, Father, because You approved it." In spite of the revolt of our pride, of the remoteness of our comprehension, these words state another precise truth. This universe, its ontological modes, its biological series,

THE KINGDOM OF GOD

which seem to us as if they could not be otherwise, are such only because the Father wanted them so. He could have given us a thousand arms and legs, or reduced space to our dimension, or built a world according to unimaginable schemas. The law of nature is nothing else but the will of God—but scientists see through these clouds only with great difficulty.

Such words as infinite, smallness, inexistence, unreality, do not describe the true aspect of creation face to face with the Creator. Because creation is real, it exists, and is immense. Human languages have no expression to designate this relationship between the relative and the absolute, since they express but relative concepts. Nor can we conceive it through meditation; we can do so only through contemplation, through admiration followed by adoration.

These three inner acts are the only ones that give us a slight insight of what the Son is. The Father is unknowable. Some day, when we will have become free-men, when the greatest gods of the time will obey each of our words, perhaps we will catch a glimpse of the Father for a fraction of a second. Until then, it is from Jesus alone that any glimmer about the Being of beings comes. As to the Son, the secret of his existence is held by the Father, who has never divulged it to anyone in this universe. As for the Spirit, he is unseizable, still less graspable, because he dwells in the biological procession between the uncognizable Father and his unknown Son.

Recalling the great number of prophets and ancient kings who were consumed with the desire of seeing the Messiah—not only in Israel, but in Egypt, Persia, India, Greece, and in the Celtic lands—demonstrates how these things we speak of have been known from time immemorial, and how the life of a race develops progressively, in a logical sequence.

The Word calls all beings through diverse and marvelous words. Those who hear him best are the poor, the unfortunate; he gives them the means of drawing closer to him, and the justification for these means.

To come to him, one must shoulder his yoke, and comply with his commandments.

Those who have labored—which means, have been maltreated by life—must sustain the struggle with meekness. Those who carry heavy loads will bear them by means of humility. Jesus gives them some of his strength. Thus, by not resisting our enemies, by not claiming our apparent due, by making ourselves insignificant, help comes and our soul finds peace.

What causes us worry, anguish, and anxiety is due to pride and a lack of faith in God. He who feels the Father's benevolence accepts to obey, accepts all disciplines, and has patience. He who feels his own unworthiness, smiles graciously and accepts tests, responsibilities, and difficulties. Thus, "The yoke of Jesus is pleasant and his burden light."

Pity

THE UNIQUE, the great, formula that applies to the smallest circumstances as well as to universal problems, the one that suits the radiant genius as well as the lowest among men, is the love of God and love for one's fellow man.

All men do not have the notion of God. Among those who do possess it, most try to set it aside as much as possible. A great number among the others think of God only at times of great distress, with fear. Very few feel some affection toward their Father, which is why the religious initiators have never requested from their faithful anything more than love for their brothers.

Love is a wonderful bloom. Only the Land of the Living in its essential purity can nurture it. Therefore our loves, even the loftiest, are nothing but the shadows of essential love—and even these reflections require several centuries of cultivation to reach their full development. By placing man upon this planet, nature provides him, through his sexual instincts, with the lowest ferment of love. Woman experiences maternal love readily. Primitive man requires a few incarnations to feel paternal love. And the filial feeling of protecting their elderly parents demands approximately fifteen rebirths on the part of the robust children. Meanwhile, adults are making innumerable experiments in passionate love, sensual love, sentimental and esthetic love.

Men and women fall in and out of love in spite of the sorrows, furors, and deceptions that last from thirty to fifty incarnations. Then, the individual destinies having finally been spent and the number of partners decreased, there comes the blessed day when the bride and groom find each other again, after hundreds of years of passionate impulses, unsatisfactory pleasures, of hopeless tears.

Contemplating the dazzling flames and flares between these two hearts engulfing each other, it is not surprising that neither the ardent souls of ancient Kabbalists exposed to the arid winds of nocturnal invocations nor that the delicate soul of the great broad-shouldered Plato, have conceived the ingenious and illusory theory of "soul mates" to justify such rapture.

All of that takes at least a hundred incarnations. Simultaneously, the human being has developed within familiar affections under their varied aspects. But, as soon as a man and a woman have been able to live a lifetime in perfect, constant harmony, in sexual, sentimental, platonic love—passion loses its charm. Fraternal love is born. Altruism takes root, and a few incarnations suffice for the angel of all-pure and all-candid charity (love) to accustom our spirit to accept it for longer and longer sojourns.

After another fifteen rebirths, the ineffable floweret—divine love with its mysterious perfume—sends out its first sprig. Now the man is on the path leading to the Father—he is a "soldier."

How can we get there faster? All religions freely reveal the wonderful secret, the ineffable arcanum. So true is it that God is good, that he desires the happiness of his children; so true is it that hidden things are merely superfluous. Just as bread and water, indispensable to the body, are the two most common substances on earth, so the necessary spiritual foods have always been named everywhere.

Each minute offers us an occasion of loving our brothers as ourselves; what is difficult, however, is forcing ourselves to swallow that food. "Not to do unto others what we would not have done unto us" is but the passive element of the precept. What we should do is "to do unto others what we wish were done unto us" under all circumstances—deliberately as well as in action, in sympathy as in antipathy, in indifference as in compassion—whenever we decide to feel, to speak, and to act so that our interlocutor, our neighbor, or the collectivity, will be happy. When we decide to behave in this manner it is to the detriment of our own pleasure. It is then that one loves one's neighbor as oneself.

This "neighbor" does not refer merely to mankind; it means all beings, because each creature is close to us. The eccentric minds who study and prefer Eastern doctrines regard their ethical system as being superior to Christianity because of the respect they have for their "inferior brothers." This respect inspired a touching gentility on the part of the candid Francis of Assisi. But this compassion, which we must not reduce to sentimentality, is an evident consequence of the gospel precept—because how could he who of his own free-will makes himself the servant of just one of his brothers, brutalize a dog, kill a bird, or break a twig without reason? How could anyone who accepts the text of John, "Nothing that exists could have been made without the Word," behave foolishly and abuse, outrage, maim, or suppress the most minute existence with which he comes in touch?

Let us always remember that the gospel does not make use of long discourses, or didactic teachings. It lays down a few universal laws in their absolute form; it is then left to the reader to deduce the particular results and the relative adaptations that are easily discernible to a guileless heart.

Let us have some intellectual courage. Let us follow the consequences of a principle to their ultimate end. Since my neighbor or fellowman is everything to which I am related —whether it be matter, fluids, mental world, social world, or spirit—my love must spread not only to the visible creatures and their bodies but to their inner being; not only to individuals but to the collectivity (our city or country); not only to substances but to their essence (social laws, ideas, and arts). Understood in that manner, our charitable attitude will extend our actions' limits into immensity and stretch the limits of our being to the lofty heavens. There is no better school, none as healthy or knowledgeable—none more arduous.

The Faithful Heart

But let us leave aside these heights so difficult to attain, and instead apply ourselves to more concrete acts. This describes very well the secret thought of Jesus in the story he relates about the man who, having been attacked, was left lying in the ditch by the Levite and the sacrificing priest—they who should by rights have been models of altruism. Meanwhile, the Samaritan of the disdained race, the scorned outlaw, is the only one who picks up the victim, dresses his wounds, and pays his expenses. As for us, if one night we were to find the victim of a criminal assailant on the street, would we pick him up without fear of losing sleep, soiling our clothes, undergoing the suspicious interrogation of the police? Would we have the courage to entice a reluctant chauffeur with our own money to drive the wounded man to a hospital as fast as can be?

When we will be able to perform those little efforts, we will have enabled cells to evolve within us that will in turn reveal to us intuitively that there exist still loftier charities, that the personages of the parable might signify definite esoteric entities, esoteric operations, or definite cosmological dramas—as secret and as generous as the level of the point of view to which our thought was able to attain.

Death

WHAT WOULD it take to know death? An abyss separates our earth from its kingdom; and nothing the earth has provided for us can cross that chasm. In fact, when the physical body has finished its time, the human composite dissociates; the directing spirits of each of the three kingdoms take back what they had loaned; the spirits of the magnetic and mental currents do likewise. This is why the double, memory and thought, remain here-below during the interval between two incarnations.

The only true death is the loss of light; all other deaths are but transformations. Just as our intellect is unable to evolve if it does not pass from one opinion to another, so our self cannot reach its own abode unless it has experienced a multitude of transitory organisms.

Banish the fear of death from your heart. To understand the mechanism of the phenomenon of death thoroughly is another story. The position from which we study it does not permit us to grasp more than a few of its exterior details. When I say "we" here, I mean to say everyone, even the mystics of our countries, even the old rabbis guided by the Shekinah, even the subtle Brahmans, even the Asiatic ascetics absorbed in their Tao. Christ alone knows the enigma of this snub-nosed Sphinx, because it is he who sustains its existence.

All we can see is but an assemblage of contradictions. For example, a death is at the same time a birth. It is one of our greatest sorrows as well as an inestimable grace. It is the most radical of separations, yet our ancestors remain close to us. It is a long voyage, but it takes only a single step to accomplish it. The departed go somewhere else, though they are occasionally still attached to the corpse for an extended time. Everyone must undergo death, and there are beings who have not known it yet. Lastly, it is the implacable form of fatality, yet it is possible to overcome it.

You well know a few of the reasons against any artificial prolongation of life. In reality, we never leave before the appointed hour—even the elderly who lead but a vegetative life; even children who die very young. Therefore, he who has an awareness of the kindness of the Father never finds

The Faithful Heart

anything he has to ask of the Father, unless it be the light. And yet, resurrections do not occur without incentives.

Death is not an infallible goddess. She might even have ideas of vengeance; she might even mistake the door. Doubtless, this seems improbable to you, yet such errors on her part are not very grave in comparison with her function—it is not a worldwide catastrophe when one or two extra stalks of grain are cut off accidentally among the million scythes serving death blows! However, it is necessary to warn the Reaper and prepare her for the centuries she will be forbidden access to the earth.

This is why only those who have overcome Death on their own behalf can stay her arm—I mean those who carry life in them, who stand erect on the right of the Friend.

CHAPTER VII

Christian Initiation

HEN JESUS had finished his discourses, he left Galilee so as to reach Judea, which lies across the Jordan. Great multitudes were following him, and he healed many people. The Pharisees came to him, putting him to the test by asking: "Is it permissible to repudiate one's wife for any reason whatever?" He answered: "Have you not read that the Creator made a man and a woman, and because of that, the man shall leave his father and mother to cling to his wife, and both of them will become one flesh? Hence, let no man put asunder what God has joined together." They asked: "Then why did Moses prescribe to give his wife a writ of separation and to repudiate her?" He responded: "Moses allowed you to repudiate your wives because of your hard-heartedness. But it was not so in the beginning. So, I am telling you: Whoever disavows his wife, unless it be for infidelity, and marries another, commits adultery. And if a woman after disavowing her husband marries another, she too commits adultery." Hearing this, the disciples asked him: "If such is the stand of a man toward a woman, then it is better not to marry." He told them: "Everyone is not capable of making such a resolution, but only those to whom it has been given. There are some eunuchs who are such from birth, from the womb of their mother: there are others made so by man: finally, there are those who made themselves eunuchs for the sake of the kingdom of God. Let him who has the strength to reach that stand, do so!"

THE KINGDOM OF GOD

Someone approached him and said: "Master, what good shall I do in order to have eternal life?" He answered him: "Why do you question me upon what is good? Only One is good. If you want to enter into life, observe the commandments." "Which ones?" said he. Jesus replied: "These: thou shalt not kill; thou shalt not commit adultery; thou shalt not steal; thou shalt not bear false witness; honor thy father and mother; thou shalt love thy neighbor as thyself." The young man continued: "I have done all that; what is still missing?" Jesus fastened his eyes upon him and lovingly, he added: "You are still lacking one thing; if you want to be perfect, go sell all you have to give the money received to the poor; so you shall have a treasure in heaven; then come and follow me." Upon hearing these words, the young man went away sorrowfully, because he had vast holdings.

Jesus then told his disciples: "Believe me; a rich man has difficulty to enter into heaven. Yes, it is easier for a camel to pass through the eye of a needle than for a rich man to enter the kingdom of God." At these words the disciples were filled with consternation; they said: "Who can then be saved?" Jesus, looking at them, answered: "Such things are impossible to men, but everything is possible to God."

Peter addressing him directly said: "What about us, we have forsaken everything and have followed you; what will happen to us?" Jesus answered: "I promised you that at the rebirth of all things, the Son of Man shall be seated upon the throne of his glory; you too, those who have followed me, shall sit upon twelve

Christian Initiation

thrones to judge the twelve tribes of Israel; and whoever will have forsaken his brothers, his sisters, a father, a mother, children, lands and houses, in my name shall receive even now the value of a hundredfold; in the midst of persecutions, and in the centuries to come, he shall inherit life everlasting."

✠

Someone in the crowd asked him: "Master, tell my brother to share our inheritance with me," and he answered: "Man, who has appointed me as judge or to apportion the shares between you?" Then addressing himself to the others: "Be wary of the dangers of avarices; because no matter how well off we are, life does not depend on one's possessions." Then he told them this parable: "A rich man's field had yielded a very large crop, so he was asking himself: 'What I am I to do, as I do not know where to store my crops? This is what I shall do, I shall put down my granaries and will build larger ones, and in there shall I amass all my harvest and the goods I possess. Then I shall tell my soul: Soul of mine, you have here a lot of goods, for many years; rest, eat, drink, and rejoice!' But God told him: 'You poor fool, it is this very night that your soul shall be recalled. And who is to own what you have amassed?' Thus shall it be for anyone who hoards for himself and who is not rich in the eyes of God.

"Let your loins be girt and your lamps lit. Emulate the men who are awaiting their master returning from a wedding feast, so as to be ready to open the door as soon as he arrives and knocks. Blessed are the servants whom the master finds watching when he comes. I tell you truly that it is he that will gird himself, will sit them down at his table, and who, going from one to another, will serve them. Whether he returns at the second quarter of the night (from 9 o'clock to midnight), whether he returns at the third quarter (from midnight to 3 a.m.), blessed are the servants whom he finds still watching! Know this: if the master of the house knew at what time the thief was to come, he would be on watch, and would not let anyone break into his home. You too must be ready, because the Son of Man shall come an hour when you are least expecting him."

Peter asked him: "Lord, are you relating this parable for us or for all other people as well?" The Lord answered: "Who is the faithful and prudent steward whom the master shall appoint over the servants, to give to each, at the right time, his measure of wheat? It will be the one whom the master will find acting in this manner upon his arrival; blessed be that servant! I am telling you truly that the master will put him in charge of all his assets. But were this servant to think in his heart: My master is late in arriving; and begins chastising valets and women servants, eats and drinks and gets drunk, the master will surprise him upon a day the servant least expects him, at an hour he knows not; he will tear him to pieces and treat him the same way he would infidels. This servant who, aware of his master's wishes, had not prepared anything and who had not followed his directives, will receive several beatings. As to the one who, being unaware of the master's directives and who has done things which deserve beatings, will receive but a few. To whom much has been given, much will be expected; and from the ones to whom much has been entrusted a great deal more will be expected.

"I come to spread fire on the earth! Oh, how I wish it were already kindled! There is a baptism which I must receive; how anxiously I await that it be performed."

⊕

In a village which Jesus entered during his journey, it was a woman named Martha who received him in her house. She had a sister called Mary who, seated at the feet of the Lord, was listening to his words. However, Martha was absorbed with all kinds of household chores which she stopped doing to complain: "Lord, are you not concerned that my sister has left me to serve you alone? Tell her to help me." But the Lord answered her: "Martha, Martha, you fret and you are perturbed about a lot of things; but only one is necessary. Mary has chosen the best part of all, which will not be taken away from her."

About this time, some people came to tell him what had happened to the Galileans whose blood Pilate had shed and added to that of their sacrifices. Here is his answer: "Do you believe that these Galileans were greater sinners than all of their compatriots because of what happened to them? No, it was not so; and unless you repent, you will all perish similarly. Regarding the ten persons upon whom the tower of Silo fell and who were killed, do you believe that their debt was greater than that of all other inhabitants of Jerusalem? I declare it was not so, and unless you repent, you shall perish similarly."

He then told then this parable: "A man had a fig tree planted in his vineyard; he came to pick fruits but could not find any. 'For the past three years,' he told the vine-dresser, 'I have been coming, expecting to pick fruit on this fig tree and I do not find any; cut it; why should it deplete the soil unnecessarily?' The vine grower answered: 'Lord, please leave it another year; I shall dig around and fertilize it; it might produce in the near future; if not, you can cut it.'"

⊕

On a sabbath day, he was teaching in a synagogue. There was a woman possessed by a spirit which had kept her infirm for the past eighteen years. She was bent in two and absolutely could not straighten up. When Jesus saw her, he called and said to her: "Woman, you are rid of your infirmity." As he laid his hands on her, she immediately straightened up. As she was praising God in thanksgiving, the chief rabbi became indignant that Jesus healed on a sabbath day, and told the multitude: "There are six days during which one must work; come during those days to be healed, but not on a sabbath. The Lord answered, saying: "You are hypocrites, because does not each of you untie his ox or his ass to take them to water? And this woman who is a daughter of Abraham, whom Satan kept bound for eighteen years, should she not have

Christian Initiation

been freed of her chains on a sabbath?" These words confounded all his adversaries. As to the crowd, it rejoiced at all the marvelous things he was performing.

✠

"Many of the first will be the last, and many of the last will be first. In fact, the kingdom of heaven resembles a family man who went out early in the day to hire laborers for his vineyard. It was agreed the workers were to receive a denarius (piece of silver) per day; he sent them to the vineyard. He went out again at the third hour (9 a.m.) and saw laborers standing by and not doing anything. He told them: 'You too, go to the vineyard and I shall give you what is right.' So they went. He went out again toward the sixth hour (noon) and the ninth hour (3 p.m.) and did the same. Going out again towards the eleventh hour (5 p.m.) he found still more men assembled and doing nothing and he asked them: 'Why have you been here all day without working?' They answered him: 'Because no one has hired us.' 'Go, you too, and work in the vineyard,' he told them.

"As evening fell, the vine-grower told his overseer to call the laborers and pay them their wages, starting with the last and finishing with the first. Those of the eleventh hour having received a denarius, the ones who had come first had expected to receive more; but they too received but one denarius. Having received the same amount, they became indignant against the head of the family saying: 'The late comers have worked but one hour and you have treated them the

THE KINGDOM OF GOD

same as we who stood the heat and load of the day!' So he answered one of them: 'My friend, I am not doing you any wrong; did you not agree to work for a denarius? Take what is yours and go; I want to give this last one as much as you. Do I not have the right to do what I want with what is mine? Why should you resent my being kind?' Thus the last shall be the first, and the first shall be last."

⊕

Meanwhile he was traveling through cities and villages, teaching, on his way to Jerusalem. Someone asked him: "Lord, will there be only a few who will be saved?" He answered him and the others: "Try your best to enter through the narrow gate, because, I assure you, many will try to enter and will not succeed. When the master of the house will have gotten up and will have closed the door, and you, who have remained outside will begin to knock and ask: 'Lord open the door for us,' and he shall answer: 'I know not from whence you came.' So you will argue: 'We have eaten and drunk in your presence and you have taught in our public squares.' The he shall answer: 'I declare that I do not know from whence you came; get away from me, all of you, servants of iniquity.'"

⊕

On that day, a few Pharisees came to tell him: "Leave, go elsewhere, because Herod wants to put you to death." He answered. "Go tell that fox: 'Behold, I shall continue casting out the demons, perform healings

Christian Initiation

today and tomorrow, and on the third day my life will come to an end. But today, tomorrow, and the following day, I must journey forth, because it is not suitable that a prophet should perish outside of Jerusalem.'"

Jesus had entered into the house of one of the chief Pharisees to partake of a meal, and those present were observing him. A man who had dropsy stood before him. Jesus addressed the doctor of the law and the Pharisees, asking them: "Is it permissible to heal on a sabbath or not?" They did not reply. So he touched the dropsical subject's hand and sent him away healed. Still addressing them, he asked: "Which one of you, were his son or his ox to fall in a well on a sabbath, would not immediately pull him out?" To this, they could not answer.

⊕

Having noticed that the guests were choosing to sit at the places of honor, he told them this parable: "When you shall be invited at a wedding, do not try to occupy the first place, for fear that a guest of more renown than you be among the invited ones, so that the host who had invited you both comes, asks you to move, forcing you to have to occupy the lowest place. On the contrary, when you receive an invitation go to the lowest place so that, when the host who invited you will come, he will ask you to move to a higher place. You shall thus be honored before all guests; because whoever exalts himself shall be humbled, and whoever humbles himself will be exalted."

He also told his host: "Whenever you give a lun-

THE KINGDOM OF GOD

cheon or a dinner, do not invite your friends, your brothers, your parents, or your rich neighbors, for fear they invite you to return the favor. On the contrary, when you are to give a feast, summon the poor, the cripple, the lame, and the blind to come. Happy shall you be, because they are unable to return the great supper; and the reward will be given you when the just rise again."

Upon hearing these words, one of the guests told him: "Happy is the one who shall feast in the kingdom of God!" Jesus said to him: "A man invited many people to a great supper he was to give. As the hour came, he sent his servants to tell the guests: 'Come, everything is ready.' But all of them conspired to make excuses: 'I have just bought a field,' said the first, 'I must urgently go to inspect it. I beg of you to excuse me.' 'I have bought five pairs of oxen,' said another, 'and I shall try them out. I beg of you to excuse me.' 'I have just gotten married,' said another, 'hence I cannot come.'

"The servant returned and told his master. The master became angry and told the servant: 'Go in haste to the public squares and in the streets of the city and bring back the poor, the cripple, the blind, and the lame.'

"When the servant told him: 'Lord, we did what you ordered us to do and there is still room left,' the master answered: 'Go unto the road and along the hedgerows, urge the people to come in so that my house shall be filled, because I am telling you that none of those who had been invited will partake of my banquet.'"

Christian Initiation

⊕

Great multitudes were following him; he turned toward them, saying: "If anyone comes to me and does not hate his father and mother, his wife and children, his brothers and sisters, and still more, his own life, he cannot be my disciple. Who is the one among you who, before erecting a tower does not think of and calculate the cost whereof to see if he has sufficient means to finish it? Once having laid foundations, he would fear lacking the money to finish it. All of those who would observe such a thing would mock him, saying: 'There he is, the man who started to build and found himself unable to finish his building!' Who is the king who, going to war against another king, does not sit down priorly to reflect whether with ten thousand men he dares go against one with twenty thousand? Otherwise, while the other is still far away, he sends him an ambassador to ask for peace. Similarly, whoever among you does not renounce everything he possesses cannot become my disciple."

⊕

He then told them this parable: "If one of you has one hundred sheep and ewes and happens to lose one, will he not leave the other ninety-nine on the grazing land to go in search for the missing one until he finds it? When he has found it, he rejoices and sets it on his shoulders; he returns home, calling his friends and neighbors together and says: 'Rejoice with me! I have found my sheep that was lost.' I assure you that there will be more rejoicing in heaven when one sinner repents than for the other ninety-nine who do not need repentance.

"Does not a woman having ten drachmas and who happens to lose one, light a lamp, sweep the house, and search carefully until she finds it? Having retrieved it, she calls her friends and neighbors, saying: 'Rejoice with me, I have found my last drachma!' So is the rejoicing of angels of God for one sinner who repents!"

Jesus further said: "A man had two sons; the younger told his father: 'Father, give me the share of inheritance due me.' So the father divided his property between them. A few days later, the younger son, amassing all he had, left for a foreign land, and there dissipated his fortune in debauchery and riotous living. After he had spent his whole wherewithal, a famine came upon that land. In want, reduced to poverty, he placed himself in service to one of the inhabitants of that land, who sent him to pasture to watch over the swine. He would avidly have eaten the carob pods which the swine were feeding upon, but no one gave him any. Pondering deeply he questioned himself: 'How many hired servants of my father's have food in abundance, while I am here, dying of hunger? Therefore, I shall go, return to my father and tell him: Father, I have sinned both against you and heaven! I am not worthy of being called your son. Treat me as you would one of these mercenaries.' He arose and returned to his father.

"He was still far away when his father caught sight of him, filled with compassion, ran towards him, threw his arms around his neck, and kissed him. The

Christian Initiation

son said: 'Father, I have sinned against heaven and against you; I am not worthy to be called your son.' But the father told his servants: 'Quickly bring the finest sumptuous robe we have, put it on him; place a ring on his finger and shoes on his feet, then bring the fatted calf and kill it! Let us have a feast and rejoicings because my son was dead and returned to life; he was lost and has been found again.'"

⊕

And so the feast went on. But as the older son who had been in the field was returning and approached the house, he heard music and dancing; he called one of the servants to find out what was going on. "Your brother has returned," was the answer, "and your father has killed the fatted calf because he has found him again, safe and sound. So, he became very angry and refused to go within. His father went out begging him to enter, but he angrily told his father: 'Here I have been working for you for years; I have never disobeyed any of your orders and you have never given me a kid to make merry with friends; but when your other son comes back, he who has dissipated his fortune among harlots, you have killed the fatted calf for him!'
"'My child, his father rebuked, 'you are always with me, all that I have is yours; but we had to prepare a feast and rejoice, because your brother who was dead has returned to life; he was lost and is found again!'"
Jesus also told his disciples: "A rich man had a steward; he learned that this steward had dissipated his goods. He summoned him and told him: 'What am I

hearing about you? Give me your accounts, because it is not possible for you to administer them anymore.' The bookkeeper-steward thought inwardly: 'What am I going to do, since my master takes away the stewardship from me? To labor in the field, I am not strong enough; to beg I would be ashamed. I know what I must do after I have been dismissed from my functions, for people to welcome me in their house.' He summoned his masters' debtors one by one. From the first he asked: 'How much do you owe my master?' The answer was: 'one hundred firkins of oil.' The steward replied: 'Here is your bill, write quickly: fifty.' To another he said: 'And you, how much do you owe?' That one answered: 'one hundred firkins of wheat.' He told him: 'Here is your bill, and write: eighty.'

"The master praised the faithless steward of having acted cleverly; because the children of this century are, on their own level, cleverer than the children of light. And I tell you: Make friends among those of unearned riches, so that when they will be lacking, they will receive you among the eternal tabernacles.

"The one who is faithful in very small matters is equally so in greater ones; the one who is unjust in a very small matter is equally so in greater ones. If you could not be trusted to use the base riches you had, who will entrust you with the real ones? And if you have not been trustworthy with the goods of another, who will entrust you with what belongs to you? No servant can serve two masters; either he will hate the one and love the other, or else he will devote himself to the first and despise the second. You cannot serve God and Mammon."

Christian Initiation

⊕

The Pharisees, who were fond of money, were listening, hearing all of this, and were holding Jesus up to ridicule. He told them: "You want to pass yourselves off as upright people before men, but God sees within your hearts. For what is highly regarded by men is considered an abomination in God's eyes.

"The law and the prophets have lasted until John's time; since then the gospel of the kingdom of God is being preached and all men do their utmost to part from it."

⊕

"There was a rich man clothed in linen and purple who feasted and led a sumptuous life. A poor man, named Lazarus, covered with ulcerous sores, lay at his door. He would have been satisfied with the crumbs that fell from the rich man's table, but even the dogs came to lick his sores. When the poor man died, he was transported by angels into the bosom of Abraham. The rich man died and was buried. Being in the abode of the dead, bitterly suffering in hell, he raised his eyes and saw Abraham, and in his bosom was Lazarus. He raised his voice and cried: 'Father Abraham take pity on me.' Abraham answered: 'My child, remember that during your life, you received wealth; while Lazarus in his, suffered much, but now he is consoled here and you are in agony. Besides which, an immense chasm exists between you and us, so that is nearly impossible for anyone who would want to, either to go to you from where we are, or for you from where you are to

THE KINGDOM OF GOD

come to us.' The man continued: 'Father I beg of you, please send Lazarus to the house of my father because I have five brothers there, to whom he might attest these things: that they too will not have to come to this place of suffering.' But Abraham answered: 'They have Moses and the prophets; let hem heed them.' 'No,' Father Abraham, continued the other, 'but were someone from the land of the dead to go to them, they would repent.' Abraham then told him: 'If they listen neither to Moses nor to the prophets, were someone to resuscitate them from the dead they would not be persuaded either.'"

The apostles asked the Lord: "Increase our faith within us." The Lord answered them: "If you had faith the size of a mustard seed, you would tell this sycamore: 'Uproot yourself and replant yourself in the sea'; it would obey you." He added: "When your servant returns from the fields, either from ploughing or herding sheep, which one of you tells him: 'Come quickly and eat.' Will he not really say: 'Prepare my supper, gird yourself, and serve me until I have eaten and drunk; afterwards you too may go to eat and drink.' And because the servant does as he is bid, does his master owe him gratitude? In the same way you, after having fulfilled what was commanded of you, must say: 'We are useless servants; what we did, it was our duty to perform.'"

⊕

On his way to Jerusalem, Jesus crossed Samaria and Galilee. At the entrance of the village, ten lepers came to him: from a certain distance they raised their voices,

Christian Initiation

crying: "Jesus! Master! Have pity on us." He saw them and told them: "Go and show yourselves to the priests." On their way there, it happened that they were healed. One of them, finding himself healed, turned back, loudly praising God; then he prostrated himself at the feet of Jesus, his face to the ground, thanking him. It was a Samaritan. Then Jesus pronounced these words: "Were not ten healed? And where are the other nine? Not one of them has returned to praise God with thankfulness; except one, a stranger!" So, addressing him he said: "Arise, your faith has made you whole!"

⊕

The Pharisees having asked him when the kingdom of God was to come, he replied: "The kingdom of God does not come with external signs. No one will say: 'It is here!' Nor, 'It is there,' because, know that the kingdom of God is among you."

Then he told his disciples: "There shall come a time when you will long to see one of the days of the Son of Man, just one, but you will not see it. It will be said: 'Here he is: there he goes.' But do not go; do not look for him. The Son of Man will appear such as lightning setting the entire heaven afire from one extremity to the other. But first he must suffer much and be rejected by this generation.

"Such as in the days of Noah, so will they be in the days of the Son of Man. Men ate, drank, were getting married, and married off their children up to the moment when Noah entered the ark when the deluge came to exterminate them all. That is also what happened when Lot left Sodom; men were eating, drinking, selling, planting, and building; but at the moment when Lot left Sodom a rain of fire and brimstone fell from heaven and exterminated them all. And so will it be on the day the Son of Man is revealed.

"Let him who shall be on the house-top that day, and who has goods in his house, not come down to carry them away. Let him who is in the fields do likewise and not retrace his steps. Remember Lot's wife! Whoever shall attempt to save his life will lose it, and whoever loses it will find it again.

"On that night, I tell you, when two men are sleeping together in one bed, one will be taken and the other left. Of two women who are grinding at the mill, one will be taken and one left." The disciples asked: "When is it to be, Lord?" He answered: "There where the body lies, there will the vultures gather also."

⊕

He told them a parable, to show them that they should pray continually and never become discouraged. He said: "In a certain city there was a judge who had no fear of God nor any regard for men. In this same city lived a widow who came to him, saying: 'Give me redress against my adversary.' But for a long time, he did not want to. Finally, he told himself: 'Though I have fear neither of God nor regard for men, as it is certain that this widow is in my charge, I shall render justice so that she will not keep heaping stones upon my head.'" The Lord added: "Do you hear what this iniquitous judge is saying? Would not God give redress to his elect who are crying to him night and day! Would he postpone coming to their help! I assure you that he shall give redress promptly; but will the Son of Man, upon his return, find faith upon earth?"

⊕

He also told the following parable to some among them who were self-satisfied and convinced they were righteous, but who scorned others: "Two men went up to the temple to pray, one a Pharisee, the other a publican. The Pharisee standing upright was praying: 'Oh, God, I thank Thee that I am not as other men, rapacious, iniquitous, adulterous, nor even as this publican here. I fast two days a week; I give tithes from all my income.' While the publican, standing at a distance, did not dare lift his eyes to heaven, but beating his breast he said: 'Oh, God, be merciful towards me who am a sinner.' I assure you, that this man returned to his house justified, rather than the other; because whoever shall exalt himself shall be humbled, and whoever humbles himself shall be exalted."

Then, they brought him little children, that he might touch them. Seeing this, the disciples rebuked those who were bringing them. But Jesus called these children and said: "Let little children be brought to me; do not prevent them, because the kingdom of God belongs to those who resemble them.

"Verily, I tell you that whoever will not receive the kingdom of God as does a little child, will not enter therein." Then he kissed them, placed his hands over them, and blessed them.

After which, each of them went home. As for Jesus, he went up to the Mount of Olives. At dawn, he returned to the temple. The multitude was surging towards him. Jesus sat and began to teach.[1]

The Disciple and the Material World

WHEN OUR MASTER JESUS refuses to settle an inheritance quarrel, he recalls to mind a phenomenon common to all planes of life, particularly visible in our social life; namely, that laws founded by men or gods always leave interstices for individual liberty to pass through their mesh—interstices that constitute the test of our free will—whereas heaven limits itself to telling us through our inner voice, if not our outer voice, which is the lawful side.

In any case, one general observation can guide us: that the order of nature is movement. Everything goes through perpetual transformism. Immobilization *per se* is contrary to nature. Consequently, one must work with one's heart, one's body, one's intelligence. Do not withhold any outpouring of energy, do not accumulate any superfluous funds, sensibilities, or intelligence for your exclusive satisfaction.

---

[1] Matt. 19:1–12; Mark 10:1–12; Matt. 19:16–30; Mark 10:17–31; Luke 18:18–30; 22:28–30; Luke 12:13–21; Luke 12:49–50; Luke 10:38–42; Luke 13:1–9; Luke 13:10–17; Matt. 19:30; 20:16; Luke 13:22–30; Matt. 8:11–12; Matt. 7:13–14, 21–23; Luke 13:31–33; Luke 14:1–14; Luke 14:15–24; Matt. 22:1–10; Luke 14:25–35; Matt. 10:37–38, 16:21–28; Mark 1–7; Matt. 18:12–14; Luke 15:8–19; Luke 15:11–31; Luke 16:1–13; Luke 16:14–16; Luke 16:19–31; Luke 17:5–10; Luke 17:11–19; Luke 17:20–37; Luke 18:1–9; Luke 18:9–14; Luke 18:1–8; Luke 19:13–15; Mark 10:13–16.

Christian Initiation

We have the right to retain a reasonable and necessary amount of all that our work, our destiny, and the kindness of the Father have brought to us. But the surplus must be returned to the general analogous current, either by making it bear fruit, or by distributing it. Therefore, neither the scholar nor the scientist has any right to keep his theoretical or practical discoveries to himself; the artist must produce, even if, in his time, there was but a single individual capable of understanding him; the rich man does not have the right to store his capital away in safes. We are nothing but stewards. There is no material possession that enhances a soul; neither do our intellectual, esthetic, or fluidic possessions aggrandize it either. It is the *use* we make of them that influences the spiritual part of our being.

The Word, the Master of masters, is ever present here and elsewhere. But he dwells particularly within a pure heart and an awakened spirit—i.e., in the man who masters his flesh and who holds his torch lit. Wherever he goes in the universes and within individuals, the Master dispenses a beatific ecstasy, which is to say the ineffable rapture that is the subjective reflection of the invisible theurgical ceremonies called "nuptials" in the Holy Scriptures. So, he travels the whole of Creation untiringly, so as to give himself to all beings, immense as well as minuscule, who have labored sufficiently to receive him without deceit.

This explains why it is said "watch and pray"; meaning, we must be patient. The Master may come only at the second or third watch. Two or three incarnations may pass in this nocturnal waiting. Remember that wherever the sun of spirits is not resplendent, it is night.

Blissful is he who opens the door of his heart the first time the Word knocks, because he in turn will be gladdened and served by the One at whose name all Creation bows, from whom a single word gives all bliss, all knowledge, and all power to whomever is ready to heed it.

For the second time Jesus repeats, "I shall come as a thief during the night, unexpectedly." "Unexpectedly": because his logic is infinitely broader and more complex than ours. No one can foresee the hour of his death (because the death of the body is not always the true death), or the hour when a race, a continent, or a planet will disappear. "During the night": because physical death is the disappearance of the sun from physical life; because cosmic death is the disappearance of its visible sun from a planet; because mystical regeneration is the rising of the sun of spirits in the psychic heavens. This will occur to all men regardless of the age of their soul—as Peter's question leads us to understand.

For, in nature we are all servants and masters, governed or governors. Each of us has duties and responsibilities, not only vis-à-vis our social inferiors, our families, fellow citizens, and domestics, but also toward other beings, temporarily unknown or invisible, to whom we are suns and gods. Since in us knowledge comes after the progress of wisdom, we are only conscious of that part of the world that we would be wise enough to administer with rectitude, were we willing. From which it follows that the formula of our duty as concerns all our conscious and unconscious charges would be to state that we are always to accomplish the proper and expedient act no matter what the cost might be. To be ready to withstand the shock of death is one of the signs of this mastery. This is why Christ chose the example we have just read about. And his word is to be understood literally when he affirms that "in truth the Lord will establish over all that he has the steward whom he will find

Christian Initiation

faithfully going about his stewardship." Yes, the Father asks us merely to be his honest stewards.

Were the total duration of a soul's incarnations counted, as today's Brahmans say, in billions of earth years, this figure, which is beyond our comprehension, would still not be worth a hundredth of a second in the face of eternity. But in any event, this way of accounting is simply not so: firstly, because there is only one soul, which remains present from the beginning to the end of a creation; and secondly, because existences take place in many different realms, the duration of time changes in accordance with the planets on which the soul may be for a time present. Hence, the man who, during this divine blink-of-an-eye, remains faithful is consequently made free, which really means in practice a master of future creations, a participant to the Treasure of Light. That man served his God during a minuscule duration of time, but his God will serve him all along eternity.

So it is not a question of satisfying one's own desires, however pompously the sages of this world may dress them up; the history of the monastic mysticism abounds with examples that reveal how pride, complacency, and self-admiration engender ecstatic and thaumaturgic states: the ivory-tower solitary, the hermit, is wise only for the short span of human wisdom.

It is logical that the more we know about the will of our Master, the more we have received of gifts, of auxiliaries, faculties, intelligence, and will, the more accountable we are, and thus the greater our merits or demerits will be. Hence, as we know only approximations and appearances regarding ourselves or others (except that everything we do could be done better), the prudent thing is to pray before any undertaking, before each act, each study. In this way we call upon the suprahuman Being who came to earth and into all planes of our terrestrial life, who lit his regenerative fire, who separated the light from the darkness, and who was baptized by the unique, unknown, inimitable baptism that is his own death as holocaust.

Let us call upon him at any time, in any act or desire, in any matter, that he may be the veritable workman of our works, the accent in our speech, the look in our eyes, the life in all our being. The fire we mentioned a while back that Jesus was to light has modified the general currents of the fluidic oceans upon which the worlds swim. Thus, east and north were once the beneficial and sacred cardinal directions; since Christ, it is south and west that have been given the properties of the two preceding points: one as the center of divine realizations upon earth, the other as the center of human realizations. But the twenty centuries that have elapsed since that time will only have been a period of transformation in this plan, the results of which will only become clearly perceptible later on.

The Narrow Door

WHILE PERFORMING charitable acts, the majority of you contrive to lead your inner life according to a strict practice. The narrow door that give access to the Kingdom is built just as much out of renunciations and abatements accepted secretly under the gaze of God, as out of humiliations, persecutions, calumnies, and scorn derived from the outside world. Sufferings of this kind offer no difficulty other than the one of having to endure them. But our internal, inner work demands precautionary measures.

Christian Initiation

There are two kinds of precautions—the moral ones, which are basically the struggle against our faults; and the intellectual ones, which mean the training of our attention and of our reflection, so as to concentrate them in view of provoking a pious emotion that will strengthen our will.

Meditation such as the Catholic masters understand it—the two St Victors, Cisneros, the Brothers of the Common Life, Ignatius of Loyola, Berulle, Saint Francis de Sales, the Sulpicians—no matter what the particular modalities of each school be—is only a voluntary exercise of the memory and of imagination upon pious themes in view of fomenting the emotive state requisite to obtain a greater will power. This does not resemble in any way the engendering of thought or of the mysterious engendering of love that operates at the pinnacle of contemplation.

That is why Jesus does not speak to us of meditation, but of action primarily; just as he does not refer to the phenomena one observes among contemplatives.

This is because meditation is but one means. Contemplation is another. To be ravished in ecstasy is yet another. Jesus does not teach us under diversified aspects, but only under the aspect of unity. He does not speak of body, of soul, of spirit, of psychism; neither does he speak of secret forces or particular faculties. He looks at each man, each creature, as a flame of coherent life. Or rather, knowing full well that we are incoherent, he invites us to become unified within; and to make us aware of the benefits thereof, he speaks to us as if unity were already existent.

It must be understood that these analyses, filling so many pages of ours, are studying things from the outside, for fear of disorienting our superficial and particularistic views. And if someone can leave these dissections aside, let him do so joyfully and abide simply in the vigorous simplicity of the gospel word.

In Christian mysticism there is one way that—when encountering visions, ecstasies, and thaumaturgies—lingers there, mistakenly considering them acquired results. It is a false path because it leads one to mistake a step, or an accidental means, for the goal.

There is another path, which refuses all supra-normal phenomena, and continually seeks the beyond of what is reached: austerity, obscurity, simple faith; which believes without the slightest proof and advances without the slightest indicator. This path is frightfully steep.

There is yet another path, still more arduous, in spite of its engaging aspect. This one refuses nothing, and the climber studies each incident of the journey because each thing is for him a sign of the solicitude of Christ on his behalf. The least dream, omen, spiritual impression, encounter, or notion seems to him worthy of attention. To this point, it is the easiest line. The arduous part commences with the need for the pilgrim to become unattached to any of these signs, or even appropriate them as his spiritual capital. These various experiences, from dream to ecstatic ravishment when the Trinity manifests itself, no matter what respectful care he takes in his studies thereupon, must only be regarded as provisory, approximative—in short, as something uncertain. The only rule of conduct here will be the teachings of Christ: enduring tribulations, continuous renouncements, the ever-renewed gift of self. His only strength will be faith, the impulse toward the ultimate, toward the beyond, toward the unknown.

When Jesus sees the sincere effort exerted by his servant, he sends him encouragement or warnings. Whether these

Christian Initiation

marks of his divine solicitude take on the aspect of dreams, visions, ecstasies, or some kind of mastery over matter, they must become as a pearl of great price for him who receives them. But, let the recipient beware not to become attached to the gift and forget the giver. Let him observe, let him note—then he must go forward. The greatest of saints and the purest of souls on earth will always remain an immense distance from the eminence of Christ and of his purity. Divine apparitions can never be anything but veils of God, and even the most resplendent of these are still exceedingly abstruse.

God is the inconceivable and imperceptible. The disciple serves a being he cannot visualize, since God surpasses any concept; a being he does not even feel, since our heart is only capable of understanding the reflections of the divine. The stubborn march towards the unknown, the ungraspable, the unrevealed, the invisible, the ineffable, the inconceivable, the impossible—this is called faith.

The same rule will govern our contemplative life as controls our active life. One must love, undertake anything, study everything, but one must love only in God, undertake anything only to help our fellowmen, study only so as to serve better.

Man is connected with the world:
through his physical senses; through his hyperphysical senses (activities of his double: clairvoyance and/or clairaudience of the subjects magnetized or initiated in esoteric training exercises); by his mental faculties (his intellect's activity); through his spiritual heart.

On the other hand, the world is connected to man:
through his sensations of physical objects; through sensations of hyperphysical objects (telluric fluids,

THE KINGDOM OF GOD

invisible creatures indicated in our tradition); through ideas; by agents who are pure spirits of light or of darkness.

Let us note that the hyperphysical objects may also provoke physical impressions and sensations in the case of:
ideas: in hyperphysical and physical impressions; pure spirits: in ideas, in sensations and impressions.

Whatever he may feel (given that at the beginning of contemplative life the five senses are usually invaded by inebriating delights), the disciple must be content merely to accept and register the phenomenon, to give thanks, and then to abandon it—even to the point of forgetfulness. This is the only means of progress. No matter how pure they might be, these physical beatitudes are situated at a great distance from the spirit. Hence, as soon as the disciple experiences aridity during the exercise of cogitating upon pious subjects, or when he ceases desiring these reflections, and especially when he loves to feel alone and peaceful in the presence of God, without mental activity, devoid of any feeling save that of a calm, profound, and reposeful sweetness—as soon as these three signs occur, the disciple knows he is entering into the contemplative life, and consequently can sally forth upon the path of pure naked faith.

All along this road, the traveler feels himself bathed in the light of the divine presence surrounding him. This presence is that much the more effective and intimate in that he is unable to analyze it. This is so, because we can only feel and analyze substances sufficiently dense and complex to enable our sensorial or mental faculties to take hold of them. The rays of the sun become visible owing to the shadows against which they stand out conspicuously. When we have become

Christian Initiation

empty, pure, translucid, the spiritual sun illumines us without our being aware of it, because our conscience has no more darkness upon which to lean. This is how he who lives in the Kingdom has become a little child again: he has learned everything and has forgotten it all.

From a certain height the disciple perceives, understands, operates—or at least, everything happens as if it were truly he who is the author of these things. That, however, is an illusion: rather, in the exercise of the most prestigious miracles and magnificent revelations, he must escape, prostrate himself, and take stock that it is God who operates through him. Otherwise, he suffers a redoubtable collapse.

Another trap, just as dangerous, happens when during the inner desert of contemplation a dialogue commences between our self and an interlocutor whom we have the tendency to believe divine, while in reality it is but an unknown faculty of our deeper self. The spirit of man contains a whole world: just as in our normal physical life we are not conscious of the individualism of our stomach or our liver, so in our inner life we must first have climbed very high in order to notice that each of our psychic, moral, and intellectual faculties is an individual being—each living in a certain measure for its own advantage. That is why, during the times of a national crisis, one believes one sees an immense homogenous collective movement, while in reality each citizen acts in full consciousness and liberty, especially the best of them.

At the point when the disciple enters into connection with the invisible world, his life becomes a series of delicate problems that he must solve immediately. In everything he feels, in any vocation he undertakes, he must discern the principle thereof: something of himself; something from darkness; something from God. He extricates himself from these several complexes only through pitiless moral discipline, renunciation, and ever more profound humility.

Illusions of Piety

ANYONE CAN, if he eats sparingly and spends long hours immobile and with his mind tense, obtain visions, auditions, or other extra-corporeal sensations—the origin of which does not emanate from the physical world. But what is not material is not automatically divine: between terrestrial matter and pure spirit there are thousands of unknown matters, creatures, and worlds, to which we may also add our imagination, which can excite all sorts of contacts and images in our nervous system. Beware of people who believe themselves to be interpreters of God. They are mostly those who speak to themselves. Beware of visionaries. Vision can be useful only in very rare cases. True dreams that our spirit does not deform are also rare. Guard against the attraction of external things.

It is an error to attach any importance to a prayer formula. The Father understands all languages. Neither Hebrew nor Latin nor Greek have any more value for him than one's local dialect. To attach any importance to place, hour, body-posture, or gestures during one's prayer is also an error. If humility impels us to prostrate ourselves upon the ground, that is fine; but if we rail at the hardness of the flagstones, our kneeling will be of no avail. Doubtless, in certain dynamic centers galvanized by the crowds, at certain hours when the currents are favorable, prayer seems to ascend more easily; but that is only an external impression. Heaven is everywhere independent of hours, places, formulas, or rites. These things help, of course, but let us beware lest they end up by hiding spiritual realities from us. Prayer is solely a colloquy between our heart and the divine Persons. And to be heard by them, we must simply conform to their law. Nothing else.

Set your mind at rest that all of this strictly conforms with Catholic teaching. I could even cite saints who condemned the wearing of medals, going on pilgrimages, and attending religion feasts as contrary to one's interior life.

But there are more subtle snares.

Having reached a certain stage of spirituality, the disciple often draws the attention of the adversary, who watches for his slightest weaknesses and draws him into ambush. That is why we should never stray, even one step, away from the narrow path of total self-renunciation and patience. Mere complacency towards one's self may open the door to the tempter's seductions. What the disciple needs to remember is that the slightest breach of our ideal renders our will anemic, clouds our conscience, dulls our intelligence, and renders our sensibility obtuse. Not only the fault, but an involuntary omission, to the moral code vitiates the disciple's entire being in all of its facets.

When we turn toward God, let us be aware that he is infinitely above all forms, and inaccessible to any devotional, psychological, or scientific more or less secret artifices. He alone who is empty of any of the created will receive the uncreated within. Jesus exhorts us to seek the quietest room in the house. He gives us a formula that enumerates all our needs, and many other things that we will never comprehend. Why seek further? Among the millions of Our Fathers and Hail Marys recited each day, how many have been said properly? Even we, are we able to recite the

THE KINGDOM OF GOD

Our Father from one end to the other without distractions? Can we even enunciate one among the seven petitions realizing fully in our mind and heart all of the plenitude of its significance? Hence, when attacking difficult and dangerous works, why risk mistakes of itinerary, collapses, that are far more grave in the spiritual than in the material world?

The small tasks of everyday trace the best path to follow in our desire for perfection. Nothing prevents us from accomplishing them from a heart having taken refuge in God, devoid of the selfish angle that makes us cantankerous towards whatever we do with the idea that this belongs to us, and that merit and honor are due us. However, Christ never stated that we must disdain what this world possesses—which is luminous, alive, beautiful! His will is at the origin of each masterpiece, of beautiful landscapes, of the majestic mountains or fertile plains; it is his will that knots family ties as well as those of a country; it is his will that authorizes nature to reveal its secrets and that commands some of its forces to obey us. Thus the true disciple admires and loves all things as representations of divine favors, but considers none of them as his property or conquest. He makes use of them, and gives thanks. And when benefits derived therefrom are forbidden him, he still gives thanks, because he finds in each pleasure or privation a lesson to be learned.

To the pure and limpid disciple everything refines his inner guilelessness. Everything for him is a sign from God, and a source of peace, mirth, fraternal love, and powerful energy. By not linking any of these marvels to his self, the still more magnificent marvels that the Father offers his servants will be reflected in his translucid heart and be conceived through his renovated spirit. And if, pursuing his

Christian Initiation

ascension toward faith, this disciple, while recognizing the inestimable value of the experiences that heaven enriches him with, does not attach himself to these ravishments, Christ will confer upon him new treasures endlessly, since his kingdom has no frontiers, and his light no limits.

Here, disregarding the puerility of the observation, we might say: the spirit that stops at any plateau of knowledge, of esthetic enjoyment, or of the will, ceases to advance.

To prevent these falls and errors, there is but one means known: to live in the scintillating night of faith. Is there a pious person who, upon hearing about a healer, does not hasten to consult him? Those who act in that manner do not have faith, and they call themselves Christians. Whoever needs proof to believe does not have faith. But to describe the forward march of the true mystical feeling: it is not the spectacles of nature that lead it to God; it is, rather, in God, from the standpoint of heaven, that it perceives the real beauty and the real significance of nature—the beauty, if the disciple has a poetic lyrical mind; the significance, if he is a thinker.

Man can love God. He may feel the divine influx. But as far as understanding God, or understanding his lights, he cannot. His intelligence accepts and registers nothing but the shadows of God, nothing but the partial and obscure refractions of his splendor. That is why one must advance with faith.

The renunciation Christ asks of us in order to follow him is not one, but triple. St Ignatius of Loyola wants us to become indifferent to all created things (see his *Spiritual Exercises*, First week, Principle—which deals with material indifference to food, clothing, and lifestyle). When St John of the Cross wants us to forget (to let go of) everything cre-

THE KINGDOM OF GOD

ated, he speaks of a more profound metaphysical indifference. But neither the one nor the other are possible or living, if, in the bottom of our heart, we have not liberated ourselves from the lure of our temperament or of our mentality for all these things. It is this third renunciation, the one of desire, the most central and hence the most difficult, that Christ asks of us. Here again, we note that the gospels consider any problem from its center, any difficulty from its crux, while the greatest human masters stop at one relatively external aspect or another.

In short, it is the self that has to be transplanted, that inner fire which wants to devour everything: concepts, things, and the beauties of creation. One must remove from it all the nutriments this fire would reduce to ashes, and to give it in their stead heaven and God himself. It is then that the flame of the self flickers, smoulders, and its smoke plunges us into the spiritual night. But at an unforeseen hour, when the Word comes "as a thief in the night," he reanimates this expiring flame at the fresh and soft light of eternal life.

All efforts at this stage must be actuated by love. Yet, love of God is not like ordinary love that incites us toward temporal beauty; changing the goal of that kind of love is the preparation for love of God. The senses engender perceptions; the psyche engenders passions; intelligence engenders thought; but will alone engenders the sole veritable love—the love of God.

Love of God does not mean love for any one thing, no matter how sublime. Love of God is our projection out of ourselves and out of all nature through our will—because nothing that the will may reach is God, and any sympathy enchains us to its object. Only when the will tears itself

Christian Initiation

from everything in order to soar to the beyond, will it go to God, and will it give birth to love.

Such is the narrowest arch of the narrow gate.

Having reached this place, the disciple has conquered all desires and broken his chains. He has no thirst or hunger, save for God. For his own sake, he still has to invent the best means to be satiated and to quench his thirst. The experiences undergone by his predecessors or his companions can only be beneficial to him in a general way.

The summit of perfection is reached when the Holy Spirit adjudges the human creature worthy of receiving the true baptism—after which, he becomes free.

Before receiving the baptism of the Spirit, we must have made ourselves so small, or so strong, that not a thing costs us pain or concern—whether something to be effected, or something to submit to, whether ordinary or extraordinary.

Considering the innumerable variety of actions, of events and sentiments possible to man, one understands that each method of ascetic pursuit comprises but one part of the work. Secular life is one of the experiences to pass through, religious life another; and thus, each kind of life's pursuit is but a discipline, and all disciplines have but one goal—that we fulfill the will of God with all our heart, all our mind, all our intelligence and forces.

The means of attaining this perfect state, as you know, is to become master of the self. Mastery of self comes when the intellectual, the passional, and the instinctive within us obey the light. You are well aware that the emotive center is the most powerful—the brain never remains independent from our enthusiasms or our hates, and the body almost always obeys our passions. Thus, it is that the rectification, the solidity, and the ennobling of our character, seem to be

THE KINGDOM OF GOD

the most efficacious means of attaining self-mastery and the obedience of the whole person to this chosen ideal.

The simplest nomenclature concerning the diseases of one's character is that of the seven capital sins. We know them under their intellectual and corporeal forms, but we still have to combat them under their psychological form, which is far more difficult.

Within us, but the more exteriorized, are the instincts. Further within, one finds the appetites. The former belong to the body and cannot be destroyed, the second belong to the character, and the goal of mystical discipline is to transmute them. But in fact both intermingle and reinforce each other, which renders the work quite arduous!

It is difficult to oust the noxious ferments of one's character; they are generally discovered by this sign: that they manifest themselves not so much as big isolated faults but as constant imperfections. For example, prating, manias, habitual curiosity, impatience, or scruples are organic diseases of the psyche.

By exercising one virtue, all virtues grow. Through the habit of one sole fault, all faults germinate. If, according to the strict teaching of the gospel, we apply ourselves to refusing the foods and liquids our appetites yearn for, and if we push that fast to its limits, the self weakens and agonizes. Then, at the moment when this agony is to terminate into the void, the Word arrives and restores to the self a new life according to the light, according to the spirit, according to love.

But how many bloody encounters before this triumph! In truth, the sole creature towards whom I must show pitilessness is my self. Vices, faults, temptations, are nothing, provided we combat them or refuse them. But still, we must combat unto death and give an implacable refusal unceasingly renewed.

Martha and Mary

THE REMARK THAT Jesus addressed to the "matron of the house" Martha was not, as religious writers repeat, one after another, a critique against active life and a eulogy of contemplative life. Jesus was stating that one must perform each task in its time. Martha was evidently hurrying busily to welcome her guest and honor him, although she had a host of servants to perform domestic chores. There is a time to act, a time to think, a time for matter, a time for the spirit. And, as it is the latter who is Master, it is to him we should first attend; for an hour later, Jesus could have left without fretting Martha having profited from the divine conversation.

Tradition is mistaken in making of Martha the prototype of active life, and of Mary the prototype of contemplative life, and especially by giving preeminence to Mary. Let us examine the differences.

Contemplative life consists primarily of a sortie from the world—hermits, anchorites, monks tear themselves away from their families and society. They adopt a discipline of physical austerities—rough clothing, no defenses against winter or summer; abstinence, fasts, chastisements, limited sleep; a life of introspection and long orisons, which with their whole strength they spend to extirpate vices and even the least faults from their hearts; extirpate everything that may constitute an obstacle to divine union. They experience this divine union progressively through inner peace, quietude, a feeling of the divine presence, ecstasies, rap-

THE KINGDOM OF GOD

tures, spiritual marriage—all of them experiences intersected by agonizing purifications—by detachment of the self from the physical world and even from itself.

Let us examine these sacrifices.

To renounce the joys of one's family may be a beautiful thing when one loves one's parents, when one loves family life and children. But if in fact one prefers living alone, where is the sacrifice?

Yes, the discomforts of monastic life are painful, and subjugate our corporeal laziness. But do ordinary workers have a comfortable life? Do miners, sailors, common laborers, farmers, and peasants live in immaculate surroundings, eat choice morsels, sleep to their heart's content?

To renounce one's will, to place ourself in the hands of a religious superior, is difficult by nature for active, independent characters. But how many others might rather not to have to be preoccupied with households, landlords, cooking; not have to hear children screaming or the carping and harsh words of a boss?

Long divine services, night and day, endless prayers in one's cell—this is painful only to a man of action.

Thus, we note that only the novice to whom it is in fact abhorrent to adopt the monastic life takes a definite step forward, toward God, by doing so.

⊕

As for us, we should always remain faithful by putting into effect our mystical desires through precise, just, and complete acts. If on occasion our ardor is warmed through reading books by contemplatives, let us not for that reason envy the destiny of these solitaries. Doubtless, given the excessive deviations many commit in the dense domain of

Christian Initiation

sensual pleasures and material triumphs, it is important that others counter-balance their fall through strict reduction of the life of the body and by the continual mental focus toward the divine aspects of Christianity. The Trappist, the Carmelite, the Order of St Clare, restore the equilibrium of Christianity. But we have a different role to play.

Our lifestyle is incompatible with contemplation. First, we do not enjoy the solitude, the leisure, or the calm indispensable to those exercises or to their analyses. Secondly, we cannot submit to any healthy critique the spiritual sensations that spring up during the course of our long orisons—for at the moment these contacts (feelings) spontaneously occur, they invade our consciousness and possess us. Once we have returned to our normal state, we can examine them only in the memory they left, whereas the contemplative sage may observe phenomena at the instant they occur, and not after they have vanished. Also, in the contemplative life, it is not what we are conscious of that is most important, it is what occurs beyond our consciousness—the imperceptible solicitation of grace, free from all voluntary effort, but through which the consciousness justly conquers a few portions from the subconsciousness. Rare are the contemplatives, then, who can maintain their equilibrium to the end, and who never alter the limpidity of the gospel doctrine through any sort of personalism.

Our path is different, but hardly less rocky. Left unprovided with such help as monastic life offers, we must on the one hand grasp heaven through a faith helped neither by visions nor revelations, and on the other work with matter with the same ardor as do those for whom it contains all hopes. We must immediately raise our spirit to the supernatural, far beyond all that creation offers us of encouragement, joys, and rest. We must not take refuge or rely on human affections, or upon art, or upon thought—but only on faith. Yet, when fortune smiles upon us, when we are loved, when art or philosophy communicate their noble secrets to us, we must rejoice in having the money, the honors, to enjoy such beautiful, pure joys. Finally, when and if ruin comes, when everyone attacks us, when we have no more books to study or beauties to contemplate, we still must be happy in the midst of these miseries, bitternesses, ignorances, and hideous ordeals.

When Jesus visited the two sisters, "the best part" that Mary took was not to forget everything in the presence of the Master, but to have understood that if heaven speaks to us for a few seconds, we must leave everything aside so as to better hear him. Also, if Martha seems to have the lesser part in this world, do we know what part she will have in the other world? Do we know whether she tore herself away from the beatitude of his Presence because she believed her duty was to prepare dinner?

Who Are the Disciples?

THE GALILEANS executed by order of Pilate (the eighteen upon whom fell the tower of Siloam) were not, says Jesus, greater sinners that the rest of the people; words that some terrorizing preachers would do well to remember. In fact, there is an average ethical level for a given collectivity, which very few go beyond. This is one of the reasons why we should be indulgent toward one another, why we should cure ourselves of the clinical mania to see the finger of God, the anger of God, the chastisement of God, in every catastrophe. God never punishes. It is, rather, men themselves

Christian Initiation

who through certain actions provoke climatic, meteorological, geological reactions, as also accidents and epidemics—but this is a natural process of the same order as the one in which the angry man, upon hitting a table, may sprain his wrist.

Jesus explains the benevolence of heaven very well. For instance, the fig tree is man; its proprietor is God; the winegrower is the Messiah. Man does not produce the fruit he should—he is sterile, with a frightfully obstinate tenacity; but Christ intervenes, and thanks to him, the Father's clemency is moved, and new existences are granted us to permit our ever-possible amendment.

We have already covered the subject of the doctrine of Jesus relative to the narrowly superstitious observance of the sabbath—even the kind of diseases he healed (paralysis and dropsy) having a certain rapport with the number seven. But obeying laws is far more potent than launching new ones. That is why we should pay close attention to our conduct—for we are all legislators on a small or large scale, and everyone has an innate tendency to impose his fantasies or ideas upon his neighbor, so as to take his ease. We must carefully guard against this, learn how to restrain ourselves, and try to find that narrow door through which only those who have been humble and charitable may pass. Otherwise, when the judgment day of the race comes, we would be left outside the house of the Lord, which means outside the planet or the continent where his reign will be established. Then all supplications will be in vain.

No religion gives us the privilege of being admitted to the Father's house with certitude; even the precedence of the ontological hierarchies will not be observed, because we will find souls of any and all ages therein. Indeed, not all men who are to inhabit a universe or a star or a country descend upon it at the same time; some take longer but gentler roads; others are led by shorter but steeper paths; so much so that it may be that the first to descend have put in less work, and are ranked well after those who, coming much later, have had a enormous effort to make. This is what the parable of the laborers of the last hour explains.

But let us go further.

The Father has invited the whole of humanity to his house; but the guests are tied up by their business, by their family, by all sorts of earthly preoccupations, by money, science, or sensuality. So the Father sends his servants to bring back those who have no money, no honors, no families—those who rove about the roads. Thus the rich man and the scientist are not excluded from God's kingdom because of their social function or mental qualities, but because they will not leave these fragile things to obey the Father's call.

The life of the world is different according to whether its Lord is absent or present. In the first case, creatures compete for the best places, embellishing their ambitions with such names as know-how, ingenuity, activity, will-power, intelligence, business acumen, and so on; but when the Lord comes, he re-seats his guests according to their true worth. So, let us not imitate the gossip-mongers of Jesus, who always chose the best seats at the table. Let us rather take what others refuse, on all occasions—the obscure, inconspicuous job, anonymity, the difficult task. Heaven brings down him who elevated himself, and elevates the one who took the lower degree of his own accord.

According to men's measure, the wise thing to do is to frequent those who are richer, more celebrated, or more

Christian Initiation

powerful than we are, hoping that some of their splendor will radiate upon us. Divine wisdom, however, says quite the contrary: seek the poor, from whom you cannot profit. This explains why it is written in the Book of Life that angels visit only those who previously went to their inferiors, to the needy ones.

These two parables apply to all subjects, among them: the fall of angels, judgments, individual illumination, preparation of the philosophical mercury. To receive this inner Eucharist that is the mysterious meal of the soul at the divine table, it is essential that primarily one must have chosen the lowest places in the house of nature. One must have given food, money, sympathy, of our knowledge, to our lesser brothers, have given up everything at the first call from God. And lastly, one must have become inwardly detached from created treasures of all kinds.

Jesus sums this up with supernatural vigor in a few witticisms. Let us try to understand these paradoxical aphorisms, which are so many challenges to what seems to be the best of human nature.

To become a disciple, four things are essential: to come to him, to hate seven kinds of beings, to carry our cross, and follow him. The first condition is self-explanatory and easily accepted. But the second? To hate, whom? A father, a mother, wife, children, brothers, sisters? Everything that makes life worthy to be lived, everything that renders it pleasant, honorable? And is this the same God who orders this when he blesses large families? As for the seven kinds of beings, let us not seek to assign to these seven terms a mysterious meaning either in the psychic or spiritual sense, but rather be content with and satisfied with common sense. Have you ever felt you loved your family for yourself and not for them? Have you been aware that these affections were anchored within us with all the obscure roots of our flesh and blood? Hence they are not meritorious, since the pains we experienced take on an indispensable character. All that ties us, restrains us, in this world, all that attracts us sufficiently to make us forget the Law, no matter how sublime our motives might seem from a human viewpoint, must be pushed aside, and we must detach ourselves from it. "To renounce the self and any ownership, while having full confidence in God; to accept anything as if it came from the Creator and not from a created being; to be kind and patient"—such is the maxim of Meister Eckhart. Here is the maxim of his initiator Jean Fugger: "The greatest pain of the just, and the most meritorious, is to find himself abandoned by God, to become selfless and do violence to the self to the extent of being resigned to remain without the help of God as long as it pleases him."

Lastly, to refer to a formula better known than those of the two great protagonists to spiritual life during the Middle Ages, let us say that the disciple is he alone who in all circumstances adopts the most repugnant, the most antipathetic course, with a smiling heart.

To hate one's parents and one's own life does not mean one must be a bad son, or a wretched mother, or that one needs to commit suicide—the life of the body (our corporeal life), the passional life, is not our true life. It is, rather, our selfish, self-engrossed life, our self-centered will, our selfish hunger, that we must hate in all its manifestations.

The third condition is to carry our cross. What is our cross, if not the instrument of our expiatory torment, of payment of our debts and atonement for evil committed? The formula at this stage is—patience and resignation.

Christian Initiation

The final condition is to follow Jesus. No longer merely to undergo, but to act on his deeds, to undertake as he did, to radiate, in our infinitesimal sphere, as he radiated on the universal orb.

This does not indicate merely desiring Jesus and remaining passive, as the next parables of the builder and warrior indicate, because the disciple in the deeper sense of the word is a builder and a soldier. His share in the buildings of the divine city is reserved for him; a post awaits him in the cosmic battle. Therefore, whoever wants the ends finds the means. Before one can build, stones are needed; before a combat, forces are needed. We amass both through observance of the second and third formulas just cited. It all adds up to renouncing everything we possess. When we have drawn to ourselves all the cells we had piled up on the sands of natural desires—only then will it be possible for the soldiers who fought for the conquest of idols to build our spiritual abode, or to be enrolled among the soldiers of heaven.

We can see the difference here with what the Far Easterners let show of their secret ethics. Their ascetics who are of the highest degree first recall within themselves all those of their strengths and powers that family, social, and intellectual life had hitherto absorbed. But they use this core, which is all their own, to draw new forces so as to become pure and perfect that they may help others with efficacy. They do not seem to realize that, no matter how good a purpose we may have for taking what doesn't belong to us, nature always forces us to return what we have unduly acquired. Instead, the gospel puts man to work as soon as he has proven his goodwill.

In this way, the propagating force of sacrifice radiates as

soon as possible; the disciple finds himself under the central radiance of his Master as soon as he can bear its brilliance, and does not commit his future to such complications.

Apologetics

THE SCIENCE that connects intellectual understandings to God is called the apologetics of the theologians; the art of bringing love to God is called the apologetics of the mystics. And the sole master of that art is the Holy Spirit. To induce man to research for the kingdom of God, one must know how to manipulate him such as he is: in his physical state, with all his faults, powerlessness, delicacies, and grandeurs. One needs a little of the gift of knowledge and a lot of the gift of tears, because one knows only what one has wept for. One must know that in himself man is not good. One must know—in spite of Rousseau, in spite of the rationalists of the 18th century, the socialists of 1848, and the humanitarians of today—that man cannot become good by himself, and realize that Christ alone can ameliorate the essential root. One must differentiate between what is natural or supernatural within us, and dispel the prestige of greatness that seduces the crowds. Sesostris, Alexander, Caesar, Napoleon, Pythagoras, Dante (and other thinkers and geniuses such as Giotto, Leonardo, Poussin, Pierre de Montereau, Shakespeare, and all artistic geniuses) are great because of their inborn and human greatness; they are small before God by the very greatness of their intelligence, their will, or their sensitivity, unless secret and humble sacrifices have opened the door of the kingdom of heaven for them. I am well aware that it is God who permitted the gods to give these giants their genius, and that, therefore, we the mediocre ones owe these great men admiration and deference. But let them not hide our Father from us.

Reason and the testimonies of the sacred books, the words of the great disciples of Christ, may lead us to faith, which means to the kingdom of God, but they cannot open the door. This kingdom is beyond and above all demonstrations, and may even appear opposed to them. To enter, one must will to do so, and yet it is not will that opens the door. As soon as one crosses the threshold, one possesses certitudes upon supernatural subjects and, when the whole person is acclimated, one also receives certitudes upon natural subjects.

This does not mean that the human being is entirely corrupt; it is simply that he is more matter than spirit, more selfish than altruistic—which is why he becomes addicted to evil rather than to good. We must not execrate ourselves either, but, using moderation, know that we must recognize any encroaching vices as well as any tiny virtues, and because of this enormous disproportion discipline ourselves pitilessly, without permitting either despair or overweening conceit to encroach.

The Father's Goodness

THE SHEPHERD who feels happier at having found his lost ewe than having kept safe the ninety-nine others, the woman who feels happier at finding a lost drachma than having kept the other nine; the father who warmly welcomes his prodigal son while giving nothing special to his virtuous son—are all examples of the love of the Father for man. The metaphysicians will claim that this is not right. Well, of course not: it is not justice; it is love. Nothing exists within us unless its prototype pre-existed in heaven; were we to be treated according to mathematical justice we would never be able to make amends for our sins, and we would be unable to fulfill our work. Because he is merely doing his duty according to justice, the virtuous man does not win any personal merits; but love awards him merits and recompenses him, just as love greets the penitent with open arms.

It is incomprehensible, unheard of, that the Being, one minute particle of whom suffices to fill the immense creation, involves himself with us with more solicitude than would the tenderest mother; that he heeds and listens to our stammering prayers. Do we know, in its innermost essence, what sin is? Do we know what evil lies in its spiritual root? How many abysses do we pass by daily? Very few men have sufficient mental resources to scrutinize certain mysteries. Let us be content knowing that the Father loves us. Were we able to respond to even a fraction of that love, we would all of us be extraordinary saints.

The Doctors of the Church, St Irenaeus and St Ambrose, among others, teach that the ninety-nine ewes represent the good angels, and the hundredth, humanity. Humanity is symbolized as the prodigal son and the tenth drachma; the woman is the community of the celestial court, Zion; the father of the family is Jesus; but the eldest son denotes a race of beings unknown to all mythologies, a race that lives close to us nevertheless, and that works—but not according to the same mode as ours.

Though he loves us—or rather, because he loves us—the Father wants us to work; it is the second aspect of his love demonstrated by the parable of the faithless steward.

The rich man is the Father, or living providence. The steward is man, to whom organs were entrusted that he might act upon all planes, that life might increase and spiritual seeds fructify—seeds that were deposited in his innermost being, or in the outer domain attributed to him from the very beginning.

By acting badly, he squanders his forces; hence, he does not sow. To escape punishment, he tries to come to terms with other beings who are not his dependents, although they are subjects of the same Master. Although illegitimate, these contracts that he enters into, either by force or ruse, become obligations. The result is that his creditors—the gods of wealth, of glory, and of science, for example—always make a profit out of these deals.

This is how men conduct themselves in general; but it is not in conformity with true wisdom.

Therefore, this advice: "make friends with unjust riches." According to the primary plan of creation, temporal enjoyments should concord with true spiritual merit. But men and devils have twisted this correspondence, so that the aforementioned prerogatives are now reefs upon which the virtue of men usually founders. Riches, health, success, glory, are usually unjustly repressed by Mammon. If we faithfully administer the gifts the *Moirae* (Fates) award us—I mean, if we look upon them as not being our acquisition or property, but as simple loans—we will enable our brothers to profit from them. Moreover, if the disciple is courageous, he will seek tests and adversity as a means to lessen the load of his brethren. But he must attempt this only out of love, because "whoever wants to save his life loses it."

The friends we make in this manner are the invisible servants of heaven, not only those the Church calls "the good angels," but many other beings unknown to esotericism.

THE KINGDOM OF GOD

These ordeals, no matter how horrible they may seem, are really "little things." In truth, glory, wealth, and science are but little things. Our faithfulness in fulfilling these modest tasks will, however, permit us to be conscientious in the "great things" that our Friend will entrust to us later: meaning a power, a secret, or a mission. These are the "veritable riches" we are called upon to distribute. Let us be well aware that "what belongs to others" is all we possess upon all planes; that "what is ours" is the spark of divine light.

Here you have to choose. To want to be both light and dark is chiaroscuro, equilibrium. But nothing in nature remains in stable equilibrium unless it is immobile. And immobility is the anti-vital state, the real hell, the gateway to nothingness.

Stay away from men who preach this immobility and who claim to have achieved it in order to secure for themselves possession of the highest prerogatives it is possible to conquer. Listen to the author of the *Interior Church*:

> By going against our own will, by subjugating it, we seek no other goal but to find therein nourishment for our spiritual pride and a powerful desire to accomplish our own desires. Today, we can find a startling example in one of those clever manipulators of magnetism. They tell you to hold yourselves in a state of perfect inactivity. But do you not see that they make use of this inactivity to reach the goal they had envisaged possessing? The very goal that makes them more active at the same time as they claim being just passive?[2]

The story of Lazarus and the selfish rich man demonstrates how the frontiers of the world are insurmountable.

Christian Initiation

Ecclesiastical tradition teaches that from the circumference of the earth to its center, is to be found: the limbo of the saints of ancient times whom Christ has liberated; also purgatory; also the limbo of the non-baptized children; and also hell. This cosmography is not mere imagination. For that matter, neither are the esoteric doctrines of the various peoples. But nowhere does one find the exact and complete description of the land of the dead or of the other invisible worlds that are close to our planet.

Besides which, such knowledge would be of little use to our culture. However, we may well state that the paradise, purgatory, and hell of the Catholics do exist; as do also the *scheol* (the well of the abyss of the Hebrews), the fourteen cosmic planes of the Brahmans, the numberless heavens and hells of the Buddhists. A theology is always the natural history of one aspect of the invisible, and not a simple philosophical symbol.

Special Rules for Disciples

REGARDING DISCIPLES, Jesus discusses a point of moral law from their standpoint.

A scandal is, as a whole, an unexpected and bad example that, owing to its exceptional character, has a peculiarly grave importance. We are responsible not only for any act and its direct consequences, but also for subsequent acts that ours has called forth among those who witnessed it. The stone hurled upon the ocean of the world determines

---

[2] A reference to the well-known mystical text *Some Characteristics of the Interior Church*, by I. V. Lopoukhin (1756–1816), published in Russian in 1798, and in English translation beginning in 1912.

ripples that spread to the furthest shores. Moreover, there surges in the bottom of the heart of the one we have scandalized a kind of surprise that wounds him mysteriously, or rather that poisons him—vitiating the influx of light and spiritual life at its sources. This corruption encumbers the scandalizer and binds him to an implacable fatality.

The false beggar who steals the money of the true beggar rivets himself to a chain and ball. And the one who does not overcome his rancors does an analogous thing. We are sufficiently aware that all our acts have an invisible counterpart. At our side, day and night, stand our good angel and our demon, who are our constant witnesses, and as well a temporary guide who changes from time to time. They perceive, not so much the physical forms of our actions, but the feelings from which they sprung. They recall everything, regardless of deaths and rebirths. A conversation or argument does not occur between two interlocutors only, but among four: the two men and their two guides. More particularly, the good and bad angel intervene in our inner awareness. But once we have made a decision, the two guides follow it. And, as we change guides several times in a lifetime, were we to meet our enemy at a later date, both of us would not have the same guides—meaning: the reconciliation that should have taken place then cannot be complete. It will be necessary for us to wait sometimes several lifetimes for each of the adversaries to find the same guide he had at the time of the altercation, and also that they meet and face each other on this physical plane. From this, we see immediately how important it is to spare no effort in making peace between us as soon as ever possible.

Setting a good example and forgiving are not the entire work of the disciple. He must also act as an intermediary between the crowd and his master; he must make the master's requests heard, and he must heal and relieve misfortune through prayer, when he cannot do so materially. It is for this last purpose that the apostles ask Jesus to increase their faith; and he responds by explaining the difficulty of their wish.

We usually see moral virtues as abstractions devoid of biological influence, lacking any organic form. In particular, three among the moral virtues qualified by the Church as theological—faith, hope, and charity—seem rather vague soul states that produce merely personal opinions and "reasonable enough" results. But they are much more than that; they are the spiritual powers of the mystically regenerated man, in the same way that feeling, thinking, and will are, for classical psychology, the faculties of ordinary man. Just as these latter are localized in certain organs of the physical body, so are faith, hope, and charity localized in other parts of the body, and their development creates the seeds of future material organs unknown even to the most learned esotericists. The Father, the Son, and the Holy Spirit are but one God, just as these three virtues are but one virtue. And if we want to elucidate this theological interpretation further, we might say that faith corresponds to the Father, charity to the Son, and hope to the Spirit.

Let us not forget that virtue means power. Hence, faith is not a state of soul but a power of the soul, an organ of the glorious body, whereas what we usually call faith, even the most ardent we may sustain, is only a vague, uncertain, powerless desire. Jesus was not using a rhetorical figure when he said: "If you had faith as though it were a grain of mustard seed, you might say to this mulberry tree: uproot thyself and plant thyself in the sea, and it would obey you."

He merely expresses a simple, positive reality: the domain of faith is precisely the impossible, the unprecedented, the new, the inconceivable. To say, as for example Boehme does, that faith is the essential operative force of the will, simply does not suffice.

Let us say I have a family, a business, friends, but I go bankrupt and panic—that means I do not have faith. If my children become ill and die and I lose courage—that means I do not have faith. If my beloved wife passes away and I lose all energy, all dignity—that means I do not have faith.

Were I to bear all these ordeals without complaint, still it would not be faith; yet I would be some kind of saint were I happy that those ordeals fell upon me rather than upon another—only then would I be able to tell myself that within a lifetime or two of going through the same things without faltering or flinching, perhaps I would feel in my heart the first tremor of a tiny seed of faith.

How can the attitude of a soul influence the course of nature? What is the mechanism of gospel magic? Take an example we could use as an analogy for all other imaginable cases. Let us say we are in business and a disloyal rival ruins us. Here, however, we must recall to mind that from one of the gods, which the Brahmans call Lords of Karma, our offending rival could have received permission and power to wrong us because we ourselves had been similarly guilty in the past. If we bear this shock with courage and resignation, we will be liberated from the debt, and have cleansed the stain—but even so, nothing spiritual will have germinated in us on account of that ancient wrong committed. Let us say, then, that another ordeal strikes, one not due to a past life; it came by means of a visible or invisible being especially tasked to test our strength of character. If we bear it with the

Christian Initiation

inner joy of a courageous soldier, all the forces, fluids, thoughts, and impulses that we will exert during the struggle (born from the inner and outer shocks) will cut a path to our will, and attract those forces and beings disseminated in the world that have the same tendencies. Hence within the sphere of our individuality we will come out of the battle with all sorts of additional vigors. On the other hand, if the situation we find ourself in seems to be without issue, if no friend or any other human help can rescue us and—in spite of all this—we keep hold of the unwavering certitude of the presence of the Father, then all of the energies we deploy will pierce through the spheres of nature up to the very gates of heaven, and our faith will gather what we need: thought, intuition, therapeutic or magical dynamism.

Faith is not (as certain occult schools erroneously teach) the immense will power of an adept; the will is only the means of obtaining it through the realization of trust in God, and courage. No matter how lofty it is, the will is nothing but a natural or human force. The definition of faith, however, is supernatural and superhuman. Magic provides the means of producing extraordinary things, but it acts only by bringing unknown natural laws into play. Faith surpasses creation. It requires neither studies, nor rites, nor place, nor time. It operates anywhere, anyhow, because, coming from the Absolute, it participates in the spontaneity and liberty of the Absolute.

Yet the disciple who executes these three enormous tasks must still fulfill an indispensable condition for his work to last: he must remain humble to the point of nothingness in the face of the all-powerfulness of the Father. Jesus explains it forcefully: "You are worthless servants because you accomplished only what you had to do." Heaven owes us no salary. The recompenses it awards us are but favors. And the most evident sign of his particular solicitude for one of us, is when that one never has a day free from a test. That is why man's only hope to become a soldier of light is when he attains the stage of always doing more than his duty.

Everything I am telling you are things we already know, but that we seldom extract from the limbo of our memory. We must beware of all the spiritual insights we have received, but leave unproductive. How many men around us, maybe among those that our religious fanaticism or pride of caste look down upon, are yearning for these lights? Look at the ten lepers Jesus healed: only one of the ten retraced his steps to thank him; and that one was a Samaritan spurned by Israelite orthodoxy.

Man is despairingly ungrateful—the proof is how nettled we are at the dart of another's ingratitude. Yet, are we not ingrates toward the Father? We never remember heaven unless we are distressed. And how pitiful and wretched is our prayer! If some initiates obtain such startling results through mental concentration, what would we not obtain on the social, scientific, artistic, or moral planes, by means of the concentration of our heart, which is the prime source whence the mind receives its life? Never can we gather and bring our desires, feelings, and affective centers sufficiently back to God. If only we were to do so, we would gain that spiritual health which is the source of all health.

We do not know how to be thankful. Worse yet, we forget to be thankful.

To make amends for this forgetfulness is the concern of the will; to remedy this ignorance is the concern of feelings. I cannot will in your stead: it is you who must want to will. But I might help you clarify your feelings.

Man is so naturally ungrateful that gratitude only serves as a veil to his incurable vanity: "God, I thank thee for having granted my prayer," often means: "My God, I was worthy for thee to grant me (this or that)... that my patient was healed in response to my prayer; I know it is not I or my prayers that healed him, but I sent for the physician and bought the prescriptions." From that stage, the belief that we are exceptional beings is but a step!

True thankfulness is the spiritual state of gratitude. It is also the inner attitude wherein ends the effusion of gratefulness. To render thanks is to thank twice. It is the cry of thanksgiving in the ecstatic beatitude of love. It is to render thanks for what we know we have received; to render thanks for what we are unaware of having received; to render thanks for everything in us that knows how to receive; to render thanks for everything within us that rectifies the miserable gesture of pride against divine alms. Being thankful denotes the broken, wounded heart lying in the dust, which surrenders unconditionally to the victorious arrows of love under the shower of the Father's blessings.

But to pronounce the words of veritable thanksgiving, it is essential that our heart feel everything it receives, even when it seems not to be receiving anything. Moreover, our heart must know that beyond the perceptible, palpable, visible gift—escorting it beyond, above, and on all sides of the little sphere of our conscience—it still receives ceaselessly from a superabundant and inexhaustible stream.

This is the state in which you must first settle your souls, your spirits, even your bodies, before rendering thanks. Attend to this: notice, once more, that the preparation for an act is the more difficult part, and consequently more important than the act.

THE KINGDOM OF GOD

We will then comprehend how "The kingdom of God is within us." Not, as some false mystics of great renown state nowadays—that God exists only in the soul of man and that all man has to do is to be exalted in order to become a veritable divine Word. The kingdom of God is really, objectively, in our midst, it is imperceptible to us in the same manner spirits remain invisible to our sight, although they nevertheless fill the space we move in. Were we to desire this kingdom with as much constancy and logic as we apply to contacting spirits, we would see it—and more easily.

This is because the Shepherd seeks his sheep with inextinguishable ardor. The spiritual space in which our heart lives is almost always a region of hell—it is up to us that it be a corner of heaven. Once we have attained that result, it will be useless to search hither and yon for secret teachings or scamper after mages—for just as the worshiper of Mammon meets and joins with other worshipers of Mammon, so, by dint of ordinary circumstances of his life, the servant of heaven will find himself inevitably in the presence of the physical person of his blessed Master.

Or, better said, this servant will not need this external presence, for he possesses the internal presence made constant by faith. Thus, if perchance while extending help to the unfortunate, you are the witness to catastrophes and panics announcing the last days, you must abide in the immutable calm of your spiritual certitudes. Heaven does well what it does: if you are designated to take such or such a direction, its angels will be fully aware of where to find you, no matter in what garret or hamlet you reside.

For, this judgment of the last days will come suddenly despite of all its warning signs; but the supernatural horror of cataclysms should neither alter our composure nor slow

Christian Initiation

our work, because everything will be planned and regulated, down to the least detail; and it will take place in the most corrupt country, for "eagles gather where the corpse is."

The Disciple as Intercessor

THE PARABLE of the unjust judge makes us understand that we must persevere in our prayers: whatever we have not obtained at the end of a week, might be obtained at the end of a year; if our voice has not been heard within a year, our call might be answered in thirty years. To supplant a simple god, the ancient Hindu rishis would make penance for tens of centuries. We, then, who are certain that the Master of the gods himself yields at our voice, even after a lukewarm bout of distractions—surely, we can repeat our request even if to do so may mean depriving ourselves of some sleep during the night.

Another condition for prayer that we know to be essential is humility. As soon as any action (be it even heroic or sublime) is performed on account of, or accompanied by, pride, it becomes a setback instead of progress. Heaven leaves the prideful man totally alone. Those puffed up with pride, believing they act and conquer (no matter in what field) because of their own merits, blind themselves, limit their horizon, soon believe they have nothing further to accomplish, and end by falling into most woeful pitfalls. There are various types of pride, since each of our qualities can make us vain: least dangerous of these is that of the man seeking glory (because the Tarpeian rock is closer to the Capitol); most dangerous of these is false humility. There are other forms, of course, but we need not describe them here.

THE KINGDOM OF GOD

In short, let us not imitate the Pharisee and look at the good we have done; let us, rather, do as the Publican did: look at the good we omitted doing, at the evil we committed. *That* is an excellent exercise to learn to know ourselves.

This is what Jesus taught the accusers of the adulteress when he wrote out their sins in the sand and forgave the sinner. The publicity of her fault relieved her of this responsibility, because of the contempt of her fellow citizens; this is a very curious mechanism, which explains the auricular confession, of which the ancient custom of public confession was an excellent application. Similarly to certain monstrous creatures dwelling in caverns and subterranean lakes, that when brought to the daylit surface devolve into blind, powerless, massive bulks, so also is evil's venom drained when made known. Evil can grow and propagate only in the shadows, which is why we should always confess it publicly, in full daylight: at first this shames us the more, but in the spectators' judgment our opprobrium will for this reason be the less.

The lack of simplicity always burdens our lives; and Christ teaches us a lesson when he offers us as an example the unawareness of the lilies and the innocence of little children.

In the esoteric language of the ancient synagogues, the term "little children" referred to initiates. The Egyptians, Orientals, Hindus, and Greeks likened initiation to a second birth. In fact, there can be no initiation without a special connection with a second plane of consciousness. To adepts, the Sanskrit word *dvija*, usually translated "twice-born" or "reborn," seems to mean "living on two planes." Each religion is the product of a hierarchy, of a special invisible world: the majority of its faithful is conscious only

Christian Initiation

of its rational, physical, and visible aspect, and receives only intermittent lights from its invisible world; the initiates perceive in addition a greater or lesser part of its invisible collectivity. But it was necessary, either by themselves, with the help of a superior, or with help of a god—or rather, and in most cases, through the cooperation of all three factors—that the seed of a particular light (esoteric knowledge or devotion, for example) that had been deposited in their spirit would grow therein, and, having reached its term, issue from its fluidic matrix to live consciously in the secondary atmosphere of the religious *egregore* to which this initiate belonged. This is a genuine birthing.

In passing, note that no religious system contains within its spiritual framework the totality of invisible nature. Catholicism, however, being closest to the center, contains the greater share of truths.

All initiatic training exercises served to nurture this spiritual seed. The innumerable lives of the human monad likewise serve to feed what at the hour of the final salvation will be our "body of glory." Just as the neophyte is unable to cross the gap separating the visible and the invisible part of his religion, so the disciple of the divine Word is unable to cross the abyss separating the created from the uncreated without the help of the Master.

And so the kingdom of God is accessible only to those who are naked, as naked as the newborn child. Still better, after having studied everything, experienced everything, suffered everything, one should renounce everything—and above all, forget everything. As the root of memory lies in the body, one cannot forget; something outside us, beyond us, must remove that memory: this something is the water of the baptism of the Spirit.

THE KINGDOM OF GOD

Thus, in order to receive the teaching of the gospel fruitfully, as well as the lively force emanating from it, one must be stripped free of all other theories, all other desires, all preconceived judgments, and any diverging preoccupation. It is not sufficient to have cleared the table of our mental world, one should have cleansed one's heart and senses as well. Due to the difficulty of this preparation, man often comes to Jesus only after having passed through various material, sentimental, philosophical, and religious experiences; after having undergone all sorts of setbacks and disillusionments, serving to cleanse idols and tinsel-foils out of his inner being. As we ourselves never would have the courage to rid ourselves of all these things (which we had sought after with such passion) in cold blood, it is heaven that shows us how empty they really are, and untethers us from them.

In any case, to understand the doctrine of Jesus, to receive the kingdom of God, we must wholeheartedly give ourselves over to it, body and soul. Neither intellectual pursuits, dilettantism, nor the expectant attitude of the eclectic philosopher procure us that knowledge. Candid simplicity, total ardor, spontaneous admiration, are needed to feel deeply the convincing freshness of the divine word.

I must insist upon the essential difference distinguishing human initiations from divine initiation. The former can give access only to the more or less sublime planes of nature, whereas the latter alone can give access to the kingdom of God.

Leaving aside Hindu Yoga (which some would have us believe to be very ancient, but which undoubtedly goes back no further than Krishna, and which provides, not liberty, but escape), the methods of ancient Brahmanism,

Christian Initiation

Osirism, Mithraism, and the Orphic mysteries only act on the natural faculties. No being before Christ had been able, in his investigations, to go beyond our zodiac; no master had therefore been able to teach more than he knew. This is what occultists do not want to comprehend; they will have to face up to the evidence the day their astral and mental senses are stopped in their tracks.

How to Become a Child Again

ALL OF THIS and many other things come to us from Jesus. Man flees from God; yet Jesus goes towards man, follows him secretly, in all of the aberrations of his uncertain steps. Why does Jesus refuse to be called "good"? To teach us a lesson in humility and unity. The Son considers himself as a naught before his Father; he does nothing without the Father's command or without his permission; he relates all of his triumphs and his sufferings to the Father; he wants to remain a simple intermediary between us and his Father. And this absolute self-effacement of the Lord of Creation tells us how indispensable must our humility be, and to what depths we must resort to probe within ourselves.

The conquest of a *paradise* is humanly feasible; observing the five principles suffices: no adultery, murder, stealing, or bearing false witness—and lastly, filial piety. The conquest of *heaven* demands two other conditions: to be poor and to follow Jesus.

This, however, is so difficult that, on this subject, Christ answers Peter in this way: "What is impossible to man is possible to God." For wealth is only the expression of our selfishness. Wealthy is not only the person with a large fortune, but also the person who has won many honors, whom many friends cherish, who possesses a vast intelligence, who feels within himself vigorous passions, and afterwards, who is endowed with extraordinary faculties, or finally whose will is always master of the others; provided, of course, that the beneficiary of these various riches is attached to them from the heart—that he considers them his inalienable possession, and believes in them.

All this occupies, internally, faculties, organs, and chambers and, externally, physical cells; the lights from the Kingdom find no available place and cannot be assimilated. This is why the disciple must be as naked as a poor man and as simple as a little child.

Then he must clear his slate, make reparation the for evil he has done in the past, by resigning himself to the ordeal; finally, he must restore light where his evil deeds had brought darkness. So do we carry our cross and follow the Word.

When we can take that road, or rather when heaven judges us sufficiently resistant to lead us thereon, we find rewards. Whoever has forsaken home, parents, or children for the kingdom of God "already receives benefits a hundredfold, here on earth." Let us remember: it is not merely possessing a stack of titles and degrees that immobilizes us in the spiritual world; it is that we have attached too much importance to these paper credentials, and to have put our heart and the depth of our being in them.

The work of the disciple necessitates a constant collaboration with an army of invisible auxiliaries. He doesn't think or act by virtue of a pre-established system; but at every step he needs to know what is true at the moment, what is actual, what is opportune, so that he can accom-

Christian Initiation

plish the act of the moment—that is, the best, the most fruitful one. Hence (since he believes himself to be a mere cipher) he needs messengers, helpers, servants, couriers, errand-runners to keep him informed, and who work according to his wishes. He needs invisible parents, meaning the secret presence of his ancestors. He needs an invisible spouse, meaning a spark from the uncreated Wisdom. He needs invisible children, meaning works that radiate the force of which he is the seat. He needs invisible treasures, meaning merits to pay the debts of others, to comfort the unfortunate and change for the better their paths. He needs an invisible home, so as to rest from time to time. He needs invisible fields, so as to restore his over-burdened spiritual body. He needs invisible brothers and sisters, which means occasionally meeting a field-worker of the great Farmer, a soldier of the great King.

After that difficult lifetime, his Lord grants him eternal life.

One final comment. The "good" man, who is on the magical, voluntary, personal path—in a word, in nature—sees his good deeds automatically rewarded by this play of backlash, the mechanism of which Eliphas Levi has shown us. But if this man is on the divine path, he does not consider himself entitled to a reward; and when out of pure grace and love the Father offers him a favor, the soldier's humility gives him the strength to give up his share of the bounty for the benefit of the community for which he has already endured so much fatigue. This ultimate sacrifice earns him an extraordinary privilege, the nature and *modus operandi* of which it is impossible for us to understand at present.

www.ingramcontent.com/pod-product-compliance
Lightning Source LLC
Chambersburg PA
CBHW020048170426
43199CB00009B/213